COOKERY

RHETORIC, CULTURE, AND SOCIAL CRITIQUE

COOKERY

Food Rhetorics and Social Production

Edited by Donovan Conley and Justin Eckstein

THE UNIVERSITY OF ALABAMA PRESS TUSCALOOSA

The University of Alabama Press
Tuscaloosa, Alabama 35487-0380
uapress.ua.edu

Typeface: Scala Pro

Cover design: Mary-Frances Burt/Burt&Burt

Cataloging-in-Publication data is available from the Library of Congress.
ISBN: 978-0-8173-2049-2
E-ISBN: 978-0-8173-9280-2

To Tryst, Airalia, and Cailix (the future)

Contents

Acknowledgments

EDITED VOLUMES ARE COLLABORATIVE ENDEAVORS from start to finish, and ours has been an especially rewarding one. *Cookery* began as a panel on "Dirty Rhetoric" at the 2016 NCA convention, failed at becoming a special issue, and wound up finding favor with Dan Waterman at the University of Alabama Press as a result of a conversation initiated by Justin.

We therefore wish to thank Dan, first and foremost, for his warm reception, his clear and unfussy editorial guidance, and for providing a welcome balance of rigor and flexibility as we worked through our various drafts. Similar gratitude is extended to the anonymous reviewers who read our manuscript and subsequent revisions, always without delay and in a spirit of collegial supportiveness. And we offer a special thank you to Greg Dickinson for agreeing to write an Afterword, thereby christening our project with his wisdom and humanity.

The ideas in this volume have taken shape through conversations with friends and colleagues over the years and across the discipline. As such Donovan and Justin both wish to acknowledge the invaluable insights of Nathan Stormer, Diane Keeling, Jeremy Engels, Dustin Greenwalt (who also provided comments on Donovan's chapter—thanks again, Dustin!), Jamie Wright, Harry Weger, Anjali Vatz, Gabriela Tscholl, Amy Pason, Darrin Hicks, Tyler Snelling, Stephen Hartnett, Lisa Keranen, Patrick Dodge, Betsy Brunner, Benjamin Burroughs, and Damien Pfister.

Along the way we received invaluable assistance, in the form of research and/or editorial support, from Matthew Salzano, Kate Hall, and Stephanie Willes. Thank you so much, each of you, once again, for providing crucial support and helping us hit our deadlines.

We also wish to extend a mournful note of special gratitude to our friend, colleague, and mentor Rob DeChaine. Rob was a champion of our project early on and throughout its development. For his brilliant editorial insights, sage professional advice, and kind disposition, we express heartfelt thanks. We miss our friend Rob.

Donovan also wishes to extend thanks to his colleagues at UNLV, an unfailingly supportive, generous, and decent group of human beings who also happen to be brilliant scholars and teachers. Thank you to David Henry for the years of mentorship, to Sara VanderHaagen for professional integrity and intellectual troubleshooting, to Jenny Guthrie for comradeship in winning ugly, to Tara McManus for time shared in the post-tenure service foxhole, to Randall Bush for the gifts of intellect and heart, to Tara Emmers-Sommer for encouragement and illumination, to Erika Engstrom for way too many high calorie tokens of support, to Emma Bloomfield for raising the game through shared interests, to Philip Tschirhart for rhetorical brilliance, to Brian Cozen for the many fresh and stimulating exchanges, and to the one and only Jacob Thompson for countless cooking sessions filled with conversation and laughter around tables with friends and families (love you, buddy).

Donovan also wishes to extend a heartfelt thank you to Michael Bruner, for cheering this project toward completion, and for offering every form of support imaginable in the process; to Donna Ralston for providing administrative backing at every level, from purchasing books to arranging travel, and for making the general business of scholarship a far less onerous one than it could be (thank you, Donna!); and to Rob Ulmer, dean of the Greenspun College of Urban Affairs, for cultivating a vibrant and fun workplace atmosphere like no other.

Finally, Donovan reserves his sweetest thank you's for Mums, Shelly, and Amy for infinite love, support, patience, encouragement, laughter, and grace. But the most thankful of all thanks goes to his wife Amy, for the gift of new life.

Justin wishes to thank his amazing colleagues at Pacific Lutheran University, Amy Young (who, in addition to writing with him for this volume, listens to him ramble and read countless drafts of everything), Kate Hoyt for chatting about ideas, Mike Bartenan for support and helping him develop as a scholar, Peter Ehrenhaus for teaching him the value of a table for an article, and Marnie Ritche for being always willing to chat about ideas. Justin also sends his appreciation to PLU provost Joanna Gregson and Arts and Communication Dean Cameron Bennett for awarding him and Amy Young a Karen Hille Phillips Grant which enabled them to undertake research for the project. Justin also wishes to thank his wife Lisa Korby for her support, her love, her wit, and her wisdom. And, he cannot forget her infectious love of food.

COOKERY

Introduction

Soiled

Donovan Conley and Justin Eckstein

If Plato's rhetoric-as-cookery analogy is the foundational provocation that gave rise to rhetorical theory, it is worth recalling that this crucial sequence unfolds toward the end of what is essentially *Gorgias*'s exordium. If all rhetorical theory bends back toward this inaugural critique, what does it mean that the cookery insult is dispatched, never to return, merely a fifth of the way through the dialogue? Minimally, we may note that rhetoric-as-cookery is not *Gorgias*'s culminating argument, nor is it Plato's final word on rhetoric itself. While it has become conventional to characterize *Gorgias* as Plato's "base" rhetoric and *Phaedrus* as its more "noble" sequel, in fact both dialogues feature disputes over rhetoric as the entry point to discussions about knowledge, goodness, justice, right living, pleasure, power, and thus the very composition of the social. Indeed, the formal dimension of these dialogues reminds us that to disagree about rhetoric is nevertheless to have already invested in the fate of civic life, for debate as such affirms an investment in togetherness. *Gorgias* uses oratory as a way to dramatize a more fundamental question: How best to ground communal values in order to fertilize civic life? *Gorgias* thus dramatizes the battle over politics's richest soil. Socrates offers sharp distinctions and clean cuts in a fantasy of nonrelationality. A world of static forms, tidy and reliable, is enunciated through his dialectical theatrics. Callicles, by contrast, plays the recalcitrant interlocutor who refuses to be boxed in by Socrates's abstract rigidity.

During what is perhaps the key moment in the "cookery" exchange with Polus, Socrates proclaims:

> Thus, cookery puts on the mask of medicine and pretends to know what foods are best for the body, and, if an audience of children or of men with no more sense than children had to decide whether a confectioner or a doctor is the better judge of wholesome and unwholesome foodstuffs, the doctor would unquestionably die of hunger. Now I call this sort of thing pandering and I declare that it is dishonorable—I'm speaking to you now, Polus—because it makes pleasure its aim instead of good, and I maintain that it is merely a knack and not an art because it has no rational account to give of the nature of the various things it offers. I refuse to give the title of art to anything irrational, and if you want to raise an objection on this point, I am ready to justify my position.[1]

We raise no objections about the cluster of terms Plato is problematizing here—pretense and authenticity, indulgence and wholesomeness, obsequiousness and honor, pleasure and goodness, habituation and education, artistry and rationality, convention and nature, the popular and the political elite—but the way he stacks them invites refutation. Indeed we embrace James Kastely's masterful reading of Plato's philosophical rhetoric as, at bottom, a provocation to further thought: "What Socrates'[s] refutations open up," writes Kastely, "are the constructedness of any individual or state and the web of entangled commitments that any individual or society inherits and acts upon and must accept responsibility for."[2] Kastely's emphasis on the commitments and responsibilities of our historical entanglements cues the presence of relationality lurking behind the tidy creases of Plato's avowedly nonrelational epistemology. And this very tension, between the fecundity of *Gorgias*'s concerns and the rigidity of its conclusions, illuminates the "deep" or "primary" or "always-already there" nature of ecological relationality. We cannot but notice the presence of "moreness" pushing through the seams of Plato's hermetic formalism.

Kastely must be right; otherwise Plato's arguments fail too easily.[3] For all their formal brilliance, Plato's conclusions about rhetoric must be accepted at face value to be acceptable at all. This is likely why Socrates acts the bully throughout the dialogue, frequently seizing control over the exchanges with his interlocutors. Immediately preceding the cookery moment, for instance, Socrates loses patience with Polus and begins forcefully directing the conversation:

> Socrates: Just ask me, will you, what sort of art I take cookery to be.
>
> Polus: Very well; what sort of art is cookery?
>
> Socrates: It isn't an art at all, Polus.

Polus: What is it then? Explain.

Socrates: A kind of knack gained by experience, I should say.[4]

Forcing an interlocutor to ask a wrong question showcases Plato's rigid formalism. Not only does Socrates badger Polus into a preformulated conclusion on oratory, he drags the pupil through a series of dialectical hoops along the way.

On its face the cookery analogy looks devastating. In fact, the critique is both savage and elegant—savage *because* elegant—with its cascading antitheses of body and soul, true and false, production and preservation. To summarize the core components of Socrates's argument:

- Humans are made up of two distinct entities, body and soul;
- Human endeavors either promote "true" health and its maintenance, *or pretend to*;
- Cookery is a form of pretend medicine, mere flattery disguised as nutrition; and thus,
- Rhetoric is to the soul what cookery is to the body: the mere pretense of justice.

Here is a visual layout of the argument:

TABLE I.1. SOCRATES'S COOKERY ANALOGY

	Body	Soul ("Government")
True Arts	Training (production)	Legislation (production)
	Medicine (preservation)	Judiciary (preservation)
Counterfeit Arts	Beauty Culture	Sophistry
	Cookery	Rhetoric (pretend justice)

Socrates proclaims his formalism in the starkest terms, announcing, "I will put the matter in the form of a geometrical proportion . . . and say that cookery is to medicine as beauty culture is to physical training, or rather that popular lecturing is to legislation as beauty-culture to training, and oratory to justice as cookery to prejudice."[5] A revealing tension lurks within this series of analogies, however. All of these *"is to-as"* constructions signal the presence of relational awareness, but Plato labors to ensure his relations dissolve between firm ontological boundaries. Indeed, Plato uses analogies less to show how things are alike than how they are either exactly the same or utterly distinct. He does not use analogies to highlight the gaps between terms, but rather to transcend and negate those very gaps. Definitions—clean, unflinching, vertically stacked, and determinative—are the ultimate goal.[6]

But analogies make sense only because of the gaps between terms, in the charged middle space of interpretive interplay. As Kenneth Burke puts it, "To tell what a thing is, you place it *in terms of* something else."[7] Plato is attempting to resist this naked empirical fact, to utter forth his ideals through the sheer power of form. For the cookery analogy to stand, however, we must accept Plato's overwrought articulation of pleasure with deception, on the one hand, and medicine with justice on the other. According to these alignments, chefs, by definition, cannot promote physical health and strength because Socrates has already defined cooking as deception through flattery. Chefs promote mere pleasure and, as Jessica Moss notes, Plato regards pleasure with deep suspicion: "Pleasure is dangerous because it is a deceiver. It leads us astray with false appearances, bewitching and beguiling us, cheating and tricking us."[8] Extending the logic of this claim, the pleasure-danger articulation quickly grows absurd. Countless exceptions could be offered by way of refutation. Katie Zabrowski observes, for instance, "Anyone who has added a pinch more salt and a sprinkle less of sugar to a cake batter knows that every granular element matters for all the others, and therefore likely sees the error in Plato's understanding of cooking. No ingredient is, for cooking or for rhetoric, mere garnishment. In Plato's ontology, however, ornamentation (rhetoric) does not play a co-constructive function but rather serves as deceptive flattery, distracting from the 'real' or 'true' construction. Frosting as flattery, then, would be said to distract us from the real taste of the cake, without itself being a constructive element. It is, however, an element no less real than the others; after all, frosting makes the cake."[9] Cookery is what emerges when random ingredients are combined in the presence of heat, producing a transformation of the parts into a new whole; hence the absurdity in Socrates's definitional stacking of cooking on top of flattery, medicine on top of justice, legislation on top of the soul, or beauty culture on top of deception, and so on. Definitional boxes are but portraits of ecological relationality frozen in time. They are wishes. Plato's ontology of longing ignores the historical fact that real structures have fuzzy edges and cracked folds.

The final exchange between Socrates and Callicles dramatizes the tension between Plato's strict formalism and the ecology of relations spilling through its cracks (Plato would insist, *no cracks!*). As the younger student, Polus fares badly in his exchange with Socrates, but Callicles is not so easily pushed around. When the two of them square off in the dialogue's final exchange, it quickly becomes clear that Socrates cannot bully Callicles into submission. Here is a sampling of their tension:

> Socrates: But you have agreed that it is possible to feel enjoyment when one is in pain.
>
> Callicles: So it appears.
>
> Socrates: Then enjoyment is not the same as good fortune nor pain as bad fortune, and pleasure is a different thing from the good.
>
> Callicles: I don't understand your quibbles, Socrates.
>
> Socrates: Oh yes you do, Callicles; only it suits you to feign ignorance. Just carry the argument a little further.
>
> Callicles: What is the point of continuing this nonsense?[10]

This exchange encapsulates the dialogue's core struggle over the optimal grounding of communal life. Socrates is arguing on behalf of nature/*phusis*, and Callicles on behalf of social convention/*nomos*—Might and Right, respectively. Their contrasting positions play out in this brief back and forth, with Socrates laboring to sew up a definition and Callicles dodging every attempt to be hemmed in. Refusing to play by the rules of Socrates's rigid formalism, Callicles embodies the messy moreness of social relations and the elastic nature of communal values. When, in a moment of exasperation, he exclaims, "Couldn't you finish the argument alone, either in a continuous speech or answering your own questions yourself?," Callicles hits on the fatal flaw in Plato's approach: its formal hostility toward difference, otherness, and change.[11]

Socrates concludes the dialogue by threatening Callicles with eternal damnation—*when the moment comes for you to stand the trial of which I have just spoken you will be quite unable to defend yourself*—never allowing his opponent a chance to reply, and this is precisely the kind of formal closure that James Kastely seizes as an opening for refutation.[12] The abrupt coldness of Socrates's last stand conjures an ethical injunction for audiences to step into the breach of communication, to respond and take up, *to refute*. Kastely writes, "In a Platonic universe, the true and good do not triumph, even theoretically; rather, the irremediable fact of his universe is that injustice is ineradicable. The philosophic problem is how to live responsibly in such a world; Socrates's answer is that one must use rhetoric to indict one's own loved ones."[13] If this is accurate, Socrates's final indictment of Callicles takes on a wholly different character, possibly even that of our first "invitational rhetoric."[14] And it is precisely this tension, between the Apollonian enclosure of Socrates's epistemic formalism and the Dionysian excess of Callicles nagging its every fold, that Plato's dialogue ultimately dramatizes. *Gorgias* stages a debate over rhetoric as a false dichotomy between immaterial purity and material pollution. While Socrates may technically "win" for scoring the last word on eternal damnation, the dialogue itself constitutes an open invitation to further engagement. One simply must respond in the face of such lousy options. History has been very generous to Plato in this regard.

Plato's abstract formalism, in other words, is trespassed by the inevitable and often recalcitrant moreness of actual historical bodies, practices, voices, and desires. As Alexis Shotwell notes, "the world always exceeds our conception of it."[15] *Gorgias* enacts a fundamental tension between epistemic rigidity and ecological fluidity; between, it should be said, a longing for purity and an embrace of dynamism. It thus frames political life as the ongoing process of carving, publicizing, and defending a shared ground (Conley picks up this thread in chapter 6), and "grounding" as such is an inherently contaminating enterprise. Another way to say this is that Socrates and Callicles are jostling over "dotted lines," carving the social into comprehensible units of meaning and utility. As Timothy Morton puts it, "It is not so easy to draw a dotted line between the physical and the semiotic. Such lines are nowhere to be found on the surfaces of frogs, poems, clouds, and permafrost. Yet since Plato, as Heidegger and Derrida both explored, Western philosophy has been in the business of trying to find these dotted lines."[16] What are these dotted lines? They are real abstractions and useful fictions, the discursive extension of thought that constitutes the social landscape out of the lifeworld. Words, symbols, technologies, logistical operations, and institutional formations: where order and meaning are engineered discursively, we find these dotted lines coproducing thought and history together.

As we have seen, Socrates devotes his efforts in *Gorgias* to carving lines around concepts, stacking terminological siblings according to rigid internal logics, and then assuming the stacks fell from the heavens. This is how the abstract becomes realized, rhetorically: through a formalizing process where matter is given shape through dotted lines such as coded expressions, normalizing practices (habits), technological applications, logistical operations, and spatialized designs. *Cookery* approaches rhetoric's generalized influence through food, and thinking about food rhetorically involves reckoning with its systematized production, hence reckoning with the behemoth of modern industrial agriculture. In so reckoning we arrive at what Morton calls *agrilogistics*, a very deep place in human history where the word meets the world in the form of dotted lines and folding structures. Food is central to understanding rhetoric's generalized influence because modern industrial agriculture touches virtually every body on earth and, as we detail in the next section, rhetoric constitutes the unique character of bodies encountering one another.

This approach veers somewhat from recent work in rhetoric that centers on the ways food mediates the cultural processes of identity formation and preservation.[17] An oft-cited example of the intersections between food and identity is fried chicken, which as Camille Bégin suggests, is "loaded with tension and racist imagery."[18] Fried chicken is raced in part because it is tied to the Great Migration after the Civil War, when freed slaves brought their culinary habits with them to the North. Even though many whites ate fried chicken in the South, it became a moniker of southern black identity that persists in complex ways today. However, as Certeau, Giard, and Mayol explain, "Stated differences are often attributed to a *regional cultural history* with obscure particularities, when it is really a question of material necessities established little by little through tradition, a way of adapting to local agricultural production."[19] In other words, that which constitutes identity takes its particular character through the preliminary confluence of history and geography. Indeed, as Bégin adds, "once associated with a region, the taste of fried chicken became linked to race."[20] An ecological approach to questions of identity and food would emphasize the social practices that coalesce around specific historical relations tied to a given agricultural reality. Indeed, Young and Eckstein remind us in chapter 2 that the distinctiveness of cultural identity is tethered to the available resources of place; hence the importance of "terroir" in understanding the unique quality of a given way of life. As Jane Bennett notes, "Food is an active inducer-producer of salient public effects, rather than a passive resource at the disposal of consumers."[21] *Cookery* shares this view as it asks us to examine the historical relations that crystallize in a specific place—oftentimes in strange ways, as Jeff Rice examines in chapter 4—giving rise to new structures of meaning and sensation that come to be known as identity. Far from a passive resource, the edible matter we call "food" operates rhetorically within various strata of polyvalent production. By polyvalent production, further detailed in the next section, we mean food's inventional capacity exceeding its conventional usages and habituations. As is well known, corn's caloric density and starchy hardiness make it an ideal commodity for transforming into sweeteners in one instance and ethanol in another and fish food in yet another (and so on). Food's rhetoricity emanates from edible matter's seemingly infinite compositional malleability.

AGRILOGISTICS: GENERALIZED INFLUENCE AND SEDIMENTED AGENCY

Kenneth Burke already scouted the conceptual terrain we are carving out, although his focus was on language as such. In the discussion of scene in *Grammar of Motives*, he considers the original doctrine of materiality, atomism, and isolates the conundrum of origins and directionality. How might we trace the course of human action when scene itself is said to be determinative? How might we distinguish the arrow of influence from the generalized swirl of environmental factors? Burke has this to say:

> [Lucretius argues that] regardless of their differences in weight, the [atomic] particles would all fall through empty space at the same rate of speed, and so would remain forever out of touch with one another, except for the presence, within the atomic seeds, of a slight tendency to *swerve*. And in thus swerving, they collide, rebound, and variously combine, to cause the endless evolution and destruction of worlds, things, and beings. . . . But the Epicurean physics is the basis for an ethics. Hence, we are dramatistically admonished to look for the "seeds" of an ethical principle in the physical terminology itself. Or, otherwise stated, we are admonished to examine this "inclination" of the atoms on the possibility that it is a device for transcending sheer motion and opening towards the wider realm of action and agenthood.[22]

Contained in these observations is an implied progression from scenery to agency. Burke is seeking an ethics of action from a terrain of pure motion, and so he lands on the concept of the *swerve*. The notion of *clinamen*, or swerve, illuminates the element of contingency present within our physical universe: indeterminacy, chance, serendipity, and creativity but also their stranger cousins surprise, mystery, the uncanny, and the virtual.[23] As Conley notes elsewhere on the swerve, "A democratean universe of linear movements is a deterministically static and rational space, whereas an epicurean universe of swerving movements is an endlessly mutating and hence *aesthetic* space."[24] An aesthetic, swerving historical plane of bodily collisions is a space of kinetic interaction, relational jostling, and mutual affectation. In such a universe rhetoric is best characterized by Burke's notion of *courtship*, which he describes as "the use of suasive devices for the transcending of social estrangement," adding, "there is the 'mystery' of courtship when 'different kinds of beings' communicate with each other."[25] Language exists comfortably in such a space of aesthetic courtship, as it fills up the gaps between bodies with various proddings and inducements. And, of course, Burke saw within language itself the seeds of action, as he took pains to distinguish motivated action from unmotivated motion. He suggests in the above quote, for instance, that ethically motivated action might transcend "sheer motion."

But to what extent is language itself the originator of influence, and to what degree is sheer physical motion qualitatively distinct from motivated human action? This longing for the origins of action as emerging from the dynamic motions of the lifeworld, and for discovering the pivotal role of language in the plane of historical transformation, cuts to the heart of rhetoric's historically conflicted self-understanding. In a notable recent example, George Kennedy proposed an account of rhetoric's generalized essence as a form of energy expenditure not unlike a calorie. As he puts it, "Rhetoric in the most general sense may perhaps be identified with the energy inherent in communication: the emotional energy that impels the speaker to speak, the physical energy expended in the utterance, the energy level coded in the message, and the energy expended by the recipient in decoding the message. In theory, one might even seek to identify some quantitative unit of rhetorical energy—call it the 'rheme'—analogous to an erg or volt, by which rhetorical energy could be measured. I leave that to the experimentalists."[26] This approach reduces rhetoric to a level "below" language, below thought, possibly even below sensation itself. Energy moves through all the lifeworld's bodies, human and extra-human alike, so Kennedy is postulating a universal mode of influence that finds expression not simply in words but in gestures, shapes, sounds, tastes, smells, and colors.

We offer no experimental results in rheme quantification, nor do we wish to identify rhetoric's essence once and for all. Instead, we join a chorus of critical scholars working at the edges of communication studies, food studies, cultural studies, and eco-philosophy in developing a robust account of rhetoric's constitutive materiality.[27] Our commitments are more empirical than definitional, so we are happy to follow the direction of Nathan Stormer who has already tilled this conceptual terrain.[28] In particular his brief but superb "An Appetite for Rhetoric" lays much of the foundation for the framework we are developing. The driving premise of "Appetite" is that rhetoric and food are mutually mediated through the living, historical force of hunger. As Stormer puts it, "My only point, ultimately, is that an appetite for rhetoric does not deserve autonomy from hunger, given that any rhetoric is immanent to hunger and hunger is always, everywhere immanent so long as that rhetoric is enlivened by bodies that eat. The consequence of hunger's particular immanence/imminence is that it shapes rhetoricity in ways different from that of other appetites."[29] Such "other appetites" might include those for syllogistic predictability or consubstantial oneness; Stormer's point is that hunger pushes rhetoric beyond the familiar terrain of *doxa* and identification into new realms of inventional expressiveness. Extending the argument in a way that begins to establish our own position, he adds, "Or, to the extent that rhetoric is understood as creative forces that mobilize affect, hunger is 'the wild' at the heart of civility . . . a gaunt power that both obliterates *and* compels other forms of invention."[30] Here Stormer points to wildness as the moreness of actual historical bodies, voices, and desires we first noted in *Gorgias*. Rhetoric takes us beyond food in certain ways, but food, through hunger, takes us beyond rhetoric in many more. Thomas Rickert echoes this view in *Ambient Rhetoric* when he states, "we can see rhetoric as evolving systems, or ecologies, of theories, practices, (social) relations, and technologies that *continually outgrow* current frames of practice and theoretical orientation."[31] This notion that rhetoric's materiality engenders surplus modes of invention is what we mean by its polyvalent production. Rhetoric's fecundity is wedded to its physicality, which is why Stormer also notes that "farmers have been repeatedly valorized as the bringers of civilization; cultivators come before culture."[32] This sentiment reminds us that rhetoric is more verb than noun, that its agency is distributed throughout the inventional process and not compressed into a finished product. Indeed, rhetoric precedes the fruits of culture, a fact which inevitably carries us back to farming and agriculture, which in turn takes us back to the fuzzy discursive intersection between human thought and natural history Timothy Morton calls agrilogistics.

Accepting the fact that rhetoric's productive richness stems from its deep materiality entails tracking the dynamics of social influence back to a distant moment in human history—roughly twelve thousand years ago in the "fertile crescent" of what would become Mesopotamia—that generated the conditions of possibility for agriculture itself.[33] If agriculture involves the techniques and practices of food production, agrilogistics involves the underlying epistemic and discursive patterns—the *logic*—that gave rise to those very techniques and practices. The key to understanding agrilogistics is its generative blindness; it is a logic of production constitutively incapable of recognizing its own historicity. Indeed, agrilogistics is precisely the mode of social production that forges distinctions between an "inside" (like "Culture" and "Us") and an "outside" (like "Nature" and "Them") and that aims to calm an individual's anxiety about her or his place within a seemingly infinite mesh of object relations. Agrilogistics is the metaphysics of presence applied to the entire object domain of the lifeworld.[34] It uses dotted lines to produce cones of meaning, such as "Environment" or "Home" or "Nation" or "Self" out of the churning mass of stuff that surrounds and bewilders us. It discursively folds a churning mass of raindrops, for instance, into a thing called "Rain" for which songs and shelters are built.[35] Agrilogistics is the original social constructionism.

Even the discourse surrounding "Wildness" is agrilogistical, a way of folding structures of meaning around that which is abject, perverse, and/or unknown. We have wild mushrooms, wild animals, wild rice, "Man versus Wild," and so on, but never wildness as such. Morton writes, "Why does the attempt to find wildness outside of agrilogistics, which is to say Nature, always fail? Because the idea that there is a definitive outside of agrilogistics *is itself agrilogistical*."[36] Drawing distinctions between here and there, present and absent, real and false, pure and spoiled, and then folding social structures to comply with these distinctions—this is the fundamental agrilogistical maneuver. If agriculture sought to close the gap between humans and their means of survival, agrilogistics first sought to close the gap between humans and the surrounding lifeworld by dotting lines and folding matter into cones of meaning. Morton adds, "Why do we think of Nature as opposed to the human? Or underneath it, or beyond it—deep inside me, happening despite me, and so on? It's because a ten thousand-year long agricultural project, which began in Mesopotamia and is still in effect, was wildly (pun intended) successful at doing what it implicitly set out to do: *establish thin and rigid boundaries between the human and the non-human.* So successful was this project in the Fertile Crescent that it now covers an awful lot of Earth's nonoceanic space. So successful was it that the vast majority of vertebrate biomass consists either of humans or of their domesticated animals."[37] This quote establishes the history of agriculture as equally the history of Man and Nature as discursive concepts and social categories. Agrilogistics arranges these categories, distinguishing human from nature by folding the former on itself—with the rhetorical assistance of barbed wire fences, lines on maps, shotguns, thou-shalt-nots, folk songs, commercial transactions, Walt Disney films, frozen food packaging, countless reality TV programs, and so on—while keeping the other at bay, "over there." Dotting and folding are the basic moves in this productive process, and rhetoric provides the adhesion.

Thus, agricultural production historically has as much to do with the forging of social distinctions as with the cultivation of crops; distinctions between where Man ends and Nature (God or Creation) begins; distinctions between what counts as property versus mere land; distinctions between the social and cultural versus the merely biological; distinctions (as Jeff Rice explores in chapter 4) between the familiar and the strange; even, as we have seen, Platonic distinctions between terms like pleasure and deception. This agrilogistic process stabilizes distinctions by establishing "thin and rigid boundaries between the human and nonhuman." These boundaries—Morton's dotted lines above—give shape to our most basic notions of social order and communal value. We have established thin/rigid boundaries around dogs and cats, for instance (Pets), which do not apply to pigs and chickens and cows; and we have established thin/rigid boundaries around pigs-chickens-cows (Food), which do not apply to insects and critters (Bugs). We establish lines and boundaries when we designate *this* as "organic" over here and *that* as "processed" over there, or when we define "local" as *this* fifty-mile radius, or "global" as *that* invisible set of practices, etc. Thin and rigid boundaries are what hold the sheer mass of object relations together in a complex assemblage we call the social. It is agrilogistics all the way down, and rhetoric is the bonding agent that holds everything together—imperfectly and provisionally, but functionally.

Summed up, Morton's account of human history is a tale of the ways in which agriculture grows the fortunes of both crops and sociality together. Agriculture is the world's largest generator of social influence, but agriculture itself is the expression of a more primitive form of world-shaping influence called agrilogistics. Where thought, via discourse, interrupts the world in the form of dotted lines and thin/rigid boundaries, yielding to and generating new affordances for action, we find the presence of rhetoric. In his "Definition of Man," Burke describes ideology as a spirit inhabiting a body, adding, "it makes that body hop around in certain ways; and that body would have hopped around in different ways had a different ideology happened to inhabit it."[38] Shifting focus from immaterial to material inducements, we might say that wherever an object/body bends in a particular direction when it might have bent in another, we find the gravitational warping of rhetoric in action. The swerving motion of bodies in relation to other bodies is the characteristic ground of ecological activity, and this activity could be considered rhetorical insofar as those bodies might have swerved differently. We thus second Thomas Rickert when he asks, "Why tether persuasion *only* to argument, judgment, and praise, as opposed to other forms of inducement?"[39] Rhetoric inscribes the full range of gravitational inducements and proddings—from reason to deception, seduction, intimidation, flattery, arousal, nudging, and so on—that fill up the gaps between and among swerving bodies that might have swerved otherwise. Again, courtship best describes this terrain of activity, where bodies draw on any available resources (persuasives) to overcome the mysteries of their mutual estrangement.

What remains is the question of Big Rhetoric versus small rhetoric(s).[40] Returning to Burke's reflections on scene, how can we isolate meaningful forms of expression from within the gargantuan pile of shifting influence that an ecological approach requires us to contemplate? Given the deep materiality of an agriculturalized rhetoric, we propose treating questions of action and efficacy—of agency—as matters of sedimentation and intensification. As a starting point, consider what David Depew says about "hierarchical agency" in reference to Richard McKeon's architectonics: "McKeon wants to redeploy Aristotle's distinction between architectonic and subordinate arts. House roofers and drywall installers are subordinate artists. An architect is, paradigmatically, an architectonic one. The former achieve their ends only if they are under the direction of the latter. For this very reason, Aristotle argues that as one goes down this hierarchy agency is reduced. A nurse is less active than a physician. An ambulance chaser is less active than a partner in a law firm with oak paneled offices."[41] Acknowledging that for McKeon rhetoric remained a verbal and cognitive process, we take inspiration from the notion that agency *intensifies* and *extensifies* as we move up and down layers of activity. Why not dispense with its corporate associations and replace "hierarchy" with "layers" or "strata," then extend the logic in both directions? Within the context of agricultural production—starting from "the bottom"—it is plain to see how a specific choice of crops produces a certain kind of output rather than another; how the use of specific chemicals and technologies bend harvest yields in certain ways rather than others; how particular laws, policies, regulations, and market trends foster certain kinds of harvests rather than others; how particular knowledges, skills, talents, trade secrets, traditions and innovations hasten certain kinds of results instead of others; and how specific voices, movements, tactics, and agitations achieve certain kinds of pressures and obligations rather than others. An agitation is more politically active than a new crop rotation, but the agitation is not necessarily more influential for that reason. Both activities yield varying degrees of influence and produce differential outcomes. Indeed, all these forms of influence swirl atop, beneath, and between one another. Rickert says as much when he writes, "[rhetoric] coalesces out of multiple cultural, material, and semiotic strands that are mutually entangled and coevolving."[42] What emerges from all of this is the social itself, interwoven by the signifying practices of culture and out of which political formations take their shapes.[43]

An ecologized rhetoric, with its sedimented notion of agency, will embrace all these layered forms of influence *as* influence—just as Dickman and Rivers describe influence herein. We see no need to make categorical distinctions between the linguistic and nonlinguistic, symbolic and material, intentional and unintentional, cognitive and corporeal, or the rational and affective. Whenever an object (like a body) swerves in a particular direction rather than another, rhetoric will have been deployed. And yet not all swerves are alike. We thus find utility in making relative distinctions between the intensification and extensification of agential force: distinctions between deep (micro) versus shallow (macro) planes of activity, between dark (weak) versus bright (strong) degrees of bodily attraction, between rigid (Platonic) versus plastic (Calliclean) modes of discursive enstructuring, and between corporeal (embodied) and incorporeal (abstract) mediums of operation.[44] A modified genome in a plant seed is a much "deeper" form of influence than a protest outside of Monsanto's headquarters, but the former needn't be dismissed merely because of its relative invisibility. What distinguishes a coding sequence from a protest, ecologically speaking, is their relative degrees of intensification and not simply their proximity to the linguistic or symbolic or rational. What matters is not determining whether speech ought to be privileged over algorithms in terms of rhetorical salience but rather the unique design of a given entity (speech, code, object, technology, etc.) and the nature of its operation in relation to certain historical outcomes. Rhetoric oriented in this way would seek to account for the particular shapes that bodies assume as they court one another across the ongoing mystifications of class, race, ethnicity, gender, age, ability, regionality, and the rest.

EDIBLE ARRANGEMENTS

The layout of chapters in *Cookery* reflects the layered ordering of agential sedimentation, from a "deep" ontological stratum of generalized influence in the first chapter "up" to a political one of antagonisms and articulatory practices in the last. Beginning at the deepest level of analysis, Katie Dickman and Nathaniel Rivers's "Brewing Influence: The Mixology of Morals" explores rhetoric's ecology through the prism of inebriation. Postulating influence as a form of intoxication, and vice versa, they accentuate the fuzziness of bodily boundaries and thereby render persuasion a matter of corporeal vulnerability. As they write, "We focus on rhetoric as a dirty, sensuous aggregate of influence. Alcohol helps us to trace the yeasty ways that influence works as a risky, vulnerable and already compromised (if not contaminated) process of becoming." Through concepts like "abstract machine" and "meshwork," Dickman and Rivers's chapter enriches and extends the polyvalent ecological dynamics we have tracked herein. As they note, "Influence aggregates. Influence is a contaminated network in which we cannot help but participate." With the second chapter, by Amy Young and Justin Eckstein, "The Terroir and Topoi of the Lowcountry," we move "up" a layer of agential sedimentation with the culinary productions of superstar chef Sean Brock. Brock's interventions with and into dirt signal for Young and Eckstein the concentrated rhetoricity of place, specifically the ways soil can function as a site of rhetorical invention. The authors track Brock's novelty in producing new dotted culinary lines out of old dirt, emphasizing the ways terroir affords new sociocultural distinctions. As they write, "Our argument is that Brock draws from the symbolic and material resources from the Lowcountry to introduce distinctions that make it difficult to say that all food is the exact same, and thus interrupts the assumption that food can easily be exchanged with one another." The notion of "heritage" itself generates an intensification of activity, a sense of purpose and directionality that adds incorporeal "brightness" to mere soil.

The third chapter, "Food Pornography" by Casey Kelly, takes us "up" another agential layer as it considers the hyperintensive impact of food corporations as they have transformed the social landscape of cooking and eating by deploying pornographic visual tactics in their marketing appeals. As Kelly states, "the rhetorical work of pornographic food images is to addle the consumer with ineffable desire and, thus, generate affective attachments to the kinds of excessively indulgent and visually spectacular foods that are manufactured by industry for mass consumption." Pornographic visual tropes are made into enthymemes by corporations seeking to lure consumers away from their own kitchens; Kelly demonstrates how the neon allure of "food fetishism" bends bodies away from the home and toward ready-made foodstuffs. His emphasis on the affective dimension of foodporn is where this chapter's conception of agential force resides.

The fourth chapter, "Rhetorically Strange Foods" by Jeff Rice, takes us further "up" with a historical and cross-cultural mapping of culinary strangeness. Rice's concern is with the cultural line-dotting that determines how and when one particular food counts as tasty and familiar versus another that is labeled weird and foreign. Whereas Kelly's chapter emphasizes the over-coded tactics food corporations use to influence consumer choices, Rice's chapter enacts a form of critical divergence within the plane of cultural signification. In a move that resembles Timothy Morton's notion of *ecognosis* ("it is like becoming accustomed to something strange"), Rice seeks to "dislodge" familiar readings of strangeness in a critical act of attunement to the sheer weirdness of *all* culinary distinctions.[45] As he puts it, "I explore a number of supposedly unfamiliar food practices to ask how their rhetorical construction might allow for an unheimlich intervention on my part, a defamiliarizing gesture that contrasts traditional focuses such as exoticism or critiquing otherness." Rice wants to show how what might seem strange is already familiar, and vice versa, and in doing so offers a conception of agential intensification in the form of critical attunement.

Building off Rice's culinary cartography, *Cookery*'s fifth and final chapter, by Donovan Conley, "More than a Membrane," grapples with the question of the political in light of the conundrums raised by agrilogistics. Beginning with the premise that most of what happens socially (ecologically speaking) happens "off stage," Conley wrestles with the phenomenon of invisible influence. Acknowledging the social power, and creative allure, of invisible influence, he nevertheless argues for a notion of the political that rises above the undulating meshwork of the social itself. Conley's chapter insists that any notion of the political must organize itself around real antagonisms—the social space where discourse and conditions clash—and must hazard new articulations, or dotted lines, as aesthetic bids on alternative futures. The political work of social change, Conley argues, emerges from the untenable contradictions between how things are and how they might otherwise become. To echo Stormer, the political is born out of a collective drive to resolve hunger's blockage.

Together, the chapters in *Cookery* illuminate various strata of an ecologized rhetoric. What emerges from the layers is a portrait of influence that accentuates delivery/style (the modalities of contact) and arrangement (the contours of form) as the featured terms of an agriculturalized rhetorical canon. The countless ways that bodies touch, affect, impinge, inhibit, accelerate, and compel (etc.) one another, giving rise to new social formations and "structures of feeling," is the central work of rhetoric operating ecologically. Food exhibits these dynamics in an especially potent way, which is why modern industrial agriculture is the dominant ground of so much that counts as social influence today. Amazon's acquisition of Whole Foods, for almost $14 billion, reminds us that modern industrial agriculture is itself hungry for ever greater levels of commercial saturation. Omnipresent-yet-reflexive consumption seems to be the goal of the emerging relations between Amazon's home delivery juggernaut and Whole Foods' ethos of conscientiousness. Through the matrix of technology, geographical distribution, digital commerce, and the utopian promises of individual convenience, we may predict the hastening fragmentation of food's social terrain.

The Amazon-Whole Foods merger raises the stakes of home delivery as the increasingly prevalent domain of commercial exchange. The trend toward consumer capitalism and the experience economy means that corporations are seeking ever more intimate connections with potential customers, jostling to invent new schemes that close the gaps between producers and consumers; here, delivery becomes the privileged mechanism by which new eyeballs and stomachs are courted. The recent history of media content delivery tells us everything we need to know about the shifting ecology of bodily contact. Back in the early 1980s, we used to rent both VHS machines and movies together; then the machines became affordable enough for home purchase. Then we drove to the nearest "mom and pop" video store to rent our movies, but because each store was independently owned, we had to obtain rental cards from each one, which entailed bringing along three forms of ID every time we wanted to rent from a new store. Eventually Blockbuster came along and streamlined the process, as a result of which we spent weekend nights strolling through the aisles of Blockbuster searching for titles; we rented our movies, drove them home, and then drove them back four days later when they came due. Then Netflix came along, with the sole initial purpose of unburdening consumers of the driving part of movie renting, instead shipping envelopes with DVDs directly to our homes through the mail. More recently, of course, everything changed with the advent of online streaming; and now, with Amazon Prime—in conjunction with Netflix, Hulu, and iTunes—we can watch movies and TV shows in our homes, on multiple devices simultaneously, in between purchasing virtually anything that exists for sale on planet earth—delivered to our front doors tomorrow or possibly even later today.

If the legacy of agrilogistics is a social landscape saturated by the rhetorical contours of polyvalent production, and if modern industrial agriculture's cheapening logic of quantification results in ever greater levels of commercial saturation, and if saturation is a form of influence, then the Amazon-Whole Foods merger establishes *delivery/style* and *arrangement* as the primary canons of an ecologized approach to rhetoric.[46] The question of rhetoric is ultimately the question of any given form of influence, as Dickman and Rivers elaborate in chapter 1, and influence is a form of touch. Hence rhetoric is fundamentally a matter of the ways in which bodies and objects (including the objects we call subjects) touch and sway and bump into and impinge upon—that is, court—one another. Our inventions mean little if they remain stored in the garage, undelivered, unseen, unused. Morton helps establish this point when he notes, "To deliver anything so we humans can see it you need rhetoric. You need some kind of glamour. . . . I'm going to suggest that rhetoric isn't just ear candy for humans, or even for sentient beings. I'm going to suggest that rhetoric is what happens when there is an encounter between any object, that is, between alien beings."[47] Rhetoric as an encounter between alien objects, including the objects we call subjects, brings us back to Socrates and Callicles and the civic drama of relationality. Rhetoric describes the manner of influence that emerges between bodies and things, and the task of eco-minded rhetorical scholars is to describe and explain the particular quality and distinctiveness of a given emergence; to account for the particular shapes that bodies come to assume in common, and to spy out new openings for shapes untaken. Indeed, Stormer and McGreavy make this assertion when they write, "Rhetoric's ontology, approached ecologically, considers how the qualities of relations between entities of all sorts, not just among humans, enable different modes of rhetoric to emerge, flourish, and dissipate."[48] *Qualities of relations* is the standout idea here. Both rhetoric and ecology take shape through the unique and particular ways that bodies and entities deliver "goods" back and forth between themselves; goods like intoxication (Dickman and Rivers, chapter 1), or terroir (Young and Eckstein, chapter 2), or desire (Kelly, chapter 3), or strangeness (Rice, chapter 4), or invisibility (Conley, chapter 5). Each chapter in this volume takes up the task of describing and explaining emergent relational qualities. We rarely forge distinctions in the rigidly formal manner of Socrates, in *Gorgias*, but the business of social change and political reformation, however understood, entails the labor of re-dotting and reconfiguring the boundaries that constitute the stakes of shared living. What we hope to have shown is that this activity emerges from a layered foundation of material formations that count, rhetorically speaking, at least most of the way down.

NOTES

1. Plato, *Gorgias*, trans. Walter Hamilton (New York: Penguin, 1960), 46.

2. James L. Kastely, *Rethinking the Rhetorical Tradition: From Plato to Postmodernism* (New Haven: Yale University Press, 1997), 7.

3. Here we are indebted to Brian Vickers's reading of Plato. See his *In Defense of Rhetoric* (New York: Oxford University Press, 2002), particularly the second chapter, "Plato's Attack on Rhetoric."

4. Plato, *Gorgias*, 43.

5. *Gorgias*, 47.

6. Richard Weaver expounds on the definitional method of discovery: "To define is to assume perspective; that is the method of definition. Since nothing can be defined until it is placed in a category and distinguished from its near relatives, it is obvious that definition involves the taking of a general view . . . perspective, detachment, and capacity to transcend are all requisites of him who would define." See his *Ethics of Rhetoric* (Davis, CA: Hermagoras Press, 1985), 108. Kenneth Burke provides additional insight when he writes, in *A Grammar of Motives* (Berkeley: University of California Press, 1969), "In both Platonist and neo-Platonist versions of transcendence, the dialectician begins with the particulars of the senses, with the images of imagination—and he subjects these to progressive transformations whereby their sensory diversity is thoroughly lost in generalization, the structure being completed in the vision of the One" (429). Generalizing outward from sensory diversity toward the formal unity of the One is precisely the move we wish to underscore and trouble.

7. Burke, *Grammar of Motives*, 24.

8. Jessica Moss, "Pleasure and Illusion in Plato," *Philosophy and Phenomenological Research* 72, no. 3 (2006): 504.

9. Katie Zebrowski, "Alinea Phenomenology: Cookery as Flat Ontology," in *Rhetoric, through Everyday Things*, ed. Scott Barnett and Casey Boyle (Tuscaloosa: University of Alabama Press, 2016), 56.

10. Plato, *Gorgias*, 99.

11. *Gorgias*, 114.

12. *Gorgias*, 148.

13. Kastely, *Rethinking*, 14.

14. See Sonja Foss and Cindy Griffin, "Beyond Persuasion: A Proposal for an Invitational Rhetoric," *Communication Monographs* 62, no. 1 (1995): 2–18.

15. Alexis Shotwell, *Against Purity: Living Ethically in Compromised Times* (Minneapolis: University of Minnesota Press, 2016), 4.

16. Timothy Morton, "Where the Wild Things Are," *LA+: An Interdisciplinary Journal of Landscape Architecture* 1 (Spring 2015): 5.

17. Some notable works include Melissa A. Goldthwaite, ed., *Food, Feminisms, Rhetorics* (Carbondale: Southern Illinois University Press, 2017); Casey Kelly, *Food Television*

and Otherness in the Age of Globalization (Lanham, MD: Lexington Books, 2017); Ashli Quesinberry Stokes and Wendy Atkins-Sayre, *Consuming Identity: The Role of Food in Redefining the South* (Jackson: University Press of Mississippi, 2016); and Carlnita P. Greene and Lynn M. Walters, eds., *Food as Communication/Communication as Food* (New York: Peter Lang, 2011).

18. Camille Bégin, *Taste of the Nation* (Champagne: University of Illinois, 2017), 13

19. Michel de Certeau, Luce Giard, and Pierre Mayol, *The Practice of Everyday Life Volume 2: Living and Cooking*, ed. Luce Giard and trans. Timothy J. Tomasik (Minneapolis: University of Minnesota Press, 1998), 177.

20. Bégin, *Taste of the Nation*, 13.

21. Jane Bennett, "Edible Matter," *New Left Review* 45 (May/June 2007): 134.

22. Burke, *Grammar of Motives*, 159–60.

23. Jane Bennett has written some wonderful books about this very phenomenon. On the concept of ecological "weirdness," see also Timothy Morton, *Dark Ecology: For a Logic of Future Coexistence* (New York: Columbia University Press, 2016).

24. Donovan Conley, "The Good Body, Skilled in Eating," *Pre/Text* 21, nos. 1–4 (Spring–Winter 2001): 9–34.

25. Burke, *Grammar*, 208.

26. George Kennedy, "A Hoot in the Dark," *Philosophy and Rhetoric* 25, no. 1 (1992): 1–21.

27. Key recent works include Thomas Rickert, *Ambient Rhetoric: The Attunements of Rhetorical Being* (Pittsburgh: University of Pittsburgh Press, 2013); Barnett and Boyle, *Rhetoric through Everyday Things*; Christian Meyer and Felix Girke, eds., *The Rhetorical Emergence of Culture* (New York: Berghahn Books, 2011); Douglas Robinson, *The Deep Ecology of Rhetoric in Mencius and Aristotle: A Somatic Guide* (New York: SUNY Press, 2016); and Bridie McGreavy et al., eds., *Tracing Rhetoric and Material Life: Ecological Approaches* (New York: Palgrave Macmillan, 2018).

28. Some of Nathan Stormer's key pieces include "Thinking Ecologically About Rhetoric's Ontology," written with Bridie McGreavy in *Philosophy and Rhetoric* 50, no. 1 (2017): 1–25, and "Rhetoric's Diverse Materiality: Polythetic Ontology and Genealogy," *Review of Communication* 16, no. 4 (2016): 299–316.

29. Nathan Stormer, "An Appetite for Rhetoric," *Philosophy and Rhetoric* 48, no. 1 (2015): 100.

30. Stormer, "An Appetite for Rhetoric," 102.

31. Rickert, *Ambient Rhetoric*, xiv. Emphasis added.

32. Stormer, "An Appetite for Rhetoric," 102.

33. Timothy Morton, "Dark Ecology," 42–44.

34. Morton identifies three principles of agrilogistics as: 1) The Law of Noncontradiction is inviolable; 2) Existing means being constantly present; and 3) Existing is always better than any quality of existing. See Morton, *Dark Ecology*, 47.

35. This example comes from Morton's essay "She Stood in Tears Amid the Alien Corn: Thinking through Agrilogistics," *Diacritics* 41, no. 3 (2013): 95.

36. Morton, "'Where the Wild Things Are,'" 6.

37. Morton, "Wild Things," 4.

38. Kenneth Burke, "Definition of Man," in Burke, *Language as Symbolic Action:*

Essays on Life, Literature, and Method (Berkeley: University of California Press, 1966), 6.

39. Thomas Rickert, "Rhetorical Prehistory and the Paleolithic," *Review of Communication* 16, no. 4 (2016): 355.

40. See Edward Schiappa, "Second Thoughts on the Critiques of Big Rhetoric," *Philosophy and Rhetoric* 34, no. 3 (2001): 260–74.

41. David Depew, "Revisiting Richard McKeon's Architectonic Rhetoric: A Response to Richard McKeon's 'The Uses of Rhetoric in a Technological Age: Architectonic Productive Arts,'" in *Reengaging the Prospects of Rhetoric: Current Conversations and Contemporary Challenges*, ed. Mark J. Porrovecchio (New York: Routledge, 2010), 38.

42. Rickert, "Rhetorical Prehistory," 353.

43. Bryant writes, "There is no distinct sort of stuff that composes the social. Rather, the social is nothing more than the way in which different types of machines are bound together in an assemblage. The social is power lines, roads, mountain ranges, rivers, people, animals, factories, microbes, computers, spirits, money, satellites, soccer balls, gods, signs, laws, liturgies, sporting events, television shows, fluorescent lights, buildings, groups, institutions, flees, and rats. . . . The social is not a specific sort of stuff, but is another word for the 'ecological.' A social assemblage is an ecology." See Levi Bryant, *Onto-Cartography: An Ontology of Machines and Media* (Edinburgh: Edinburgh University Press, 2014), 190–91.

44. These "machinic" qualities are culled from Bryant, *Onto-Cartography*, 28–29.

45. Morton, *Dark Ecology*, 5.

46. Modern industrial agriculture operates according to a "cheapening" logic of quantification. This logic is superbly captured in Raj Patel and Jason W. Moore, *A History of the World in Seven Cheap Things: A Guide to Capitalism, Nature, and the Future of the Planet* (Oakland: University of California Press, 2017).

47. Timothy Morton, "Sublime Objects," *Speculations II* (May 2011), 208–9.

48. Stormer and McGreavy, "Thinking Ecologically," 3.

1

Brewing Influence

The Mixology of Morals

Katie Dickman and Nathaniel A. Rivers

"The essence of intoxication is the feeling of plenitude."
—Friedrich Nietzsche

Alcohol is more than the signification we pour into it. It is also a thing that pours itself into us, and we are often, as the legal designation eloquently puts it, *under the influence*, vulnerable to its effects. This influence is of course a risk (to life and limb and liver), but it is a risk that leverages and generates fruitful forms of sociality that emerge through the activity of inebriation. Indeed, when we drink, we are not so much under the influence as taking part in its generation—a drinker must drink to become drunk, and the drink, drunk, must inebriate. Debra Hawhee has written of the need for rhetoricians to "consider more deeply the constitutive roles of sensation in participatory, rhetorical acts."[1] Inebriation is such a sensation. Furthermore, sensation is but one physical process in the larger diagram of influence—a diagram of alcoholic influence that shares the same component parts with the diagram of rhetorical influence and that is mirrored in the production processes of each.

Considering the constitutive role of sensation requires engaging just how a sensation is generated among and along bodies in environments. In particular, alcohol works together with human bodies to create the conditions for a range of risky rhetorical performances. These conditions mirror the mechanisms by which alcohol's inebriating capacities are formed—namely, brewing and distilling—which include processes of "contamination" by yeast just as persuasion is a sort of contamination by influence. Drunkenness is a rhetorical force that constitutes, to borrow words from Nathan Stormer and Bridie McGreavy, "a distributed sense of capacity derived from mutual vulnerabilities between entities."[2] Tracing the collectivities of rhetorical ingredients that create and those that actualize such potentialities through shared vulnerability, we mark the effects of imbibing as a kind of collaborative, productive rhetorical contamination. Attending to alcohol in this way invites us to consider how particular sets of material relations generate specific forms of social, political production, thereby allowing us to ecologically engage and evaluate our (material) rhetorical performances, which are necessarily political. Vulnerability denotes an ontological condition, as we will show, but it likewise connotes an attitudinal stance. Vulnerability discloses itself (or we disclose it) as a mode of rhetorical existence shot through with contamination, which in turn renders rhetoric both possible and necessary. Following Stormer and McGreavy, we "start from an orientation that presumes connectedness and attachment between all manner of things and that sees beauty and value in rhetoric's unruly variability."[3]

We focus on rhetoric as a sensuous aggregate of influence. Alcohol helps us to trace the yeasty ways that influence works as a risky, vulnerable, and already compromised (if not contaminated) process of becoming. Hence, the title's nod to Manuel DeLanda's "The Geology of Morals: A Neo-Materialist Interpretation": we treat the process of making and consuming alcohol as a way of getting at the thorny moral and ethical questions of and about rhetoric, which, historically, has been deemed corrupt and corrupting. "Under the influence" refers to that which is compromised, contaminated, and underhanded. But more than a metaphorical inebriation, which is not a stand-in for rhetoric's influence, it is of a kind *with* it. DeLanda writes, "There is, no doubt, some element of metaphor in my use of the terms, but behind the appearance of linguistic analogy there are, I believe, common physical processes behind the formation of real meshworks and strata which make all the different usages of the terms quite literal."[4] DeLanda distinguishes between metaphor and physical processes with the examples of the phrases "class struggle is the motor of history" and "a hurricane is a steam motor." In the former, "motor" is being used "in a purely metaphorical sense"; in the latter, it is not: "rather we are saying that hurricanes embody the same diagram used by engineers to build steam motors."[5] Deleuze and Guattari use the term "abstract machine" to refer to this diagram shared by very different physical assemblages. Thus, there would be an "abstract motor" with different physical instantiations in technological objects and natural atmospheric processes.[6]

So too for us with alcohol and rhetoric, both of which are instantiations of sensual aggregates of contaminants that move and motivate.[7] Contamination, or as we will later discuss, intoxication, is such an abstract machine churning out the dynamics of suasion—a common physical process diagram shared by the production of rhetorical influence and that of alcohol. Intoxication speaks to a condition of vulnerability, and so Stormer and McGreavy's deployment of vulnerability activates the analogue machine in cultivating a (slightly) tipsy rhetoric of influence.

In order to come to know better the process of brewing alcohol, particularly beer, and to understand the creation and actualization of rhetorical acts as following a similar recipe, this chapter develops its argument through beer's production and consumption stages. These stages are organizational tools, certainly, but again they should not be misunderstood as merely symbolic analogies. DeLanda compares geological and social strata not simply because the notion of social strata draws upon the geological structure of layered sediments but also because that structure in both instances is created in a physically similar way. So just as mashing must follow milling in order to lead eventually to a proper boil for brewing, so too is this chapter, and all rhetorical acts, composed of contingent and effectual processes.

Influence is a compelling term in its capacity to denote a kind of persuasion ("to have influence" or "to influence") that is implicitly ecological. Influence also attends to relations in the way a friend can be a good or bad influence. Influence is a capacity rather than an instrument, and it is a capacity that is irreducible to a particular rhetorical agent. Influence directs us far more than we exert it. This distinction lies dormant in the etymology of the term, which moves away from uniquely *human* power dynamics and toward the capacity of environments to flow. Going back in time from Middle English and Old French and then to Latin (*influentia*), influence was generally sensed as "an influx" and "flowing matter." It likewise had astrological significance: "the flowing in of ethereal fluid," which affected "human destiny." Influence was wielded by humans; it crashed into them in waves. Later, in the thirteenth century, it came to designate "imperceptible or indirect action exerted to cause changes."[8] There is a compelling tension here that complicates influence in ways resonant with our inebriated focus in this chapter. Influence is a flow that is indirectly causal.

Vulnerability is openness or an opening up to influence. While we employ the term *influence*, we agree with Barbara Biesecker's critique of the "the logic of influence" that structures rhetoric. "This long-held conception of the rhetorical situation as an exchange of influence defines the text as an object that mediates between subjects (speaker and audience) whose identity is constituted in a terrain different from and external to the particular rhetorical situation. Hence, the rhetorical situation is thought to modify attitudes or induce action on the part of *consummate individuals*."[9] We mean by *influence* not the mediation of already existing subjects but rather an ontological condition of which we take and are a part. Influence flows and so us with it. We aim not merely to recoup the term but to redeploy it given its concatenation with inebriation. It's a productive influence that isn't simply the end of rhetoric but is a prerequisite for rhetoric at all. Of course, the risk of such a rhetoric that is not itself an exchange among consummate individuals is that it becomes a form of imperceptible influence upon which we cannot deliberate: it's an influence that seemingly defies reason giving. There are obviously questions of power and mastery and even wealth connoted here as well, which, admittedly, makes it troubling to revisit and maybe revive the term. A wealthy individual with *influence* does not have to provide persuasive reasons: influence already flows through them, sweeping other reasons away. Such imperceptible influence is precisely what Donovan Conley confronts in his contribution to *Cookery*. Conley puts it this way: "Rhetoric traditionally finds itself tugged in both directions, shuttling back and forth between rational judgment and nonrational sensation."[10] For Conley, dis/articulation is an aesthetic practice of bringing elements together and/or breaking them apart.

This political work of rhetoric necessarily entails troubling the clean formal boundaries rendered by Plato in *Gorgias*. Examining politically oriented food practices that seek to surreptitiously shape desires, Conley fears a turn away from agonism and the distinction-making work of dis/articulation. Vulnerability speaks to influence as rhetorical, which is to say agonistic. The influence described by Conley is one that eschews agonism in favor of a rhetoric of frictionless transmission of a priori goods and values. The vulnerability of alcohol, like Plato's *Gorgias*, dramatizes the agonism of influence, which, following Conley, we could describe as an ongoing practice of dis/articulation.

"Nonrational sensation" is certainly something our chapter tacks toward, but not, we argue, as a permanent move away from rational judgment, which Conley seeks to make or at least keep room for in rhetoric. Instead, we chart sensation as a stage in the process of being affected, an integral part in the diagram of the influence machine. We tactically pursue vulnerability as an aspect of judgment—vulnerability is an important precondition for rhetorical deliberation. We hope to show that alcohol, as an analogue, does not perform rhetoric as the kind of hidden influence Conley deftly critiques. Alcohol, its own vulnerable operation, attunes us to this ecological substrate of rhetorical activity while also generating a telltale exhaust, the hangover, that makes its influence felt.

Our claim is that alcohol registers as influence without necessarily falling back on an overly hermetic understanding of reason and subjectivity. Alcohol wears its consequentiality on its sleeve—it renders as either reward or regret, and possibly both. Alcohol is thus a way of thinking influence that partakes neither of the logic critiqued by Biesecker, which presupposes consummate, that is, invulnerable subjects, nor the wholly nonrational or invisible, sensual influence beyond all articulable reason questioned by Conley. Alcohol is a solution that dissolves any neat and tidy separation between the two. Alcohol's production, its fermentation, is marked by exposure and contamination—its version of sensation. Indeed, contamination is the central, agonistic process by which the transformation of ingredients begins, and it is made possible through vulnerability, through exposedness to influence. Vulnerability is not simply something we can come to experience; vulner-ability is a capacity (another term developed by Stormer and McGreavy) that affords reason and deliberation as such. In describing the bilaterality of argument as opposed to the unilaterality of "coercive correction," Douglas Ehninger writes that the arguer lays their view "on the line for examination and criticism."[11] In so doing, he writes, "the arguer lays himself on the line also."[12] This being on the line "places the 'person' in a position of genuine existential 'risk.'"[13] We will keep this notion of existential risk close by, and we will return to it in the end.

PART ONE: PRODUCTION

"You can never buy beer, you just rent it."
—Archie Bunker

The production of beer flows through the stages of milling, mashing, lautering, boiling, fermenting, conditioning, packing, and consuming. Beer becomes through the contingency of each step. Milling requires a particular kind and degree of exposedness or vulnerability, a kind similar to that being established in the introductory section of this chapter. Milling is the priming stage: it prepares the barley by opening it to influence through peeling back its hull to reveal the starches inside that upon being boiled become fermentable sugars. Care and precision at this stage are essential, and as beer aficionados at Chicago's The Beer Temple taproom describe it, "The key is to crush the grains enough so that it exposes the starchy center of the barley seed without damaging the grain hulls that encase them. If the crush is too coarse, not enough of the starch will be converted to fermentable sugars. If the crush is too fine, the husks, which act as a filter bed for the brew will be destroyed, and the brew will become gummy and unusable."[14] This chapter's milling stage opens readers in a similar way, as do all good arguments, priming them to receive the information contained herein according to the terms we use, to the definitions of terms to which we adhere, and to the arena in which we've placed the discussion.

Before you feel invaded, let's understand how alcohol—and, similarly, the seed of persuasion—is already inside us. In his celebrated study of the mechanics of foods and their interactions in cooking, food scientist Harold McGee wonders why our bodies are equipped to break down alcohol—this thing we only in the last few thousand years *accidentally* learned how to produce.[15] By the grace of Bacchus, our body's ability to process alcohol was part of us long before alcohol-to-be-drunk was discovered and produced, and it was there to encounter the alcohol that our own body produces. "Like the yeasts who [sic] produce it for us," McGee writes, "our bodies sometimes make small amounts of alcohol in the process of metabolizing carbohydrates. And the bacteria that inhabit our intestines excrete larger amounts, which we immediately absorb and must deal with."[16] If yeast and its eventual alcohol are contaminants, then we are, in a sense, influenced from the start. That alcohol is something we "must deal with," means that it calls for and warrants our attention but even further that it physically cannot be denied it. Alcohol, like suasion, is a call that requires response; we must affirm or deny it, but we cannot deny the part of it that already resides within us.

The analogy between alcohol and suasion is an abstract machine in the same way that hurricanes are a steam motor per DeLanda. The correspondence is physical, not purely metaphorical. In the language of abstract machines, the enzyme that breaks down alcohol, alcohol dehydrogenase (ADH), could be said to share the same physical processes with discernment—the step that follows influence but comes before succumbing entirely to it. We are always contaminated with choice. We depend upon discernment to choose. As with discerning, "Our absolute dependence on ADH to detoxify ourselves has certain unfortunate consequences. While exercise helps us burn food calories more rapidly than we would while sitting, alcohol is not available as an energy source to our muscles until ADH has worked on it: so, exercise will not sober us up any faster than sleeping will. Nor does any other food, whether coffee or some other folk remedy."[17] As with alcohol, so too persuasion: our bodies cannot be purified of it through virtuous activity or drink, i.e., the exercise of reason. Instead, reason is the effect of having been contaminated with the need to choose. It is the effect caused by our innate vulnerability to be influenced and to be influencers, paired with the seed of suasion already planted within us by our own sowing. The physical diagram that charts our influence by alcohol matches the schema by which we come to be persuaded to make and accept choices.

DeLanda draws upon Deleuze and Guattari's notion of abstract machines not only to bring home his point that analogues need not be merely metaphorical but also to make concrete the distinction he draws out between strata and what he calls *meshworks*. Strata, like the organization of rocks or social classes, are products of organization guided by homogeneity. Meshworks are less hierarchical, and yet the two are not mutually exclusive but rather often give rise to one another. An anchor point for meshworks in rhetoric is an ecological understanding of rhetoric; meshworks, like ecologies, "[link] together a wide variety of heterogenous elements . . . which are articulated through interlock, that is, by their functional complementarities."[18] Influence is a meshwork in this sense; it is, both physically and metaphorically, a conglomeration of ingredients and processes fueled by influence and extending it in turn. Their relationships with one another, their organizing themselves into a process or entity that influences beyond itself, is a matter of all parts' vulnerability. This vulnerability is mutual and as such is each entity's functional complement to all the others. That is, vulnerability functions to produce a meshwork formed by and toward the effect of intoxicating influence.

The mashing stage of brewing applies heat to the barley, continuing the transformation of its starches into sugars that upon exposure to yeast will become consumed in the name of flavor and alcohol. Starch, in this instance, maintains its vulnerability to material suasion and change but it remains—and perhaps *becomes* even more so—a pointed vulnerability. Its being is a focused response to the actors with which it interacts, heat in this case, in the name of what they are to become together, as a meshwork. This is an affirmative understanding of materiality and its suasiveness, and it is one that political scientist and new materialist Jane Bennett teaches us is a physical—and one might argue, geological—notion of the bubbling up of persuasion. She writes, "If the eaten is to become food, it must be digestible to the out-side it enters. Likewise, if the eater is to be nourished, it must accommodate itself to the internalized out-side. In the eating encounter, all bodies are shown to be but temporary congealments of a materiality that is a process of becoming, is hustle and flow punctuated by sedimentation and substance."[19] And so when we encounter assumptions about drinking alcohol as a cause for transformation of the drinker's being, or at least her personality, we must apply some degree of heat to those assumptions in order to reach a more precise understanding of the relationship between the imbiber and the imbibed.

Bennett helps us here again, affirming that material ingested and digested does in fact alter us as a result of altering itself, i.e., making itself digestible by us. She writes, "Food, as a self-altering, dissipative materiality, is also a player. It enters into what we become. It is one of the many actants operative in the moods, cognitive dispositions, and moral sensibilities that we bring to bear as we engage the questions of what to eat, how to get it, and when to stop."[20] In other words, what we ingest, how we digest it, and determining when we've had our fill are collective decisions among all the players involved—enzymes, digestibles, occasions, flavors, disposition and effects upon it, and many more of which we are often unlikely to perceive.

The process of brewing beer is a series of alterations done unto barley. We've seen already the milling and mashing that expose and then act upon the starches within it. Lautering and boiling are the next stages, and they, among other things, filter and sterilize the mixture of ingredients. In the lautering stage, sugar becomes further separated from the barley, its no-longer-useful bits now called the "spent grain." The spent grain becomes waste at this point, removed from the sugary liquid, or wort. Now cleansed of its spent parts, the wort is boiled, sterilized, and flavored.[21] But this is not the end. Instead, each of these stages is preparation for the most vulnerable stage of brewing: fermentation.

Belgium's Cantillon Brewery is a study in this pointed vulnerability. The brewery is home exclusively to lambic-style beers, those slightly sweet and tad bit sour inebriants brewed using open, or spontaneous, fermentation. Deriving yeasts from the atmosphere, brewers here forego the now more common packaged and predictable brewer's yeast in favor of specifically local, wild bacteria. Cantillon's brewing process is a drama of contamination. Owing the inception of this historical brewing process to happy accident, that is, to early beer makers lacking the wherewithal to sanitize their equipment, modern brewers actively seek out conditions that expose their worts to these wild contaminants. This openness, and even the more contained exposure to packaged brewer's yeast, is still a dance of contamination wherein things can indeed go wrong but also, through following the steps and keeping time, things can go very right.

Transformation through suasion is mostly considered a success. In the beer brewing process, contamination by yeast controls and gives focus to the mixture of ingredients, setting them on their path toward becoming beer. This is its first and molecular occasion of openness to persuasion's own self-becoming. Similarities abound in the staple adage (over)used to describe the condition of showing our true colors, the *real* us not confined to neat lines but filled in far beyond them through the release of inhibitions.

As we noted in the milling and mashing stages, the exposedness of the barley's starches is a pointed vulnerability, just as is the starch-turned-sugar's exposure to yeast—both enactments of the brewing process that give a clear focus to the mixture of the ingredients. But even the vulnerability it plays upon and expands in us is one of focus rather than derailing contamination. Ours and others' is a challenge to this notion that inebriation leads exclusively to distraction, in particular distraction of a negative sort. In his essay "Drinking Games," Malcolm Gladwell explores *how* people drink, making way for insights that expand beyond queries about what or how much people drink and why. He contends, contra most everyone's assumptions, that alcohol is a drug that sharpens and directs the focus of the drinker rather than solely blurring it. Parts of the drinker's focus are blurred, this he does not deny, but this is not the same as insisting that we drink in order to lose or forget focus. Instead, he writes that drunkenness is not the release of inhibitions but that it is instead myopia. Now this is not exactly the nearsightedness that occasions the prescribing of glasses and contacts, although goggles of a certain form have been said to accompany a beer-fueled date.[22] What drunkenness as myopia attunes us to is the blurring of the environmental influences far from us and the sharpening of those close enough to touch us. Gladwell explains it this way: "Disinhibition suggests that the drinker is increasingly insensitive to his environment—that he is in the grip of an autonomous physiological process. Myopia theory, on the contrary, says that the drinker is, in some respects, increasingly sensitive to his environment: he is at the mercy of whatever is in front of him."[23] In this way, alcohol, and all sorts of influence, serve as a particular kind of filter. That filter does less to suss out contaminants, however, and is more closely aligned with something like a condition requiring corrective lenses—focusing us more on what we *can* see, even lacking perfect sight. This sight is a creative, conditional moment wherein rhetoric emerges within a meshwork of kinds of influence that include both clear focus and myopia.

PART TWO: CONSUMPTION

"Quickly, bring me a beaker of wine, so that I may whet my mind and say something clever."
—Aristophanes

There is the *preparation* of alcohol. There is also the preparation *of alcohol*. That is to say there is something preparatory about alcohol as an influence under which we operate and in which we participate. These dual prepositions are built into Aristophanes's phrase "so that I may." The mind is whetted. Alcohol, then, continuously functions as a conglomeration of ever more ingredients, techniques, technologies, and locations. The process of brewing extends itself: it flows out and through. A group of people imbibing take in or are taken in by many circulating ingredients. People in a pub are poured into the pub as the pub is poured into them. A public house is not a container filled with drunks but an aggregate of ingredients already contaminated by the ideas of the public house and the patterns of consumption it suggests. To borrow again from DeLanda, alcohol is a "self-consistent aggregate [. . .] (or meshwork [. . .]), the result of the coming together and interlocking of heterogenous elements."[24] We take as given that the brewing of influence we are describing extends back to the places where the ingredients come from and forward into the bodies and locations in which these aggregated ingredients, as alcohol, are consumed and translated into influence (flowing through terroir to tap to table to toilet). As Ehren Plugfelder notes, "Beer is an interesting example of an increasingly persuasive constellation of humans and nonhumans, as the large network of microbreweries serving local or regional populations has blossomed in recent decades."[25] Ingredients must be grown; once grown they must be selected; once selected they must be brewed; once brewed they must be packaged; and once packaged they must be consumed. This whole, nested series of practices is influence generating influence—whetting the mind. Jeff Rice, describing craft beer, writes, "Craft is a network of influence."[26] Indeed, Rice's book *Craft Obsession* points to how the influence brewed of alcohol must necessarily include the social networks of that alcohol. The network is multiple and its coverage impressive: "With physical distribution, the networks function as trucks and pallets making their way from point (brewery) to point (warehouse) to point (retail or restaurant). Networks also function as advertising, the delivery of the message via social media to the consumer. The networks are also affective, tapping into emotions or feelings we carry over other activities and interests."[27]

Rice's use of aggregation resonates with our comprehensive cultivation. He writes, of assumptions, that they "stem from the aggregation of culture (how a beverage is thought to be consumed), habit (the kinds of bottled beverages one buys), memory (thoughts of packaging), and taste (what comes of a bottle that shares the same size)."[28] Furthermore, this means that not everyone's aggregations are the same all of the time. These aggregations are cultivated from unique sets of ingredients that are sometimes, but not always, in sync. Indeed, their synchronicity is itself up for grabs—it too is being composed under and with the influence.

Debra Hawhee's work on Kenneth Burke and the body, on Burke and drugs in particular, links rhetoric and bodily modification (and bodily influence), suggesting such aggregates impact epistemic and ethical production. With Burke, she writes, "the body is where something like beliefs and even morals are formed."[29] As such, transformations of the body are necessarily transformations of subjectivity and sociality. One of the takeaways for Hawhee and Burke and us is that drugs such as alcohol are similar to poems infused with "druggy" language, in that both "can be figured as transformative substances, [because] both induce affective change, and both tap into bodily rhythms, creating and increasing receptivity."[30] The connection between drugs and poems is an important one for rhetoric, positioning influence and dirty rhetoric as a suasive brew, an aggregate. The abstract machine hums. Burke writes, "In becoming receptive to so much, he becomes receptive to still more."[31] Burke writes of the reader, but from a point of view informed, as Hawhee's research shows, by his own research into drug use. Hawhee builds from Burke's influence, writing of "the rhythmically receptive body overtaken by new chemically induced 'rhythms,' resulting in a new sense of 'normality.'"[32]

There are then aggregates built through alcohol. Humans take part in, and even direct, but don't quite master this process: alcohol is always a surprise, drunkenness certainly is. Alcohol is never only itself but always an aggregation that is nevertheless also an actor moving in the world, which aggregates it still more. At every stage of the aggregate, the process is one defined (or defiled) by contamination; nothing is ever purely itself because whatever it is there is always some else (some other) there. Influence is then multiple and dirty, as rhetoric has always been understood. This influence is originary and presymbolic,[33] opening up both hospitality and hostility.

Influence flows everywhere. This is why alcoholism perplexes. It is morally, medically ambiguous. We see the alcoholic walking into the bar and ordering a drink all while fully aware that they are an alcoholic. There must be an indescribable influence at work that is without beginning or end. It is here that addiction comes to suggest something quite compelling if not deeply dangerous. Given how addiction can be understood, alcohol suggests that rhetoric's influence exists beyond simple cause and effect dynamics, which likewise prove distinctly unhelpful in understanding or even thinking alcoholism usefully; the causes and effects of alcoholism, like rhetoric, enfold one another if not collapse them. Recall our earlier discussion of the process of inebriation hinging on, in part, our body's prior receptivity to alcohol. The need is activated by desire, which is here nothing but a differently constructed or construed need. The body desires what it needs as it needs what it desires. Addiction discloses this influential logic, which marks rhetoric as well. Being receptive to something, furthermore, obfuscates needs and desires, or at least complicates the movement of influence. A prior receptivity would suggest some need—we tend to understand as *needs* those things "wired" into the body: something adaptive. But that it is for alcohol, which doesn't always file under food and shelter (indeed, it is subject to excise taxes otherwise known as sin taxes and enforced by excise police), speaks of *desire*. That our bodies can be primed for something we police as an excess confuses our commonsense assessments of intoxication and influence. It's hard to moralize on top of that. Cause and effect and need and desire cannot be easily used to make sense of and decide upon something like addiction because they are the exhaust of addiction, which arrives ahead of time. Alcohol does not cause addiction any more than addiction makes sense without the presence of influential agents. Addiction makes a risk, which resides both inside and outside of use as a feature of living already influenced, compromised, and contested lives. Alcohol addiction also marks the politics of vulnerability.

We certainly do not wish to elevate alcoholism or make it synonymous with rhetoric. We are not all alcoholics, and we recognize alcoholism as a real and unique influence in the world. The process of influence, the abstract machine, however, is telling. Alcoholism is a disease disclosing that even simple choices of what to drink, when to drink, where to drink, and how much to drink are always ever an aggregate. There is something telling in a child's misunderstanding of English's weird, nonstandard approach to tense: *I drunk too much* instead of *I drank too much* violates standard usage but gestures toward, at the same time, a confusion of subject and object. I was drunk too much. With the present simple passive we get *a lot of beer is drunk on college campuses.* Of course, admittedly, the slurred speech of drunks often accomplishes much the same. As F. Scott Fitzgerald once remarked, "First you take a drink, then the drink takes a drink, then the drink takes you."[34] Who or what is drunk is a question exposed by inebriation.

With the complications of alcoholism, we feel how the abstract machine of influence bears upon subjectivity: our senses of self, our own limitations, and our responsibilities—the ethics, the ethos of inebriation. It might very well be, as the trope goes, that our true selves are revealed in intoxication. While not without its appeal, however, the "inhibition" narrative speaks to our other insatiable desires to circumscribe influence. Alcohol is not doing anything to me but making me more me: taking off inhibitions and intensifying the singular "we" that lurks beneath. The workings of alcohol are far more insidious than all that. If only the drunk me was somehow a more authentic me rather than a hangover inducing acknowledgement of the lack of any singularly authentically me lurking somewhere safe from all influence, but that "true" self always feels multiple, disjointed, and confused. The contamination of inebriation changes the aggregate and generates a different set of influence. Inebriation is thus an aggregation of an always already operating dynamic. If anything, alcohol is a challenge to any narrow understanding of subjectivity. One becomes untethered from a particular formation of self rather than further yoked to one as the disinhibition argument has it. Besides, the notion of alcohol removing inhibitions on an otherwise stable and singular self is more than a little depressing. We do lots of things sober that we would like to image as *really us* during the sober light of day. Again, this is the risk and reward of intoxication: the explosion of self. Well, that and gross motor impairment, memory loss, and liver failure, lest we forget the particular material consequences of consuming alcohol in excess.

Rhetoric is ever under the influence. Again, drunkenness is certainly not an unquestioned good, nor is it some idealized state. What we mark here is that intense inebriation reveals an ontological process ever at work. That we typically describe inebriation as not about influence but as about inhibition is telling as well. We have yet to think drunkenness through enough. The self is not a kernel but an emergent aggregation. Of course, drunk me is the real me. The sober me is the real me. They are all the real me—multiple versions, each one a real one because it is shot through with a not me that is nevertheless me. Under the influence, as well as before, during, after, and next to influence is still more influence.

There can be no denying that alcohol carries with it and creates risk. Indeed, we must acknowledge that the vulnerability of inebriation and intoxication can often lead to violence and, especially, sexual violence. Jenny Rice is right to choose the word *wound*. Imagining sobriety as a shield, a prophylactic, is far from a full-throated critique. Alcohol complicates embodied interactions. The stakes are not lost on us. In his *Sexual Violence in Western Thought and Writing: Chaste Rape*, Victor Vitanza argues "that rape (sexual violence) was a, if not the, hidden founding principle for the constitution of Western cultures."[35] Vitanza writes, exposing the intensity of his claim: "I contend throughout that no act against another is more devastating than rape (sexual violence); no act is more impossible to think, read, write than rape. Contrary to arguments against my statement, I insist that we must come to think that the death of a human being is less devastating to community than the rape of, or rather acts of sexual violence against, a human being."[36] Bert L. Vallee, in his *Scientific American* piece, "Alcohol in the Western World," writes, "Alcohol today is a substance primarily of relaxation, celebration and, *tragically, mass destruction*."[37] In Gorgias's *Encomium of Helen*, language is likened to a drug in what might be an early abstract machine used to describe and defend the actions of Helen of Troy, which, Vitanza argues, is a prominent telling/version of the founding act of sexual violence and abduction.[38] Helen is moved by a foreign contaminant. There is, however, an ambivalence even here, or precisely here there is ambivalence necessarily. The language of drugs as an effective influence suggests the presence of receptors to which those drugs bind. We are not suggesting that Helen is now back on the hook, but that we are always already given over to influence. Influence is fraught: it is problematic in the most meaningful and consequential way. If the Trojans had been sober, the horse would never have made it inside the gates. But we, as Stormer and McGreavy write, "must shift [the commonplace for conceiving of action] from *violence*, imposition of one on another, to *vulnerability*, relational openness."[39] Sobriety is safety, then, but such safety surely denies the half-life of rhetoric that Jenny Rice has described (and to which we will return): "The wounds created and experienced in the sensorium can subject us to forms of social trauma. Yet, the experience also affirms our half-life in rhetoric's nondiscursive sphere."[40] To participate in rhetorical life is to be under the influence of what lies beyond us on account of its already being inside of us in the form of vulnerable exposedness.

Let's return to *intoxication* as a form of contamination, which is at the heart of this abstract machine and at the core of our collective anxiety about influence. *Toxic* means to be imbued with poison, coming from the word *toxicum*, meaning "poison for arrows" in Greek; *τοξικὸν φάρμακον*. Poison for arrows became simply poison. Intoxication then means to poison someone or to stupefy or excite with a drug or alcohol. A toxin is a poison projected. A toxin, then, is not simply a kind of passive poison but an active projection. Intoxication is a kind of attack. But, ponders Anne Pollock, "we even might find a perverse joy here."[41] Importantly, Pollock reminds us, "The contemporary presumption of an opposition between inebriation and health is not inevitable. Permanent intoxication is a reasonably common condition of human societies historically, and people may well have enjoyed that state," which is a great pun on a *state* as both a bodily and political entity.[42] Alcohol lubricates social aggregates, making them work by shifting our focus on various influences and therefore their impact on us. As Vallee writes, "Alcohol also served to distract from the fatigue and numbing boredom of daily life in most cultures, while alleviating pain for which remedies were nonexistent."[43] Intoxication does not necessarily spell doom and gloom for a collective.

In fact, the Greek symposia relied on alcohol as a sort of barometer of one's changing level of inhibition toward the welcoming of various influences. "At heart," writes Standage, "the symposium was dedicated to the pursuit of pleasure, whether of the intellectual, social, or sexual variety."[44] Furthermore, he argues, "Plato saw drinking as a way to test oneself, by submitting to the passions aroused by drinking: anger, love, pride, ignorance, greed, and cowardice."[45] And Pollock herself argues, "Being intoxicated is an ambivalent state: impaired, yes, but also released from responsibility in particular ways that can be both dangerous and pleasurable."[46] Intoxication is something to explore and even experiment through. To recall Burke, drugs create new forms of reception and response. Pollock's ambivalent state is a critical response to a certain "homophobia embedded in [. . .] ecological alarm."[47] Endocrine disruption, for instance, appears to result in homosexual behavior in birds such as male ibises.[48] Pollock is careful not to dismiss concerns about reproductive health, but she does want to mark the ways, as above, that health, purity, and sobriety are unquestioned goods: "From a queer feminist perspective, should we automatically decry the flourishing of nonreproductive male pairs of birds?"[49] She continues, "Yeah, maybe these birds are 'fucked up' by their polluted environment. But I do not think that I am saying too much about my own experiences with intoxication, or assuming too much about that of the reader, to point out that it can be fun to be fucked up."[50]

This becoming-fucked-up spans not just the biological, as we have suggested, but the social. Jeff Rice, tracing the distribution of alcohol across digital and physical networks, notes craft beer's ability to mess with our feelings of place: "To be fucked up is to be completely confused about any given taxonomic distinction. To be fucked up is to be caught in the social network of folksonomic distinctions. When we are fucked up, we have to allow our senses, tastes, and intellectual framework to open up."[51] The movement of alcohol, its distribution and consumption "fucks up assumptions."[52] And so we are back to the symposium and the practical value of imbibing: a measure of our openness to influence. Indeed, the Greeks, so devoted to the value of becoming fucked up, developed a special cup that allowed them to drink while reclining, the preferred repose for symposium. The shape of the *kylix*, from which we derive the word *chalice*, "enabled the drinker to drink whilst recumbent, as was the case in the symposia."[53] The design of the cup suggests that one can recline without pulling away from the sphere of influence and instead continue drinking it up from the vulnerable, recumbent state that makes influence possible.

The consumption of alcohol is historically woven into our collective history. Yet still we are afraid of influence. We are yet as ever troubled by influence and in particular bodily influence that appears to operate beyond the bounds of consciousness, control, and critical intervention. "When discourse abruptly loses its explanatory power," Jenny Rice writes, "and when we suddenly find ourselves undergoing experiences that *make us be*, we are within the participatory realm of sensing."[54] We have argued that alcohol—as inebriation, as intoxication—is a particular mode of what Rice would call making us be; and this form of being exceeds the discursive, the explanatory, the reasonable. In their treatment of cooking, Justin Eckstein and Amy Young suggest that that which exceeds also primes: "The resolution of difference into a meal always leaves a remainder—a residual tendency that feeds forward as attraction or aversion."[55] This calls back to Burke on drugs and poetry and gestures toward the preparatory effects of alcohol. As we are arguing with our mixology of morals, rhetoric is necessarily dirty from beginning to end. "Affectability or "response-ability" requires that things be inherently vulnerable to one another. Vulnerability is not a state of being at risk but of being entangled, which requires being at risk in varying passive-active relations."[56] Influence aggregates. Influence is a contaminated network in which we cannot help but participate.

PART THREE: HANGOVER

"Shut up, all of you. I'm dying!"
—Bernard Black

Though consuming seems to be the final stage of the brewing process, this stage can often extend beyond an evening of drinking. This final, bright-light-averse, please-pass-quickly stage is the hangover. It is of course possible, and advisable, to drink without becoming inordinately drunk. It is true, too, that the effects of alcohol consumption linger after nights both mild and wild. In fact, countless recent scientific studies outlining the health benefits of moderate alcohol intake have arrived to great non-scientist fanfare with much clinking of glasses. Even in moderation all drinking makes us drunk in some fashion insofar as it discloses something about material suasion and our innate susceptibility to it, and this is the central conviction of this section.

The material mechanics of a hangover are more complex than dehydration and the lack of (good) sleep. In many ways, the cause and effects of this feeling reveal our body to be not only susceptible to suasion but also warming to it quite quickly and even politely. Harold McGee describes it in this way: the symptoms of a hangover are the result of compensation for the general depression of the nervous system. The higher the peak blood alcohol level reached, the longer that the peak is maintained, the more drastic the effects on the body, the stronger its compensation, and the more pronounced the aftereffects. Having another drink, then, restores the conditions to which the body had become accustomed, as well as lightly anesthetizing it. But this only postpones the hours of reckoning, and if repeated may eventually lead to alcoholism and the necessity of suffering a true drug withdrawal.[57]

There are two aspects of McGee's description that reveal our vulnerability to suasion and transformation as not merely one of exposedness to Otherness, to that out-side Bennett mentions, but also acceptance and affirmation of that out-side's influence. First, in McGee's description we see that a hangover is the effect of the body adjusting to the out-side's contamination in order to accommodate it rather than to rid itself of it. Recall here McGee's description of the body's alcohol-processing enzyme ADH as the only catalyst of sobriety—neither virtuous activity nor drink can succeed in ridding the body of alcohol. Neither does ADH succeed in ridding the body of alcohol, for it instead breaks it down, consumes it, makes it a part of the body such that the effects of drunkenness subside but other effects remain still. In addition to this risky exposedness, the catalyst is also depended upon. Secondly, once alcohol and so too persuasion is inside of us—which as we learned earlier from McGee is, always, from the start—we want more of it. Having another, it restores us to the conditions to which we have become accustomed—to always being under the influence.

The hangover, then, is a condition too of rhetorical life. Rhetoric's hair of the dog is the continued cultivation of a pointed vulnerability in social agents, and it establishes a reliance upon being exposed to influence, to contamination, in order to feel and be alive again. Not to be under the influence of persuasion is to be in withdrawal, or rather is to withdraw, from social production. Both the dizzying effects of alcohol and the crushing effects of hangovers are the abstract machines of intoxication and contamination, of influence—those poisoned tipped arrows sprung on us and in us and through us. And these are often arrows we seek, placing ourselves at the brewery and the bar. We get drunk because we are already drunk, already shot through with others. We get drunk not simply because we consume alcohol but also because we are the kinds of beings who can become drunk. And so, the abstract machine hums within rhetoric as well.

All this is to say that we will always be working through influence, which we are always under. Not so much overcoming as responding to it, being tested by it, participating in it. Plato suggested that drunkenness was not so much an end in itself but a means for risky yet fruitful exchanges. These exchanges are made possible by the risk introduced by the consumption of alcohol, which surely harms and wounds us. Jenny Rice writes of the experience of this sometimes head-splitting interaction, arguing that "we reclaim the wound as a new way of coming to terms with the material, sensorial, and epistemic spheres of rhetorical engagement."[58] Stormer and McGreavy resonate with Rice, writing, "'Material vulnerability' stresses the vitality at stake in rhetorical capacitation: powers of transformation thrive and fade when enacted because wounding covaries with openness. The word 'vulnerable' comes from the Latin 'vulnus' or 'wound.'"[59] What does the hangover give us as we give ourselves over to it? We here return to Conley: "As a paradigm of rhetorical action, I argue that this venture [to surreptitiously shape the desires of fast food consumers] stands as a cautionary tale in the embrace of *invisible influence*."[60] What marks alcohol and the hangover in particular, here is its perceptibility. The influence is felt, experienced, participated in and then, if to excess, regretted and pained. Alcohol is an influence that foregrounds agonism. The stakes of influence are, in part, defined by the felt consequences of that influence. The hangover is an open wound. Alcohol is a risky practice of being under the influence that works through the wound and considers the profound role of sensation in the composing of our collective life. "The question," which we here mark as political, "is what to make of wounds when they occur?"[61] How can such vulnerability be cultivated as it is in the brewing of beer? Nietzsche, Stormer and McGreavy remind us, "famously upended the value of wounding with his motto 'spirits increase, vigor grows through a wound' (1968, 465). Wounding can be vitalizing."[62] This vitality is the fermenter of rhetoric's "unruly variability,"[63] which then, in turn, grounds any kind of political, ethical deliberation. Vulnerability isn't the end of reason, but its beginning.

EPILOGUE: THE SOBER POLITICIAN

"Oh, I pity the abstainer."
—Percy Dovetonsils

The forty-fifth President of these United States, Donald J. Trump, famously (or infamously if you ask us) doesn't drink. In the dim bar light of this soused chapter, it actually makes a great deal of sense that he abstains. That is, his temperance packs some (albeit speculative) explanatory power. It's fitting, in other words, that the POTUS who strikes many as a most volatile commander-in-chief is always sober (as he is surely sobering). It's counterintuitive surely, given that on the campaign trail Trump seemed to activate and embolden the kind of voter that we frequently describe as the "drunk uncle," but bear with us: it makes sense in light of our claims for rhetoric and alcohol under the influence. Trump presents a test case for rhetoric, which, as Conley writes in this collection, "shuttl[es] back and forth between rational judgment and nonrational sensation."[64] How does Trump's disavowal of a particularly influential form of sensation bear upon his simultaneous and counterintuitive disavowal of rational judgment?

We want to tread lightly here, of course. Seth McLaughlin of the *Washington Times* has reported, "[Trump] has said that his older brother Fred's struggles with alcohol, which led to his death, convinced the billionaire businessman never to drink a drop."[65] While, of course, Trump "has dabbled in the booze business," he "swears off the stuff personally."[66] McLaughlin reports, "'I look and I see what it does to people when they lose control,' Mr. Trump said at a campaign stop in December. 'If you don't drink and if you don't take drugs, your children are going to have a tremendously enhanced chance of really being successful and having a good life and having a happy life.'"[67]

George W. Bush, as a recovering alcoholic himself, also abstained. Only Barack Obama, in the twenty-first century, has been the president one could have a beer with. His famous Beer Summit marks the political import of throwing back a couple of cold ones to begin a difficult deliberation. That said, Trump's sobriety, at first glance, strikes one as a move a reasonable man makes, but in fact it's more akin to the wall he wants to build. Recall Ehninger, who writes that argument is "person-making" because it is necessarily "person-risking."[68] Comedian Chelsea Handler, in an interview with Bill Maher, articulates Trump's sobriety in a similar way. "Yeah, I find that very suspect. I don't like [. . .] when people don't like to broaden their horizons. [. . .] I mean, you don't have to abuse alcohol in the way that I do, but I would appreciate people experimenting [. . .] with drugs, hallucinogens, alcohol, loosen up a bit. Otherwise, there's a control factor that I don't trust, and that's [. . .] what creates a despot or somebody like a Donald Trump [. . .] You know. And it's untrustworthy."[69]

Trump's sobriety is not about his enlightened commitment to clear-headedness; it is of a piece with his constant effort to project invulnerability. If we have shown anything in this chapter, it is that alcohol, from beginning to end, is an invitation to be made vulnerable—vulnerable to the influence of others, nonhuman and human alike. The forty-fifth president's projection of invulnerability moves through his various policy commitments as well. His denial of the present climate crisis functions as an erasure of the vulnerabilities of the environment and how we remain influenced by changes in the environment. Indeed, Bruno Latour has argued that Trump's proposed border wall and travel ban cannot be understood apart from his climate change denial: "If we wish to defend our identities, we are also going to have to identify those shapeless, stateless migrants known as erosion, pollution, resource depletion, and habitat destruction."[70] Perhaps Trump has read *The Odyssey* and fears Trojan horses let in by drunken border guards. In short, to "Make America Great Again" requires a perverse form of temperance that is itself intemperate: the closing of all material and conceptual borders. Trump abstains not from drinking—though he does—but from vulnerability itself. No in*toxic*ation allowed here: build the wall and un-build the EPA.

The ethics and politics of vulnerability, then, are disclosed by the figure of Trump. We are suggesting neither correlation nor causation between abstinence (for which there are many good reasons) and intemperance. What we are doing is using one to get at the other: to think through influence and intoxication in affirmative terms—to think of vulnerability as a necessary and ethical component of politics. Stormer and McGreavy nicely capture the stakes of vulnerability in medical terms. "At its limit, resistance becomes immunity to influence, which saps strength because it is nonresilient; in medical terms, nonresponsiveness is death. Oddly, absolute vulnerability is equally immune to influence."[71] Vulnerability is thus not a fix, but a potentially productive problematic. Recall the process of fermentation, which can be understood as the most vulnerable state of the brewing process: "pointed vulnerability," we called it. The crucial takeaway there is that while vulnerability is baked into the process, it can be cultivated, which is to say at times dampened and at others intensified. For example, the brew masters at Cantillon ratchet up vulnerability in order to achieve the desired result. Analogically, what kind of commons could we compose along the lines of pointed vulnerability, so characteristic of the brewing of lambics in Belgium? Stormer and McGreavy write, "For a material ecology to persist (likewise for the rhetorics emerging in that ecology), it must absorb the consequences of its openness, which it does by being adaptive, not recalcitrant."[72] "And so the interchange continues," Ehninger writes, "each party alternately arousing himself as a result of the action by the other."[73] Rhetoric divorced from vulnerability remains unabsorbent: it provides no hangover, no regret, no bittersweet so-called "walk of shame" that can productively and agonistically mark compromise. If we want politics to persist, we must maintain it as vulnerable. Biesecker writes of the *logic of influence* (as opposed to our *vulnerable to influence*): "If any symbolic act is no more than an event that links distinct and already constituted subjects, then rhetorical discourse bumps up against the impenetrable and unalterable space of the subject, 'a threshold which none of the strategic [responses] manages to cross.'"[74]

There is no workable reason here; there is only nonresponsiveness, which is surely the death of rhetoric. We desire no last call.

NOTES

1. Debra Hawhee, "Rhetoric's Sensorium," *Quarterly Journal of Speech* 101, no. 1 (2015): 17.

2. Stormer and McGreavy, "Thinking Ecologically About Rhetoric's Ontology," 4. (See introduction, n. 28).

3. "Thinking Ecologically," 3.

4. Manauel DeLanda, "The Geology of Morals," Presentation, Virtual Futures 95 Conference, Warwick University, UK, May 26, 1995.

5. DeLanda, "Geology of Morals."

6. "Geology of Morals."

7. While DeLanda, whom we follow here, uses *assemblage*, we use *aggregate* to expose the messy mixture of ingredients that don't always add up to an assembled whole.

8. Oxford English Dictionary Online, s.v. "influence."

9. Barbara A. Biesecker, "Rethinking the Rhetorical Situation from within the Thematic of Difference," *Philosophy and Rhetoric* 22, no. 2 (1989): 110.

10. Donovan Conley, "More than a Membrane," 106–7.

11. Douglas Ehninger, "Argument as Method: Its Nature, Its Limitations, and Its Uses," *Speech Monographs* 37, no. 2 (1970): 104.

12. Ehninger, "Argument as Method," 104.

13. "Argument as Method," 105.

14. "Brewing Process," *The Beer Temple*, accessed January 17, 2017, http://craftbeertemple.com/videoblog/brewing-process/.

15. Harold McGee explains that our understanding of how fermentation works is quite recent. He writes, "Until well after 1800, brewers simply knew that whatever it was that caused fermentation could be found concentrated in the foam of newly made beer or wine . . . Each region had its characteristic yeasts, which infected beer or wine spontaneously and were then passed on from batch to batch. Needless to say, poor quality was not uncommon in these centuries when nature, through human ignorance, was allowed to take its course . . . In 1836 came the first small steps toward understanding fermentation." See *On Food and Cooking: The Science and Lore of the Kitchen* (New York: Collier Books, 1984), 434.

16. McGee, *On Food and Cooking*, 496.

17. *On Food and Cooking*, 496.

18. DeLanda, "Geology of Morals."

19. Jane Bennett, *Vibrant Matter* (Durham: Duke University Press, 2010), 49.

20. Bennett, *Vibrant Matter*, 51.

21. Joshua M. Bernstein, *The Complete Beer Course* (New York: Sterling Epicure, 2013), 22–23.

22. Malcolm Gladwell, "Drinking Games," *New Yorker*, February 15, 2010.

23. Gladwell, "Drinking Games."

24. DeLanda, "Geology of Morals."

25. Ehren Helmut Pflugfelder, "Rhetoric's New Materialism: From Micro-Rhetoric to Microbrew," *Rhetoric Society Quarterly* 45, no. 5 (2015): 454.

26. Jeff Rice, *Craft Obsession: The Social Rhetorics of Beer* (Carbondale: Southern Illinois University Press, 2016), x.

27. Jeff Rice, *Craft Obsession*, 98.

28. *Craft Obsession*, 109.

29. Debra Hawhee, *Moving Bodies: Kenneth Burke at the Edges of Language* (Columbia: University of South Carolina Press, 2009), 70.

30. Hawhee, *Moving Bodies*, 67.

31. Burke, quoted in *Moving Bodies*, 67.

32. *Moving Bodies*, 70.

33. D. Diane Davis, *Inessential Solidarity: Rhetoric and Foreigner Relations* (Pittsburgh: University of Pittsburgh Press, 2010).

34. "Great American Writers and Their Cocktails," NPR, December 15, 2006, http://www.npr.org/2006/12/15/6624971/great-american-writers-and-their-cocktails.

35. Victor Vitanza, *Sexual Violence in Western Thought and Writing: Chaste Rape* (New York: Palgrave MacMillan, 2011), xii.

36. Vitanza, *Chaste Rape*, xii.

37. Bert L. Vallee, "Alcohol in the Western World," *Scientific American* 278, no. 6 (1998): 85.

38. Vitanza, Chaste Rape, xii.

39. Stormer and McGreavy, "Thinking Ecologically," 10.

40. Jenny Rice, "Pathologia," *Quarterly Journal of Speech* 101, no. 1 (2015): 40.

41. Anne Pollock, "Queering Endocrine Disruption," in *Object-Oriented Feminism*, ed. Katherine Behar (Minneapolis: University of Minnesota Press, 2016), 183.

42. Pollock, "Queering Endocrine Disruption," 186.

43. Vallee, "Alcohol," 83.

44. Tom Standage, *A History of the World in 6 Glasses* (Toronto: Anchor Books, 2005), 62.

45. Standage, *A History*, 64.

46. Pollock, "Queering," 185.

47. "Queering," 183.

48. "Queering," 183–85.

49. "Queering," 184.

50. "Queering," 185.

51. Jeff Rice, *Craft Obsession*, 114–15.

52. *Craft Obsession*, 115.

53. "Kylix," *Wikipedia*, last modified October 20, 2016.

54. Jenny Rice, "Pathologia," 44.

55. Justin Eckstein and Anna M. Young, "Cooking, Celebrity Chefs, and Public Chef Intellectuals," *Communication and Critical/Cultural Studies* 12, no. 2 (2015): 206.

56. Stormer and McGreavy, "Thinking Ecologically," 13.

57. McGee, *On Food and Cooking*, 497.

58. "Pathologia," 44.

59. Stormer and McGreavy, "Thinking Ecologically," 14.

60. Conley, "More than a Membrane," 107.

61. Stormer and McGreavy, "Thinking Ecologically," 14.

62. "Thinking Ecologically," 14.

63. "Thinking Ecologically," 3.

64. Conley, "More than a Membrane," 106–7.

65. Seth McLaughlin, "Candidates' Disagreement on Drinking Shines Light on Presidential Temperance," *Washington Times*, October 20, 2016, http://www.washingtontimes.com/news/2016/oct/20/hillary-clinton-donald-trump-disagreement-on-drink.

66. McLaughlin, "Presidential Temperance."

67. "Presidential Temperance."

68. Ehninger, "Argument as Method," 109.

69. Handler was quick to add, "I respect people who are sober because they had a problem and they got sober." See *Real Time with Bill Maher*, episode 14:36, directed by Paul Casey, aired October 28, 2016, on HBO.

70. Bruno Latour, "The New Climate," *Harper's Magazine*, May 2017, http://harpers.org/archive/2017/05/the-new-climate.

71. Stormer and McGreavy, "Thinking Ecologically," 15.

72. "Thinking Ecologically," 20.

73. Ehninger, "Argument as Method," 105.

74. Biesecker, "Rethinking the Rhetorical Situation," 110.

2
The Terror and Topoi of the Lowcountry

Anna Marjorie Young and Justin Eckstein

"I had a gut feeling that to evolve as a chef, I had to understand the dirt."
—Sean Brock

Perhaps one of the greatest moments of modern food television is the sixth season of Anthony Bourdain's "Parts Unknown," in which Bourdain and chef Sean Brock are three-sheets drunk and eating at a Waffle House in Charleston, South Carolina. Bourdain had never been to a Waffle House and to say he was skeptical is an understatement. Brock, on the other hand, is utterly and completely earnest in his devotion to Waffle House. It is, it turns out, the place that made him want to be a chef—he watched people cooking at a quick pace for inebriated customers but saw them providing an incredible experience through a commitment to hospitality. And it is Brock's connection to place—in this case to Waffle House—that marks his authenticity as a Public Chef Intellectual (PCI) and advocate for a kind of terroir-to-table ethos of farming, harvesting, cooking, and serving food.

The Public Chef Intellectual PCI recognizes that food is a central political concern involving issues and challenges in our natural environment, our labor relations, our immigration policies, our histories and traditions, our sense of culture, and our connections to one another and larger communities. As such, PCIs educate the public about any number of food-related topics, from where food comes from (How is it farmed? How is it raised? How far does it have to travel? How is it packaged and sold?) to the histories and traditions of a particular place (Who brought this food to this place? How do people from this place prepare this food? How do they serve it? Is it part of a ceremony or celebration? Has it been appropriated by others?) to how to use what is considered garbage and turn it into dinner (What food gets labeled waste? What happens to food waste? How many people are food insecure? How could we rethink what we throw away to reduce waste?). The PCI is also an advocate for a particular approach to food and food culture. That is, PCIs do not merely describe food and its contexts but actively persuade audiences to see food differently. As Justin Eckstein and Anna M. Young write, "The PCI's established gravitas, ethos, and platforms for advocacy enable a level of persuasive and rhetorical efficacy that grassroots activists often lack. PCIs promote cuisines, define expectations, set trends, create markets, provide fodder for think pieces, and more."[1] They may write books or cookbooks, use Twitter or Instagram, make appearances on carefully selected food media, or use their own restaurants as sites of advocacy. They may do all these things. The PCI's object is to argue for a more humane, more sustainable, more just vision of food and food culture.

Like other PCIs, Brock is motivated to address ecological concerns related to farming practices and the distance food travels to reach the grocery store or the restaurant. But he is also a kind of intellectual ambassador to Southern cooking, a style of cuisine that tends to be treated as unserious or beneath the talents of someone like Brock. Brock's advocacy is very much centered on the Lowcountry as a terroir, a reclamation of forgotten seeds from foods that died out during Reconstruction, an obsession with his grandmother Audrey's cast iron pans, and an amplification of the role of vegetables on the Southern table.

Both in his restaurants and in *Heritage* (the bestselling cookbook that is the subject of this chapter), Brock amplifies his commitment to what we are calling "placed" food, to terroir. Terroir is a wine term that describes how place expresses itself as taste. Terroir is not a scientific measure, nor is it something we can see or feel. Historically, terroir emerged as a way of designating a particular plot, sometimes mere hectares, of soil as special, distinctive, and specific in terms of the fruit, the know-how, the climate, and ultimately, the wine that place produced. Initially, terroir was also a political strategy—it protected local French wine makers against a market that was burgeoning in the early twentieth century. At the same time, access to French wine through a globalized purchasing system enabled elites to exercise cultural capital; they could get their hands on the "good stuff." In response, terroir was a business decision, a node within a broader food system; at the same time, it had a significant ripple effect on wine specifically and agriculture generally. Whereas it is difficult to identify a food's origin in a grocery store, a wine's origin is visible right on the label. Yet, terroir itself is an act of polyvalent invention—while it originated from a protectionist sentiment by French winemakers, both its history and its potential is beyond the capitalist reach of agrilogistics.

In this chapter, we posit that soil offers rhetors a physical and symbolic topos to invent responses to an agricultural system that frequently displaces food's origins. As we argue elsewhere, topoi are not only symbolic places from which we invent arguments but also literal places—soils—that can situate and contextualize those arguments.[2] Terroir is generic in that everywhere has a terroir, but it is as specific a designation as one can make to get at a place's uniqueness. That is, a terroir is at a distinct longitudinal and latitudinal axis. Found at that geographical axis, we argue, are the rhetorical axes of dirt, techne, and political context. These rhetorical axes shape what is grown, how it is grown, who prepares it, how it is prepared, who serves it, and how it is served. When food's origins are opaque, a return to physical, technical, and political context offers a powerful critique of that very opaqueness. To make this argument, we show the intersections between topoi and terroir through Brock's 2014 cookbook *Heritage*. Here, we outline the ways Brock as PCI rhetor (and others like him) can use soil, literally and rhetorically, to challenge dominant narratives and practices of industrialized food culture.[3] Our chapter reconsiders both terroir and topoi as not only symbolic but also material; in doing so, we uncover place as an argument in response to industrialized food.

The next section introduces the concept of topoi as a "place" people go to invent argument. Traditionally in rhetoric, topoi have been understood as metaphors, symbolic "locations" from which rhetors create arguments. Then, we conceptualize topoi as rhetorical terroir—a physical, material place that supplies rhetors with the resources to make particular arguments. Next, we turn to Brock's *Heritage* to illustrate how his Lowcountry terroir informs his broader critique of industrialized agriculture. We conclude by thinking about how terroir offers particular lines of critique against the ecological devastation and cultural degradation wrought by globalized food.

TOPOI

In classical conceptions of argument, topoi, or commonplaces, are stock formulas rhetors use to advance a standpoint. Aristotle tells rhetors to "select the grounds from which he should make his attack; secondly, he must frame them and arrange them one by one to himself; thirdly and lastly, he must proceed actually to the other party."[4] In short, topoi are where speakers "go" to invent, rationalize, foment doubt, or advance a case. They are uniquely charged, or "nutrient dense," locations of rhetorical possibility. From Aristotle's successor, Theophrastus, up to Peter Simonson's recent attempt at reinventing invention, topoi have occupied a central place in the annals of rhetorical scholarship. Reviewing centuries' worth of literature on topoi, John Muckelbauer remarks, "As a result of these proliferating metaphors, the rhetorical concept of topos has enjoyed an indescribably diverse and complicated history. While *topoi* have been used as heuristic devices to aid in discovering an audience's beliefs, they have also been deployed to formalize letter-writing and sermonizing methods, to generate the substance of an argument, to denote recurrent literary themes, and, as in common use today, to refer to the supposed main point or 'topic' of an essay or speech."[5]

Topoi have been conceptualized as a resource-rich ground of discovery, emerging through engaged agonism—a rhetorical and political struggle over what has meaning—and generated through collective intelligence. We focus on two features relevant to our conversation on Brock's terroir: the distinction between general and specific topoi and their corresponding locations.

First, as a source of invention, Aristotle conceived of topoi as both general (*koinoi topoi*) and particular (*idioi topoi*). Generalized topoi are lines of argumentation that "apply equally to questions of right conduct, natural science, politics, and many other things that have nothing to do with one another."[6] These commonplaces are applicable across rhetorical contexts and include "places" like *more or less likely* (if one thing is more likely to happen, something else is less likely to happen), *consistency of motives* (if a person has a reason to do something, she/he will probably do it), and *analogy* (if two things are alike in obvious ways, they will be alike in other ways).[7] These lines of reason are broadly applicable to many rhetorical situations. Particular commonplaces are, on the other hand, entirely context-dependent, or as Aristotle understood, particular to certain discourse communities. Particular topoi "are based on such propositions as apply only to particular groups or classes of things."[8] Carolyn Miller further specifies that particular topoi represent "points of connection between reasoning and the particularities of practical situations."[9] Scientists have specific lines of reasoning that apply only to their disciplines and norms, for example *evolution* or *scientific method*. In discourses about food and foodways, we might invoke topoi like *local* or *soul food*. That is, discourse communities employ a lexicon that is particularly valuable in the contexts in which that community most often operates.

Yet, rhetorical theorizing on general and particular topoi highlights the tension between sites having universal appeal versus those that are uniquely discrete. Carolyn Miller explains that Aristotle's generalized and particular topoi get caught "between his own clear desire to characterize rhetoric as an art based on universal principles of persuasion and his empirical observations of persuasion as materially grounded in the resources of particular situation."[10] She maps this tension as occurring between two different concepts of rhetoric: materialist and inferential. For Miller, the materialist approach connects rhetorical practice to concrete situations, while an inferential account of rhetoric searches for universalized principles that can be systemized and taught anywhere. Since antiquity, rhetoric has migrated from a practical art to handle specific circumstances to a pedagogical practice tied to the academy. Miller continues, "Rhetorical history as a whole further suggests a general historical movement from the materialist perspective to the inferential, from the situational foundation of rhetoric in social practices to the elaboration of a coherent and systematic art."[11] Here, the movement toward the generic subsumed specific topics, because their insight is less portable and amenable to circulation. The impulse to create widely applicable "news" in our scholarship has continued this trend towards the general and generalizable. Brock, though, dissociates food from a generic sense of anywhere and associates it with a particular place, in South Carolina's Lowcountry. Brock's is a rhetorical reclamation of particular topoi, an idioi topoi.

Second, topoi are understood as a metaphor for a place. For example, Quintilian described topoi as "the secret place[s] where arguments reside, and from which they must be drawn forth."[12] Scott Consigny locates topoi within rhetorical situations, as "a device, which allows the rhetor to discover, through selection and arrangement, that which is relevant and persuasive in particular situations."[13] And even Miller finds topoi to be "conceptual places that yield arguments possibly useful in a rhetorical situation."[14] In each of these different iterations, topoi designate a metaphorical space of invention. As Barbara Warnick points out, "few authors have speculated as to where these 'places' might be. When they do speculate, they seem inclined to locate that 'place' in the speaker's mind."[15] In short, topoi are conceptualized as a metaphor for a mental category but have not traditionally been *literal* places in rhetorical renderings.

Recently, though, rhetorical scholars have begun theorizing topos as a physical place. Greg Dickinson's work on the suburbs, for instance, foregrounds the physical environment as a topos. Dickinson writes, "Constructed of concrete and lumber and constituted through rhetorical inducements, the suburbs are symbolic and material enactments of the hopes for and concerns about the contemporary good life."[16] Here, the physical and symbolic facilitate the performance of the "good life." The physical environment supplies the stage that delimits available symbolic resources, and the symbolic "good life" provides normative modules that underwrite decisions. Dickinson continues, "While we might not be explicitly referencing well-conceptualized contours of the good life when we make everyday decisions, these decisions and actions are often structured by implicit theories of goodness and, at the same time, reveal and enact whatever principles of the good life we in fact believe."[17] Dickinson's work uncovers the generalizable commonalities (koinoi topoi) that stretch across physical places like Broomfield, Colorado, Las Vegas, Nevada, and Surprise, Arizona.

Considering topoi as material places requires an account of terroir. Terroir denotes a unique physical place—the way that dirt, techne, and political context come together to express regionality. It is a kind of haecceity, a "thisness," unique because it can only exist in one geographical place and because of particular geographical and cultural know-how. If the themes Dickinson identifies in three suburbs are generalizable topoi, then terroir is a particular topos anchored in a region's idiosyncrasies. In other words, terroir is not a general commonplace (koinoi topoi), a general understanding of an abstract region, but a specific one (idioi topoi)—*this* or *that* place. We argue that this generic-specific configuration is a site for rhetors to mine for arguments. This model of topoi comes from an understanding of terroir. For Brock it is South Carolina's Lowcountry that gives him the resources to critique globalized agriculture. The next section explores how the specificity of a region offers sites of invention.

RHETORICAL TERROIR

Terroir is the viticulture term for the influence of environment on wine, but more broadly locates wine in a politics of globalization. In the nineteenth century, the French coined *terroir* to differentiate their wines from the rest of what was circulating in a globalized wine market. "The use of ideas about place to make arguments about quality became increasingly important in the late nineteenth century," Amy B. Trubeck writes, "and it became part of a serious sociopolitical movement to protect French agricultural products."[18] There is no exact English translation of terroir, but it denotes territory as the site where nature meets culture: a physical plot of land and a cultural boundary, yet reducible to neither. In common parlance, terroir is invoked to describe a wine's taste, as if to apprehend the region's specificity in a glass. Terroir is the foundation of France's *appellation d'origine contrôlée* (AOC or DOC), a system of naming (*appeler* in French means "to call" but connotatively means "to name"—if you introduce yourself in French, you say *Je m'appele*, or "I call myself") that classifies and regulates wine in and from France. The AOC system operates on the notion that a particular plot of land gives rise to distinctive flavors and tastes that are not re-creatable elsewhere. France's system of appellation and other systems like it in Italy, Germany, and Spain are designed to be exclusive. Sparkling white wine made of Pinot Noir, Chardonnay, and Pinot Meunier can only be called champagne if it is from the Champagne region and has been deemed champagne by the Institut national des appellations d'origine (INOA), the French government institute that governs appellational designations and standards.

But what exactly makes each region unique? We define terroir as the interplay of three elements: dirt, techne, and political context. Dirt describes the material soil grapes are grown in; techne encompass methods of harvest, fermentation, and circulation; and political context involves the cultural conditions of a region that confer meaning onto a wine. Consider what is involved for something to be called *champagne.* It must be grown in dirt 100 miles east of Paris in the Northeast part of France. In this regard, the sparkling white wine from Napa you drank last New Year's Eve may have been a lovely bottle, but it is not and legally cannot be champagne unless it is from those particular hectares the AOC system dictates are Champagne. Champagne uses specific techne that yield distinctive flavors. Master vintners mix specific percentages of each of three grapes—Pinot Noir, Chardonnay, and Pinot Meunier—to create an identifiably "champagne-ish" taste. The shape of the bottle and the flute, champagne's designated stemware, are unique to champagne and are thought to preserve bubbles. Champagne is also double fermented, a process particular to champagne that creates its effervescence and bubbles.

Finally, terroir concerns a place's histories that imbue it with cultural meaning. France's kings were crowned in Reims, one of the major cities of Champagne, connecting the region to royalty and power. In our modern food system, a food's origins are obscured, but with wine, we are always aware of its story. Trubeck continues, "even though selling wine is a global business, and my local grocery store sells wines from three continents; knowing where the wine comes from, the grape varieties it contains, and perhaps the natural environment from which it comes still figure in the way I discern which wine to purchase."[19]

Although terroir is a viticultural term, the concept has migrated into rhetorical scholarship to theorize the meaning of place and to account for the material relations of an ecology that defines the capacity for agents to influence and to be influenced.[20] For us, terroir supplies rhetors a generic site to invent specific reasons in favor of the quality of an object—idioi topoi, or the generation of particularity from the homogeneous and opaque. Terroir can be found anywhere in the world (California, France, Italy, Chile, etc.), but it is specific because each place has its own unique features. If French wine makers find reasons to favor their wines in the generic features of a terroir (dirt, techne, and political context), then other rhetors can also draw inspiration from the specific elements within generic categories of place to argue for the importance of that place. Terroir allows arguers to discuss the soil, weather, climate, and evaluate the potential affect those things might have. Techne supplies a rich set of culturally learned strategies for managing the dirt like irrigation, plowing, fertilizing, fermenting, and so on. And political context introduces a temporal wrinkle to account for how antecedent events (the sedimentation of previous movements, migrations, and events) affect the chemical composition of soil, the creation and distribution of techne, and the circulation of bodies and narratives. Each of these different features provides a place for a rhetor to introduce a qualitative difference into an object.

Terroir, then, is the inventional ground of idioi topoi in a most literal sense. Rhetors can always draw upon the dirt—the way certain grains come to taste when grown in *this* and not *that* soil, the allure of specific technical traditions derived from a given region, or the particular constellation of socioeconomic struggles that mark a place (water shortage in the Southwest, or the loss of family farms in the Midwest)—to (re)generate values and appeals. This is a powerful realization in the context of food because it challenges the globalized trend of erasing regionality and agricultural diversity. Invoking terroir interrupts and disrupts this totalizing trend. When you go into a grocery store and are totally unaware of any ingredient's origin, when food becomes divorced from the natural life cycle, then the particular dirt of a particular place suddenly offers a powerful antidote to the opaque homogeneity of industrialized food options. By using terroir, Brock crafts food that is also an argument about foregrounding the importance of regionality in the definition of the good life. Brock's use of Lowcountry terroir as idioi topoi performs a counternarrative to the totalizing reach of modern industrial agriculture.

SEAN BROCK + *HERITAGE*

Chef Sean Brock grew up in Appalachian Virginia. Wise County, as he describes it, looks almost identical to the geography of the film *Coal Miner's Daughter*. Brock's childhood centered around traditionally gendered notions of food—every family had a garden, every man stocked his freezer with venison and catfish he had hunted or caught, every woman pickled and preserved and put up food in her larder. Though none of this food was fancy, there was inherent status attached to this kind of self-sustaining, semi-agrarian existence so prevalent in southwest Virginia. Brock is obsessed with his grandmother's cast iron pans and a return to menus featuring crops that died out during Reconstruction—his sense of place is what, in many ways, defines his cooking.

In 2014, Artisan Press published Brock's long-awaited cookbook, *Heritage*. On the cover of the dense hardcopy volume are Brock's heavily inked forearms, his hands cupping a colorful selection of Lowcountry dried peas and beans. The cookbook is divided into sections that hew to common physical locations on a Southern farm, including the garden, the larder, and the pasture. Brock is a storyteller in *Heritage*—his book opens with his own family's story that roots him steadfastly in the South as a student-turned-practitioner of time-honored southern foodways: shelling peas and beans with his grandmother under an old oak tree; planting and harvesting cabbage to make mixed pickles, a kind of "southern kimchi"; smoking a ham and hanging it in the dark basement larder. Photographs capture both individual ingredients and finished dishes significant to the Lowcountry. Brock gives considerable real estate in *Heritage* to local farmers, food historians, and small-batch producers from whom he sources whatever he cannot grow himself in his restaurants' extensive gardens. Interspersed in the narratives, cultural histories, and highlights of local growers and producers are some of Brock's favorite recipes to showcase Lowcountry ingredients and foodways. The recipes are by no means an afterthought; but unlike most cookbooks, they also are not the primary focus of the book. *Heritage* is an unabashed and earnest rendering of soil—what Lowcountry farmers and producers plant, grow, raise, and harvest, and the culture tied to that very particular plot of land. In *Heritage*, Brock rhetorically places his food in the terroir of the Lowcountry not only to highlight that place but also to use place itself to argue for a geographically local approach to food more broadly.

There is a central irony in *Heritage*. Very few who buy or read *Heritage* live in Charleston or South Carolina's Lowcountry—the book has been a *New York Times* bestseller, won a James Beard Award for Best Book of the Year in American Cooking, won an IACP Julia Child First Book Award, and is on its third reprinting. *Heritage* enjoys tremendous circulation across the country and around the world. And yet, the central argument of the cookbook is to use Lowcountry ingredients to make dishes like Hoppin' John, mustard greens with benne, and slow-cooked pork shoulder in tomato gravy with creamed corn and roasted baby Vidalia onions. The authors of this chapter live in Tacoma, Washington, three thousand miles from locally grown and sourced benne or okra. In other words, most of us cannot actually make Brock's recipes and still adhere to the central tenet of the book. Place, though, is a dissociative strategy—in this case, a way to dissociate food from modern industrial agriculture's increasingly globalized marketplace and tether it instead to a particular terroir. While we may not be able to recreate Brock's dishes using Lowcountry ingredients, we can begin to articulate place in our own kitchens and communities, symbolically and materially grounding our culinary practices in local soil. And so, while the book is, like all other cookbooks, a collection of tested and delicious recipes, its rhetorical-ecological value exceeds this fact. Cookbooks are not merely repositories of recipes, they are rhetorical machines that cultivate and naturalize—*enstructure*—new forms of domestic habitation.[21] Brock's book is a celebration of revival and reclamation, and a blueprint for public and political advocacy through food. *Heritage* articulates a counter vision to industrialized food through an invocation of soil. In so doing, the book reinforces food's social power to etch out a larger set of political commitments.

HERITAGE AS TERROIR

Although implicit, Brock's call for a return to the local terroir occurs against the backdrop of modern industrialized agriculture. If, as Donovan Conley and Justin Eckstein explain in this volume's introduction, agrilogistics describes the logic that constitutes humanity *out of* nature, then modern industrial agriculture (MIA) is a particular expression of that logic designed to accumulate capital in the hands of a few. MIA targets those "precapitalist" processes like photosynthesis or animal digestion as a site of value production for a globalized market.[22] While a feudal expression of agrilogistics spreads, organizing and distributing food in the service of securing power for a corporate aristocracy, MIA uses natural resources to harvest, amass, and centralize capital. What makes this form of agriculture *industrial* is that its goal is to render commodities interchangeable in the pursuit of infinite expansion and wealth generation.

The reduction of food to an exchange value creates what we call a logic of substitution, which stresses similar qualities while obscuring differences. A logic of substitution allows a tomato from *somewhere* to be the same as a tomato from *anywhere*; it unplaces food. When tomatoes can be grown anywhere, at any time, the potential for markets to extract value from them multiplies. Corporations can and do circumvent both material constraints, like weather systems and availability of sunlight, and cultural ones like labor laws and environmental regulations. In this framework, "people and things become mobile assets; they can be removed from their life worlds in distance-defying transport to be exchanged with other assets from other life worlds, elsewhere."[23] Moreover, when place becomes increasingly irrelevant to the generation of value, corporations can play regions against one another, as in the great Amazon headquarters sweepstakes, where state governments promise these corporate entities sweeping tax giveaways while ignoring environmental protections and labor standards. A return to place introduces distinctions that interrupt this logic of substitution, dissociating food from "anywhereness" and instead signaling its "thisness." Animating the material capacities of *this* place entails foregrounding unique historical particularities that resist easily equivalence.

In particular, we suggest that dirt, techne, and political context offer three valences through which rhetors, like Brock, may forge qualitative distinctions. Brock's decision to locate his book within the terroir of the Lowcountry interrupts the logic of substitution by using ingredients that, in some cases, are available only in that place. Of course, anyone can make Hoppin'

John, but not everyone can make Lowcountry Hoppin' John. The red beans should hail from the Sea Islands, and the techniques should be those perfected over generations of tinkering and toil. The exclusivity of the terroir and intersecting valences of dirt, techne, and political context provide the material resources for rhetors to craft a sense of place. For *Heritage*, the good life involves small farmers sustainably growing, raising, and/or cultivating foods specific to a place, and consumers having relationships with those farmers plus a toolkit to cook the food of *this* place.

First, dirt. Brock features ingredients that can only be grown in Lowcountry soil. His appeal to taste generates difference based in the unique flavors that food produce. The rhetorical association of difference with taste interrupts the logic of substitution. There are several examples Brock elaborates in *Heritage* aside from Carolina Gold Rice—benne, okra, and farro to name a few. These ingredients from this specific place combine to create recipes representative of that land. Hoppin' John is one such dish. Hoppin' John is to Low Country what étouffée is to New Orleans. It is essentially rice and peas, which you would not think would be evocative, but it is. In the cookbook, Brock recalls having ordered Hoppin' John at a restaurant and thought it was disappointing and incredibly bland. As Brock tells it, several years ago, when a man brought Brock Sea Island "red peas" and told him they were "special," that they had been "planted originally by African slaves in the Sea Islands,"[24] his mind changed. This mystery man (Glenn Roberts of Anson Mills) also gave Brock a bag of Carolina Gold Rice, a product he was trying to bring back after decades of absence. With his hands on Sea Island red peas and Carolina Gold Rice, Brock tried creating his own version of the classic. He gushes, "It wasn't until I tasted those Sea Island red peas in a bowl together with Carolina Gold Rice that I realized what had gone wrong those many years ago when I'd first tasted Hoppin' John."[25]

We learn in *Heritage* about Carolina Gold Rice, a Lowcountry varietal that farmers stopped growing when they no longer had slaves to work the fields—the last harvest of this varietal from the Antebellum South was sold in the early 1920s, replaced by a commercial-grade rice that required significantly less human and financial resources to produce. Carolina Gold Rice is about a very specific place—South Carolina's Lowcountry. Even more specifically, Anson Mills' Carolina Gold Rice is grown on thirty acres on Prospect Hill field on the Edisto River, just south of Charleston. Rice, even the same varietal of rice, will taste different depending on where it is grown. That is, the dirt in which it is planted, the amount of sun it receives, the level of rainfall that season, the farmer who harvests it, and the cook who prepares it shape the finished product. If a farmer tried to grow Carolina Gold Rice in Texas or California or Montana, she or he would still get rice, but it would be a different rice than that grown in the Lowcountry. That is, the physical characteristics of place shape taste. Brock is making an argument that placed food, Carolina Gold Rice, is preferable to unplaced food like industrialized long grain rice. Industrialization renders commercial grade rice bland; Carolina Gold Rice is grown for flavor and nutrient density. Another way of saying this might be that because Carolina Gold Rice tastes different; it is, functionally, a different ingredient than other rice. In short, Brock interrupts the logic of substitution that rice is rice is rice wherever it is grown and whomever prepares it. Wild rice from Minnesota is not Carolina Gold Rice from South Carolina's Lowcountry, and a dish featuring one is not the same as a dish featuring the other even if we use the same recipe.

Second, Brock features several techniques common to his terroir—particular ways of smoking, salting, pickling, and preserving. Brock explains that "pickling and preserving are two techniques that anchor Southern cooking."[26] In Brock's remote Appalachian town, there were no actual grocery stores, so self-sufficiency is the ethos of that terroir. Every family had a garden and understanding what to plant and when—a sense of seasonality—was integral to eating and feeding people well. Growing food, cooking food, teaching others to cook or hunt or fish, serving food, and enjoying food are cultural inculcations of place. Sean Brock writes more about his grandmother Audrey than perhaps any other subject in *Heritage*. Brock's pictorial description of his grandmother's house notes it was a "beautifully mysterious playground" and in her basement were "bubbling vats of homemade wine and fermented ears of corn"—he admits he will never forget the smell of the basement, filled entirely with preserved food. Pickling and preserving, techne taught to Brock by his grandmother, are about seasonality—tomatoes are perfect in August. Those you do not eat should be preserved or they fall to the ground and rot, wasted and unused.

Brock relies on the local traditions of pickling to challenge the dominant logics that resist seasonality. Indeed, the logic of substitution removes any sense of timing for produce. If one can buy a tomato any time of the year, then a tomato is a tomato is a tomato (or a banana is a banana is a banana)—and in this case, that tomato is tremendously mediocre. By locating products back within the season, Brock gives reasons to value the ephemerality of fresh produce. Moreover, *this way* of pickling comes from his grandmother. It is tied to her land and her traditions. These ingredients are not just saved, but desired. For example, Brock writes "I have great memories of making this fermented cabbage with my grandmother. Each year when the cabbage was ready in the garden, we would chop it up and put it into ceramic crocks. The cabbage would sit in the basement and get fermented and delicious. Throughout the year, it made its way onto the dinner table as a side dish."[27] Brock undoes the logic of industrialized agriculture because he equips people with strategies to deal with seasonality. Whereas industrialized agriculture uses the logic of substitution to sell produce year-round, strategies of pickling indicate that there are alternative ways—better ones, even—to enjoy food. And, what's more, the techne of pickling enhances the food in novel ways. Instead of seasonality as something to be erased, it is something to be celebrated, because it facilitates novel innovations that beget new flavors.

Third, Brock contextualizes his images of the good life into the backdrop of the region's vexed history. In *Heritage*, Brock's focus on the African diaspora and its influence on the Lowcountry is notable. Charleston, the chief metropolitan area of the Lowcountry, was where many African men, women, and children taken as slaves first landed in this country, permanently marking the Lowcountry with West African influences. Brock describes over and over that the slave trade brought many of the foods we consider native to or integral to Lowcountry cuisine—gumbo, as he notes, is in fact an African word for okra.[28] Certainly, there are historians and scholars and descendants of West Africans brought to South Carolina by force who tell these stories of slavery, of brutality, of culture, and of history in a place like the Lowcountry, but white Southern chefs usually do not. Consider, for example, the way he talks about Sea Island red peas, an essential ingredient in Lowcountry cuisine: "One such variety of field peas is the one we call Sea Island red peas, and its history gives you a glimpse of the complexity of Lowcountry food. The Sea Island red pea reportedly came to America with Northern Italians from the Veneto, who were hired to build rice ditches before the arrival of African slaves skilled in the practice. The Africans then adopted the peas, and the Italian *risi e bisi* became what the Gullah people called *reezy peezy*. The story illustrates the importance of beans in Lowcountry cuisine."[29] In contrast to other red beans, the Sea Island ones are unique because they contain histories of European colonialism and because Brock bothers to tell the story of that colonialism in his cookbook.

When food becomes unplaced, it becomes unmoored from history, allowing ingredients an unearned parity. But, when Brock rhetorically historicizes each ingredient, he offers another point of distinction that gives food meaning. For him, these ingredients cannot be grown, raised, farmed, or bought from *anywhere*. Rather, they must be from the Lowcountry terroir, as they are deeply entwined within that political context. To consume this food is to participate within these broader historical trends. That is, terroir is not only a geographical boundary but it is also a cultural, historical, and political set of meanings and practices.

The Lowcountry terroir gives a generic-specific topoi that inspires Brock's lines of argument; he appeals to the dirt in the form of the specific plot of land his ingredients come from by naming growers from whom he buys food: Anson Mills, Celeste Albers, and Shawn Thackeray. For Brock, where food comes from is as important as any other part of the recipe because each ingredient *tastes* different based on terroir. Brock also talks about inherited local strategies for food preparations, like the advice he receives from the farmers who gather at the Wadmalaw Supper Club on Wadmalaw Island. Seasonality is not a deficit, then, but a resource for innovative and delicious cooking. Finally, the Lowcountry's vexed political context plays a prominent role in his writing. Brock constantly references histories when he talks about the slave trade and its importance to the cuisine he is preparing. Globalized food participates in the erasure of the violent colonialist histories that moved seeds from subjugated people to elites around the world; placed food renegotiates this erasure, calling attention to how Southern food is a "borrowed" food, its techniques claimed in the name of the colonizers. If MIA renders invisible the origins of the fruit, the labor associated with its harvest, and the environmental degradation of its distribution, then Brock contextualizes food and the underwriting relations that brought it to the plate. Dirt, techne, and political context provide inventional pathways to interrupt the logic of substitution. Namely, assigning dirt different tastes offers an easy way to create distinctions; novel techniques provide a more sustainable way to eat seasonally; and contextualization demonstrates how food is caught up within broader sociopolitical currents. Rice cannot stand as a substitute for itself if each grain tastes differently, is prepared differently, and has its own history. Hoppin' John, then, is only Hoppin' John if it is made with Carolina Gold Rice and Sea Island red peas using techniques tethered to region.

CONCLUSION

This chapter has argued that terroir supplies rhetors with the generic-specific resources to craft particular arguments. Our position maintains terroir as a physical place—constituted through dirt, techne, and political context—that helps Brock craft arguments for environmentally sustainable and culturally sustaining food. We demonstrated how Brock celebrates the Lowcountry in *Heritage* to respond to the generic logic of industrialized agriculture. When an audience is asked to consider where their food comes from, it draws into relief the opaque nature of an industrialized food system. In place of the infinite logics of substitution that suggest rice = rice = rice, Brock indicates that *this* Carolina Gold Rice is unique because it grew in *this* ground, cultivated in *this specific* way. How do we assess Brock's rhetorical invention? By placing food, *Heritage* constitutes a particular rhetorical strategy, one designed to temporarily interrupt the way we think about food.

Although it does not lead to a radical revolution in food, it does create space to rethink how we organize food and understand place.

Although Brock uses a particular topos, South Carolina's Lowcountry, to make his case against industrialized agriculture, his example points to the ways in which other rhetors might use particular topoi like *this* or *that* place to make broader claims about regionality, seasonality, environmental sustainability, and culture that are powerful, disruptive counter narratives. In fact, we would argue the chief purpose of *Heritage* is this kind of advocacy and activism—most people cannot honor Brock's vision of the hyperlocal and recreate the recipes he includes in the book. But they can use the book as a guide to *their* place, their terroir, their particular topos. We identify two additional implications of understanding terroir as a site of invention.

First, using terroir as a site of invention challenges whitewashed appropriations of culinary traditions. Outside of soul food, which is associated with black American cooking and not specifically the South, popular considerations of Southern food very often erase its West African slave origins. This erasure enables Southern food to be less fraught, less contaminated by history, politics, or culture. And more significantly, it enables white Southerners to more easily serve as emissaries of the region. In her work on *Food Network* star Paula Deen, Anjali Vats explains that popular treatments of Southern food culture feature "appeals to 'Southern hospitality' through the naming and performance of a Southern 'home' that invoke "a meaning-making story continually told and re-told about the South."[30] Deen's invocation of Southernness, though, is commonplace and marked by erasure such that her "telling of the story of Southern hospitality . . . privileg[es] a romanticized view of the region. Her sanitized portrayals of Southernness, while characteristic of the *Food Network,* ignore Southern hospitality's antebellum roots, when house slaves cooked and served while their masters and master's guests enjoyed leisurely eating."[31] It is not that white Southerners lack a stake on this food's history and culture. Rather, food media from cookbooks to television programming to blogs present an almost blank history of Southern food culture featuring a sort of neocolonial wonderland of abundance in which "the authentic experience of culture and color" are assimilated into a Eurocentric, white imaginary.[32] Just as Brock's use of terroir as both physical and cultural place offers a model for challenging globalized and industrialized food, it also blueprints a way to locate arguments against cultural appropriation. Brock's overt and ubiquitous telling of the linkages between Lowcountry food and American slavery challenges narrative whitewashings of Southern food and food culture in significant ways.

At the same time, we recognize that appeals to the local in terms of Lowcountry and Southern foodways may be read as rallying cries for white supremacy. That is, celebrations of this particular culture and history may give cover to those privileging the "blood and soil" of the Antebellum South. Again, we think this is not an either/or but a both/and situation—terroir's polyvalent potential for resistance is also its potential for exploitation by white nationalists. In other words, some critics would look at Sean Brock and say that he is in no way meaningfully different from Paula Deen, that his articulations are superficial and gloss the very real violence of Southern foodways. Or indeed that terroir as topoi could be used to undergird the worst kinds of nationalism.

The second implication of terroir as a particular topos that signals a general place for rhetorical invention is about consumption and circulation, in this case, the interrelated aspects of terroir's regional and cultural characteristics. Terroir as a rhetoric is about association to stories, to memories, to place. One of this chapter's authors has eaten at Husk in Nashville—it was a remarkable meal. It was also a meal that took place with friends very rarely seen, in the middle of a college reunion weekend—the kind of meal that will be remembered not only for the food but also for the associations we might have with the experience. If we think about *Heritage* as articulating a terroir, we must then understand what that terroir means and how it moves from the Lowcountry to destinations around the country and around the world. That is, while cooks outside the Lowcountry cannot make Brock's recipes or acquire his ingredients without dishonoring the kind of placed ethos and argument he makes, we can take his powerful lines of argument and rework them for *our* places, using *our* stories, and make similarly effective arguments against globalized and industrialized food. That kind of circulation, reliant on each of our experiences and associations, is perhaps the real key to Brock's rhetorical power. Reconsidering terroir as topos means recognizing topoi as both metaphorical and material, opening up new rhetorical possibilities of invention to create a more sustainable food system and food culture.

NOTES

1. Justin Eckstein and Anna M. Young, "wastED Rhetoric," *Communication & Critical/Cultural Studies* 15, no. 4 (2018): 275.
2. Eckstein and Young, "wastED," 275.
3. Justin Eckstein and Anna M. Young, "Cooking, Celebrity Chefs, and Public Chef Intellectuals," *Communication & Critical/Cultural Studies* 12, no. 2 (2015): 205–8.
4. Aristotle, *Topics*, trans. W. A. Pickard-Cambridge (Stilwell, KS: Digigireads.com Publishing, 2006), 92.
5. John Muckelbauer, *The Future of Invention: Rhetoric, Postmodernism, and the Problem of Change* (New York: SUNY Press, 2008), 124.

6. Aristotle, *Rhetoric*, trans. Edward P. J. Corbett (New York: Random House, 1984), 31.

7. Dan O'Hair, Rob Stewart, and Hannah Rubenstein, *A Speaker's Guidebook: Text and Reference* (New York: MacMillan, 2012).

8. Aristotle, *Rhetoric*, ed. Jonathan Barnes (Princeton: Princeton University Press, 2004): 31.

9. Carolyn R. Miller, "Aristotle's 'Special Topics' in Rhetorical Practice and Pedagogy," *Rhetoric Society Quarterly* 17, no. 1 (1987): 66.

10. Miller, "Special Topics," 64.

11. "Special Topics," 65.

12. Quintilian, book 5, chapter 10, 20–22, in *Institutio Oratoria*, quoted in Damien S. Pfister, *Networked Media, Networked Rhetorics* (State College: Pennsylvania State University Press, 2014), 55.

13. Scott Consigny, "Rhetoric and Its Situations," *Philosophy and Rhetoric* 7, no. 3 (1974): 181.

14. Miller, "Special Topics," 67.

15. Barbara Warnick, "Two Systems of Invention: The Topics in the Rhetoric and the New Rhetoric," in *Rereading Aristotle*, ed. Alan Gross and Arthur Walzer (Carbondale: Southern Illinois University Press, 2008), 107.

16. Greg Dickinson, *Suburban Dreams: Imagining and Building the Good Life* (Tuscaloosa: University of Alabama Press, 2015), 1.

17. Dickinson, *Suburban Dreams*, 20.

18. Amy B. Trubek, *The Taste of Place* (Berkeley: University of California Press, 2008), 24.

19. Trubek, *The Taste of Place*, 56.

20. For more on terroir see Anna M. Young, "Quaffable but . . . Far from Transcendent," in *The Politics of Style and the Style of Politics*, ed. Barry Brummett (Lanham, MD: Lexington Books, 2011) 263–77; Anna M. Young, "The Politics of Wine and the Style of Bullshit," *Rhetoric Society Quarterly* 45, no. 5 (2015); Jeff Rice, *Craft Obsession* (see chapter 1, n. 25). For more on terroir as a material site governing relational capacities, see Rickert, *Ambient Rhetoric* (introduction to this volume, n. 27); also see Katie Dickman and Nathaniel Rivers, "Rhetoric Under the Influence" in this volume.

21. Casey Ryan Kelly, "Cooking without Women: The Rhetoric of the New Culinary Male," *Communication & Critical/Cultural Studies*, 12, no. 2 (2015): 200.

22. Anna Lowenhaupt Tsign, *The Mushroom at the End of the World* (Princeton: Princeton University Press, 2015), 5.

23. Tsign, *The Mushroom*, 5.

24. Sean Brock, *Heritage* (New York: Artisan, 2014), 15.

25. Brock, *Heritage*, 15.

26. *Heritage*, 206.

27. *Heritage*, 224.

28. In season two of Netflix's "The Mind of a Chef," Brock explains that he travels to West Africa at least once a year to better familiarize himself with both the ingredients as well as techne of cooking and preservation in the region.

29. *Heritage*, 51.

30. Anjali Vats, "Cooking Up Hashtag Activism: #PaulasBestDishes and Counternarratives of Southern Food," *Communication & Critical/Cultural Studies* 12, no. 2 (2015): 210.

31. Vats, "Cooking Up Hashtag Activism," 210.

32. Casey Ryan Kelly, "Bizarre Foods: White Privilege and the Neocolonial Palate," in *Race and Hegemonic Struggle in the United States: Pop Culture, Politics, and Protest*, ed. Michael G. Lacy and Mary Triece (Lanham, MD: Rowman & Littlefield, 2014): 44.

3
Food Pornography

Casey R. Kelly

In 2003, photos of a scantily clad Rachel Ray appeared as a featured spread in the bawdy UK men's lifestyle magazine *FHM*. This collection of soft-core kitchen fetish photographs featured the *Food Network* star in skimpy renditions of homespun aprons converted into lingerie that left her midriff and legs exposed, her breasts accentuated and pushed together. In one photo, Ray stood in the doorway of a country kitchen dressed in a denim and gingham top and miniskirt, both laced together with red-and-white checkered apron string. Her exposed left shoulder leaned against the doorframe as she delicately balanced a baked pie in the palm of her right hand. Elbow bent to her side, the pie presented at face level, Ray smiled directly at the camera. In a second photo, Ray was dressed in a black bra and black-and-white-checked apron-style miniskirt, complete with strappy three-inch stiletto heels. Again she smiled directly at the camera as she bent over to pull a glistening fully cooked turkey from the oven. But that is not all. From there, the photos escalate and become more sexually explicit. In one shot, Ray licked runny chocolate fudge from a large wooden spoon. In another she gently suckled the end of a ripe strawberry. As if the fetishistic displacement of genitalia and bodily fluids were not yet made clear enough for spectators, the spread concluded with a "money shot," that ubiquitous feature of modern pornography in which the male actor ejaculates on his sexual partner.[1] In this photo, Ray was seated on the kitchen counter, her feet dangling in a sink of dishwater with her legs partially open. Her hands covered in soap, Ray formed her lips to suggest that she is "blowing" suds toward the viewer. Some suds were caught in her hair and lingered on the sides of her face. The dishes were done and the meal, so to speak, had concluded.

Ray's *FHM* appearance visually narrated an erotic encounter in which food and cooking were substitutes for body parts and sex acts, respectively. In the first act, Ray welcomed the male spectator into her boudoir/kitchen by seducing them with the promise of visceral pleasure, a warm pie and succulent turkey. In the second act, Ray moved from foreplay to simulated oral sex, caressing phallic kitchen tools, tasting, and pressing her lips against fleshy fruits. The third act included sexual release or the money shot, a visual confirmation of (male) pleasure that both consummates vicarious pleasure for the male spectator and demarcates the conclusion of the sex act. Yet visceral pleasure remains deferred.

Indeed, pornography is a genre fraught by substitution and lack, or what Joshua Gunn aptly calls "the mystery of *jouissance*"—a genre that evinces the impossibility of truly expressing the affect of bodily arousal.[2] This particular example of soft-core, where sex is implied or simulated, adds yet another layer of substitution: the fetish.[3] Here, food is a substitute for the phallus and simulations of eating a substitute for sexual pleasure, a displacement of desire onto edible objects. Ray plays a familiar stock character from pornographic films: the marooned horny housewife who throughout the completion of her daily domestic duties harbors hidden and taboo desires. This character straddles the virgin/whore dichotomy, an embodied male fantasy of a feminine body that is at once innocent and "frenzied" with sexual desire.[4] The husband's absence, but more specifically the absence of the male spectator, compels this character to sexualize the objects from her world of domestic duties, tasks such as cooking and cleaning. The male spectator comes upon Ray at home, who in the meantime has managed to fold sexual gratification into her daily chores; when caught looking, the spectator is not reprimanded but instead welcomed to assume the controlling gaze of the absent husband. Ray's physically expressed desires are also pure substitution, because a fetish object (food) has transformed into the surrogate object of desire and arousal. Ultimately, pleasure belongs to the male spectators; yet they are also caught in a visual and mimetic relationship in which both the voyeur and exhibitor defer the visceral experience of pleasure to an ersatz version of visual enjoyment. Food not only replaces sex, but worse, replaces it with food the audience can never eat. Pure longing is all that remains.

Frederick Kaufman observes that the connection between food media and pornography is more than incidental.[5] After spending hours on the sets of *Food Network* programs, Kaufman detailed how the producers purposely recreate stock characters, appropriate narrative conventions, and adopt camera techniques from pornographic films. He relays how *Food Network* producer Barbara Nitke—herself a veteran of pornographic filmmaking—boasted of importing the conventions of X-rated cinema to whet appetites and arouse audience desire. Indeed, specific genres of verbal and visual discourse are designed to elicit specific audience responses. What distinguishes pornography is how it acts on the body of the audience (i.e., arousal), an affect not lost on *Food Network* producers. What, then, are the implications of importing the conventions of pornography into the representational apparatus of our industrial food system? The purpose of my preceding description and analysis of this collection of photographs was to introduce the vexing dynamics of spectatorship and pleasure in an emerging genre of visual discourse: food pornography. "Gastroporn," or "food porn," designates food television or photography that appropriates the aesthetic conventions of pornography. Pornographic aesthetics are implicitly at work in those seductive close-ups that capture the curvature, sheen, texture, and succulence of a desired food object. Food is arranged and spliced into sexualized body parts: legs, breasts, muscles, mouths, and genitalia. Female models even pleasure phallic food objects, their bodies in ecstasy as the food pleasures them back. Food pornography treats food and sex as interchangeable: both are biological instincts that satiate bodily needs and produce bodily pleasure in a similar fashion. But it is the lurid label of "pornography" that designates those mediated or visual depictions of food that mirror the looking relations of "traditional" pornography and that are primarily directed at stimulating a bodily response such as arousal or the desire to imitate.[6] Food porn takes a variety of representational forms, including but not limited to portraits of excessive high-calorie consumption, images of food that mimic sexualized body parts or sexualized body parts that mimic food, visual and verbal tales of food experiences, amateur depictions of homemade meals or spontaneous eating and cooking in everyday situations, or representations of food introduced into sexual situations. The list goes on. But when and how did food become the subject of pornographic desire? Moreover, what are the implications of assimilating the visual discourse of pornography into representations of American food and foodways?

Since the launch of the *Food Network* in 1993, the unprecedented celebrification of food culture and growth of food media has led to the cultivation of a fetishistic relationship between commodity and spectator.[7] In culinary media, food is imbued with a "surplus" life beyond its use-value. Food's "usage" is no longer tied to simple nourishment or physical satiation but has become, in addition, imagery to be visually or vicariously consumed. Of course, the proliferation of digital technology and the popularity of food blogging and photo sharing via social media has in many ways permanently sutured food to the aesthetics of pornography. In our screen culture of online shareability, if you ate a meal and did not post a photo, did it really happen? Has the very practice of eating fundamentally changed? In contemporary digital culture, seemingly no culinary or sexual conquest goes undocumented.

The gleeful self-application of the once-lurid label "pornography" suggests that eating has been subjected to the travails of pleasure in virtual and visual culture. Above all, the pornographic label is one happily adopted by the corporate food industry. Hence, the central argument of this chapter is that the pornification of food is ultimately about the creation of unattainable corporate aesthetics, aligned with the mission of industrial agriculture to separate consumers from the production and enjoyment of the home meal. It is significant to note that home cooking is on a fifty-year decline, yet the time spent watching food television is consistently on the ascent.[8] There are now countless blogs, tumblr pages, and online forums devoted—either implicitly or explicitly—to converting food into a visual spectacle. And like porn, food media provides a display of *techne* that audiences would rarely imitate in their own home.[9] Thus, I argue that where food becomes a visual or pornographic spectacle it reinforces patterns of consumption that cede agency to the purported expertise of the corporate food industry. Expertly shot and lit to engender unattainable fantasies, pornographic food makes the real-life act of cooking look simply too difficult and ultimately disappointing when compared with the polished aesthetic of an industrially manufactured fantasy. Food pornography is a genre that arouses desires that can only be satiated by visually pleasurable corporate food.

This chapter addresses how the introduction and circulation of pornographic looking relations enables the corporate food system to address rhetorically the bodies of American consumers beyond signification. It illustrates how food pornography underwrites the industrial food system by channeling felt intensities toward the fetish objects it produces. Under the pressure of visual technologies of representation, food is converted into a sign evacuated of both the living labor of production and the physical gratification of its consumption.[10] Where food becomes an immaterial virtual entity, the pleasure of consumption is both vicarious and alienated from various nodal points of its production (growing, harvesting, and cooking). Food becomes a reified commodity with a life of its own to produce for consumers a deferred form of visual pleasure far removed from the physical processes of production and consumption. Our social relationship with food, then, becomes mediated by a visual economy of affective exchange in which consumers are expected to prefer the pleasures of the visual and virtual over the visceral and embodied. Indeed, the visual and the virtual are the preferred criteria of industry for mass produced frozen simulation of home-cooked meals. That is to say, the rhetorical work of pornographic food images is to addle the consumer with ineffable desire and, thus, generate affective attachments to the kinds of excessively indulgent and visually spectacular foods that are manufactured by industry for mass consumption.

Here, by *affective* I mean what Brian Massumi characterizes as a level of intensity that precipitates articulation in language.[11] Or in Jenny Rice's words, affect "describes an energetics that does not necessarily emerge at the level of signification."[12] In language, the residue of affective intensities manifests as emotion, feelings, or other expressed desires. In turning to affect theory, I illustrate how food pornography is a genre that traffics primarily in bodily intensities that reconfigure public tastes in ways that align with the corporate food industry's preferred modes of consumption. Food pornography arouses consumers to desire visual over visceral pleasure, expertly polished foods over the self-made meals, and frenzied excess over moderation. While Michael Pollan argues that food media distances audiences from the art of cooking, an analysis of food pornography as a rhetorical genre that circulates affect into our cultural foodways explains how and why polished visual portraits of sublime excess court bodily investments in an unattainable aesthetic that makes consumers dependent on industry to do the very profitable lion's share of society's cooking on their behalf.[13] I conclude that food fetishism contributes to a public culture that is disinterested in bodily nourishment and shared home meals. Moreover, such a divestment from cooking has consequences for health, the environment, and public life. This chapter explains how visual rhetorics become engines of industrial production by accessing bodily desires to craft a public willing to accept, if not demand, the ersatz pleasures of consumer culture.

AFFECT AND THE AESTHETICS OF FOOD PORNOGRAPHY

Rhetorical scholars have observed how genres are comprised not of particular elements that reside within a text but rather of recognizable forms that recur throughout public and popular culture. As Karlyn Kohrs Campbell and Kathleen Hall Jamieson argue, "A genre is composed of a constellation of recognizable forms bound together by an internal dynamic."[14] In the case of Rachel Ray's feature in *FHM*, it is the audience's familiarity with pornography that conditions their bodily response toward food. Similar to genres such as horror and melodrama, food pornography courts particular affective investments and translates felt bodily intensities into the symbolic realm through patterned repetitions.[15] Form—the structural organization of recognizable verbal or visual discourse—cultivates audience expectations and appetites in a manner that exceeds the specific content.[16] Joshua Gunn takes the perspective that the rhetorical affect of such genres is to deliver the "body-in-feeling" into language, suggesting that form is where bodily intensities meet the symbolic.[17] In rhetorical studies, affect has been employed to name those pre-discursive intensities that, when they enter the realm of the symbolic through language, are legible to us as emotion or feeling.[18]

Emotion, then, is the translation of bodily intensities into a legible form, or a rhetorical device that not only expresses but also activates, mobilizes, and aggregates bodily affect. Though not to be conflated with affect, emotion expressed in language contains the residual traces of ineffable feelings. As Erin Rand explains, "The language of emotion pins down the fluidity of affect only temporarily and partially."[19]

An examination of how food pornography generates particular affective investments lets us see how the rhetoric of sensation is also enthymematic, to the extent that a series of inferences, innuendos, and textual winks condition audiences to supply the missing subtext. Hence, I consider the relationship between genre and affect to be structured by a series of implicit demands for audience participation. In classical rhetorical theories of verbal discourse, enthymemes are truncated logical syllogisms where the audience supplies the missing premises with conventional wisdom.[20] Effective enthymemes draw from shared cultural knowledge between the rhetor and their audience to convey meaning and move people to ideas. Contemporary rhetorical theories that account for the use of enthymemes in visual culture suggest that images operate similarly in that they draw from context and presumed cultural knowledge to cultivate audience identification.[21] David S. Birdsell and Leo Groarke argue that "visual culture provides the broad master narratives of design which are the background for more specific visual (or for that matter, verbal) texts which perpetuate or challenge those narratives."[22] Visual images need not make explicit conjectures but may instead convey meaning through inferential power of representational forms, icons, and image events shared by a culture or visual discourse community.[23] But, as Kevin DeLuca and Jennifer Peeples suggest, in the ceaseless circulation of images and media discourse only stunning image events that bypass deliberative rationality can break through the public screen and mobilize audiences. This particular take on image culture suggests that a more complete and productive understanding of enthymemes would emphasize their sensory rather than deliberative qualities. To that end, food pornography is a contemporary genre of visual discourse organized not by logical inferences but via a series of *sensory* inferences, or representational codes that prompt viewers to complete a visual circuit between food and sex. Visual enthymemes are also sensory inferences that rely on audience recognition of form and, consequently, condition particular body responses that often register as emotion. In food pornography, sexualized portraits of food are sensory inferences that invite audiences to feel about food similarly to how they feel about sex. The result is an aggregation and alignment of feelings that reshapes how audiences relate to both food and visual media.

Working from this theorization of form, sensation, and affect, this chapter argues that food pornography is a visual rhetoric that circulates affect throughout the populace to organize and align audience appetites with the ideological imperatives of both a consumer economy and industrialized agriculture. I suggest that food pornography is distinct from other representations of food in that it is a genre of corporate discourse that conditions and habituates audiences to both desire the polished product of industrial food and participate in the production of surplus value for its commodities in virtual space (i.e., sharing food pictures on sites such as Instagram). The introduction of pornographic looking relations into our food system also directs audience intensities toward a series of ersatz substitutions: to exchange the quotidian pleasure of home-cooked meals for the visual perfection of corporate food, to cede agency over the production of food to the expert celebrity chef, to privilege visual stimulation over visceral enjoyment, and to desire rapid, frenzied consumption over moderation.

BODY GENRES AND INDUSTRIAL FOOD

Before turning to the operation of substitution logics within this genre, I want to position food pornography within the ideological apparatus of industrial agriculture, whose discourses must circulate not merely sympathetic attitudes but preferred feelings and desires throughout the populace to sustain its own existence. I read food pornography as part of an informal network of images and verbal discourses that organize and court affective investments in habits and behaviors that participate in larger networks of power in a society organized around industrial agriculture. It is a genre well suited to the production of docile bodies in that it encourages its audience to invest in productive notions of pleasure, nourishment, and "health."[24] In turn, audiences are assumed to not only adapt but actively participate in the management of their tastes and practices of self-care—desiring pornographic excess enough to not only consume but share in its visual reproduction. This analysis illustrates the extent to which in a capitalist society rhetoric, among its many definitions and functions, is a system for channeling affective energies and desires into activities that, as Eric Jenkins argues, ensure the perpetuation of a control society.[25]

How, then, does food pornography circulate affect to realign public conceptions of taste? As a specific form, pornography is structured by two key elements that transform the viewer's relationship with pleasure: excess and substitution. On the first point, the importation of pornographic aesthetics recasts food media as belonging to what Linda Williams calls "body genres." Like melodrama or horror, pornography is considered lurid because it incites a bodily response: stimulation, or worse, imitation or the desire to imitate. Williams argues that body genres are so often maligned on account of the "perception that the body of the spectator is caught up in an almost involuntary mimicry of the emotion or sensation of the body on the screen."[26] Gunn suggests that body genres are "systems of excess" that "stimulate the bodies in the audience," a kind of affective apparatus that translates felt bodily intensities and desires into the realm of the symbolic.[27] Hence, the label of pornography is typically used to denote excess and exploitation. For example, "disaster pornography" is an overstimulation of our sense of sympathy, while "organization pornography" (images of excessively organized offices and closets) fires up our obsessive-compulsive urges. The list goes on. The audience is positioned as a voyeur, reveling in excess, or worse, the suffering of others.[28] In terms of food, excess is conveyed by images of overwhelming portions of meat and cheese that excite the audience by stoking fantasies of extraordinary caloric intake without consequence.

Second, pornography involves a series of troubled substitutions, namely that the audience must exchange physical pleasure for visual pleasure. For food, this requires that the audience reduce the sensory pleasure of eating to the visual—forsaking taste, smell, and texture, not to mention nutrition. Moreover, the audience cannot have access to the food depicted on screen. In terms of identification, and drawing from Laura Mulvey, we might say that the gaze of food pornography is voyeuristic in the sense that food is primarily to be looked at and its pleasures are more virtual than tactile.[29] The relationship is fetishistic to the extent that food is a substitute for "the lack," or the impossibility of truly expressing the affect of bodily arousal. Yet pornography provides proof that sex (and pleasure) has occurred with shots of penetration and release, as much as food pornography provides proof of the physical pleasure (eating) that it displaces. Presumably, flesh-and-blood costumers have entered a Burger King and eaten the BK Super Seven Incher. Surely, someone ate the dish captured in an Instagram photo?

As both Williams and Gunn observe, the mimetic trouble with pornography is that it might induce the spectator to masturbate or at the very least contemplate doing so. This is where pornographic depictions of food diverge from both traditional pornography and nonpornographic images of food in terms of purpose and effect. Although food pornography stimulates bodily arousal, there is not a similar mimetic response available to spectators, no form of self-pleasure that substitutes for the "real thing." A spectator could simply eat to satiate their hunger; however, they cannot have the fetishized object that initially aroused their desire, at least not in its exact form. One could purchase a mass-produced version of an advertised food product that in reality can never match the fantasy stoked by the airbrushed portraiture of the original. The consumer could try to replicate other spectacular and visually stunning meals at home but ultimately will be disappointed unless they possess the culinary acumen, time, and ingredients to successfully navigate their kitchen like a professional chef.

What food pornography *can* and perhaps *must* promise that traditional pornography cannot is compensation through fetishistic consumption: the spectator can enjoy the same experience through their purchasing power. For a small price, the spectator can live out their pornographic fantasy. They can go to the same restaurant Rachel Ray visits in *$40 a Day* and order the same meal they had previously consumed vicariously through television. Although there is a large market for illicit sex work in the US, pornography cannot make a similar promise, at least not explicitly. The spectator can seek out a sexual encounter, even purchase sexual services, but it is unlikely to be the same experience with the same "actor." As food pornography often takes the form of advertisement or promotion—even amateur photographs shared to make others jealous—mimicry is at a minimum a welcomed, if not the desired, goal. Food is a commodity dissimilar from sex, and even purchasing extravagant high calorie indulgences is not subject to the same set of taboos and legal prohibitions. Thus, food pornography stimulates bodily arousal in ways that are consistent with the norms of consumer culture and offers compensation for displacement through acts of mimicry that are socially sanctioned and even encouraged.

Thus, food pornography is also characterized by a third element: compensation. Food pornography is a form of advertising, and as Sut Jhally observes, one that makes the spectator do labor in exchange for pleasure.[30] In other words, like advertising, food pornography stokes and then offers to satiated bodily needs but at a cost: the money, time, and effort required to obtain the "real thing" simulated in the image. Thus, I want to not only account for how food pornography moves bodies through form but also to what larger purpose it organizes bodily affect. Indeed, as Carolyn Miller contends, "a rhetorically sound definition of genre must be centered not on the substance or form of a discourse but on the action it is used to accomplish."[31] Of course, I have argued that form matters particularly in relationship to how genres court bodily intensities, but I am also concerned with the consequences of form for how spectators collectively relate to food. Here, I suggest that the compensatory element of food porn aligns with the objectives of both the corporate food industry in particular and consumer culture in general. Spectacular images of food suggest to the spectator that the most pleasurable cuisines are beyond replication in the home kitchen. Without the luxury of time and expertise, it is much easier to purchase the same item made by someone with culinary skills and knowledge, both of which are steadily on the decline. The home-cooked version is thus more than likely disappointing when compared to the original. At the same time, this lack also leaves room for celebrity chefs to lend their name to prepackaged frozen versions of their originals. While the store-bought version of Wolfgang Puck's "Pizza with Smoked Salmon and Caviar" looks appetizing on the packaging, this ersatz substitute is missing the flavor, texture, and nutrition of the original and contains preservatives to ensure a longer shelf life. Nonetheless, the fantasy structure of food pornography drives consumer demand for cheap and easy fixes.

Food pornography also creates a very profitable marketing feedback loop between industry and consumers. For instance, food chains such as Applebee's encourage their customers to share photos of their meals on the restaurant's Facebook page with the hashtag "foodporn."[32] Here, consumers do the work of advertisers but with a greater degree of authenticity than would a professionally produced sales pitch. Above all, food pornography fetishizes spectacular high-calorie indulgences over nutrition. What chance does the home-cooked meal with fresh fruits and vegetables stand against the visual pleasures of excess found in a stunning plate of fried appetizers? One index that monitors social media conversations about food tracked 270 million food hashtags and found that 67.6 percent favored unhealthy foods.[33] The foods that are most share-worthy or speak to the norms of a visual culture are those that index the pleasure of extraordinary indulgence. As Herbert Marcuse argued, bodily desires and pleasures are shaped by historical and cultural forces.[34] Food pornography is a product of advanced industrial capitalism, one that like other instruments of the "productive apparatus" shapes and organizes bodily affect to ensure its own reproduction.[35] It is a corporate genre of visual discourse that directs our palates to be aroused by that which is not only high in calorie but high in profit. The examples I analyze in the remainder of this chapter elaborate on this corporate aesthetic: a form that arouses desires that cannot be satisfied without the presence of a corporate food industry. In other words, food pornography necessitates a market of fantasy wish fulfillment in which corporations offer to do all the cooking for us.[36] In what follows, I briefly analyze several different examples of food pornography in order to elaborate on the relationship between the form and consequences of the corporate aesthetic.

AMATEUR

Instagram is a mobile photo and video sharing service that allows users to share digital content through a mobile application and other linked social platforms, such as Facebook, Twitter, and Flickr. Surpassing Twitter's 285 million active users in 2014, the site has 300 million registered users and is

Figure 3.1. Instagram's food pornography catalogue. Screen capture by author.

owned by Facebook, which reports 1.35 billion users.[37] The popular hashtag "foodpornography" aggregates Instagram photographs labeled as such by users of the application.[38] As of this writing, the hashtag contained an astounding 388,906 posts.

Instagram posts organized by #foodpornography include the accounts of professional food bloggers, restaurants, aspiring chefs, and amateurs who post more than just photographs of their meals. Followers can "like" and comment of individual posts, view other posts organized under the hashtag or made public by the individual poster, and follow hyperlinks to the official Instagram pages of restaurants or professionals (if made available). Professional pages range from those maintained by independent restaurants and culinary experts to corporate chains such as Applebee's. While art historians observe Western culture's fascination with visually recording extraordinary meals, Instagram has become the world's primary vector for both amateur and professional documentations of visually stunning meals.[39]

For the restaurant industry, Instagram has surpassed Yelp as the preferred data mining tool for discovering consumer trends.[40] Recognizing its uses as a marketing instrument, some restaurant owners, particularly in large markets like New York City, have sought out "influencers" or Instagram users with over ten thousand followers to eat at their establishment, photograph their food, and share their impressions over social media.[41] Restaurateurs also use Instagram as a straightforward promotional tool by posting photos of dishes from the menu or creating hashtags for users to tag the restaurant in their own independent posts. The mix of amateur users and paid professionals makes it difficult to discern between posts expressing personal enjoyment versus those reflecting professional or guerilla viral marketing.[42] Thus, Instagram is where food pornography meets subversive corporate aesthetics. In another sense, Instagram is where desire is both indexed and aroused, then aggregated and directed toward the sources of fantasy wish fulfillment. Moreover, photo-sharing sites invite users to do immaterial labor on behalf of industry by both valorizing the polished product as the highest form of visual pleasure and providing virtually instantaneous customer feedback about the product.

Although Instagram is clearly a promotional tool for industry, images of food that appear on the site appear to be spontaneous, improvised, and about-to-be consumed by a real person instead of a paid actor. They are shot live at a real dinner happening at a restaurant possibly right near the spectator. With access to a smart phone, the spectator can even shoot their own pornography, food or otherwise. Do-it-Yourself (DIY) food porn appears natural and unscripted, as though meant to titillate a viewer peeping in on their neighbor's meal. In fact, however, the demand for DIY food porn has prompted professional producers to appropriate its unpolished aesthetics in order to compete. At the same time, the quality of digital photography and video enables contemporary DIY producers to mimic the production qualities of professional pornography. The confluence of these trends makes it increasingly difficult for spectators to discern between DIY and professional productions. Which food images represent spontaneous and quotidian expressions of culinary pleasure and which are merely crafted by the restaurant industry as a form of subversive advertising? The collapse of this boundary may not diminish the visual pleasures enjoyed by the spectator; however, the blurring of amateur and professional aesthetics does affect the dynamics of proximity. Spectators can expect the same degree of closeness to their fetishized food object from both an amateur eye and high-quality production values. Instead of worrying about questions of authenticity, the spectator has, in either case, plausible deniability that they are not looking at an advertisement but a spontaneous and improvised culinary encounter. What this means is that as DIY food porn has the capacity to look more polished and as professional food porn struggles to look more authentic, they converge into one aesthetic form that contains both the visual stimulant and the remedy for arousal. Ultimately, Internet food porn mimics the aesthetic conventions of another genre: advertising.

How does DIY Internet food pornography transform the spectator's relationship with food? First, in terms of proxemics, the cultural work of the Instagram food portrait is to routinize the pornographic gaze. That is to say, every encounter with food has the potential to produce spectacular visual pleasure, even at Applebee's. Moreover, when one actually encounters food, the physical act of eating becomes secondary to producing vicarious pleasure for others. Put differently, if pornography is primarily about the exchange of visceral for visual pleasure, DIY food pornography compels individuals to cycle affect into the cultural production of food, or to reproduce visual pleasure for others before they actually consume their own food. While individuals will no doubt go on to physically enjoy their visually pleasing dishes, it nonetheless becomes imperative that they seek out dishes that are most fit for a pornographic gaze, those dishes that visually stimulate in accordance with the generic demands of this recognizable form. DIY Internet food porn privileges excess, with meals visually conveying overindulgence to spectators. Of course, dishes that revel in excess make for the best pornography even if they are not physically pleasurable to eat. Excess can produce intense short-term pleasure in some circumstances and physical pain in others. Moreover, excess can produce visual pleasure for the voyeur but simultaneously provide no physical enjoyment for the diner. The same could be said of pornography in general, where the production of a visual spectacle can produce pain and discomfort for the actors, including acts of cruelty and sadism. In terms of authenticity, "amateur" implies that the producer is not a professional; yet the food that best conforms to the genre is that which is expertly composed to maximize both visceral and visual enjoyment of the meal. Amateur homemade meals generally lack this quality even if they are quite enjoyable. Unlike traditional DIY porn, spectators of this genre generally do not enjoy the gritty aesthetics and acceptable imperfections of home meals. In other words, spectators are unlikely to be "turned on" by the less than artful meal construction that takes place in the everyday kitchen. Thus, we must turn to chefs, the restaurant industry, and advertisers to provide for us what they do best: visual spectacle.

PORN WITH A STORYLINE

For foodies interested in a storyline, something less explicit than Instagram foodporn but nonetheless titillating, contemporary food media offers programs about culinary exploits, sumptuous travels, and exotic delights. These programs are qualitatively less gratuitous than their lurid digital counterparts and are more accessible to a mass audience. Indeed, Internet food porn is a graphic text that leaves nothing to the imagination and reduces acts like cooking and dining to an ineffable moment of climax, a graphic rendering of jouissance. On the other hand, televised food porn contextualizes eating as a process rather than an event, reveling in the sensual and erotic details of how polished food is produced and consumed. Food television cultivates both physical and cerebral arousal through storytelling, where eating is part of a larger narrative and sensory experience. In programs such as *$40 a Day*, *Bizarre Foods with Andrew Zimmern*, *Diners, Drive-Ins,* and *Dives*, *No Reservations*, among dozens of others on the *Food Network* and the Travel Channel, hosts treat the audience to an immersive culinary and travel experience, complete with backstory, plot, and character development. The meals are sometimes comprised of foreign and unfamiliar ingredients that arouse the spectator through tropes of mystery and exoticism.[43] Some meals are from places spectators are unlikely to visit and thus require the host to provide thick description and sumptuous detail. This kind of food pornography is less explicit and more imaginative. As in the case of erotica, the ideal audience here is one capable of using and being "turned on" by their own imagination. Food television does not rely solely on the kind of visual stimulation engendered by explicit imagery of indulgent overconsumption. Instead, it requires the audience to envision themselves as part of the story, to adopt the subject position of the host, and to immerse themselves in a thrilling narrative that concludes with an arousing act of consumption.

For my purposes in this chapter, of especial significance is the presence of textual innuendo that demands audiences of food television imagine what is not made explicit. Televised food porn excites its audience through restraint. In other words, food television invites the spectator to invest in the narrative before delivering sexual content. Anticipation is its own form of arousal. When sexual content is delivered, it is incomplete and contrived, demanding the audience imagine its reality in place of a graphic visual spectacle. An audience familiar with the norms of Instagram would have no problem doing so. Take for instance the *Food Network*'s *The Best Thing I Ever Ate*, which draws its inspiration, at least at a formal level, from the genre of erotic confessions complete with real-world dramatic reenactments alongside first person narration. Reminiscent of magazine forums and letters to the editor in porn magazines, *The Best Thing I Ever Ate* narrativizes the intimate details of an extraordinary dining experience. The program's confessional logic offers first-person proof that this *really* happened to them—real enjoyment converted into vicarious pleasure for the audience. Of course, the stories are spectacular, covering culinary situations that occur outside the kitchen of the average consumer and consisting of extraordinary and unexpected experiences of professional cooks and TV hosts. Where do the professionals get off? The program's point of emphasis is the narrative: how the storyteller unexpectedly discovered an incredible meal in an unlikely place, how they remembered something delicious from their childhood, how they went to extraordinary lengths to track down the best version of a popular dish, and the list goes on. This form of food porn begins with a slow and intriguing build toward an eventual climax. But as a visual medium, the narration of erotic conquest is only part of the experience. The audience is also treated to a visual reenactment where the original meal is restaged to provide visual proof that the experience took place. The host revisits the scene and performs bodily arousal and satisfaction after a long and detailed story.

In one episode featuring stories about the best food found "on a stick," chef Claire Robinson recounts stories of her encounters with the corn dog served at Shake Shack in New York City. At the outset of her narrative, the camera gives spectators a series of brief close-up shots of the sumptuous phallic shaped meal. But the shots are merely a tease. The camera quickly returns to Robinson, who recalls her food memoir in vivid detail before delivering on the promise of the big reveal. Robinson reminds the audience that the corn dog can only be purchased three times during the year, making it a rare and exotic delight. The spectator is meant to feel anticipation and excitement in the food's temporary absence. In short, the audience is primed for delayed gratification. Next, the creator of the corn dog supplements Robinson's personal narrative with a demonstration of how it's made. Analogous to foreplay, the cook teases the spectator with details of its construction, complete with an instructional demonstration of hot dogs being slid onto skewers, repeatedly covered in thick batter, and submerged in viscous cooking oil. As the dish comes together, the camera oscillates between Robinson and the cook's narration. This drawn out narration builds anticipation for the moment of consummation, when, finally, Robinson consumes the dish and recounts for a second time her feelings of enjoyment. This emphasis on narrative stimulation diverges from other forms of food pornography that seek to arouse primarily—if not exclusively—through voyeurism. The affective though seemingly cerebral aspects of such depictions give the text the alibi of artistic expression. The spectator is witness to a tasteful seduction, and thus, the context surrounding the text's more gratuitous representations of food can no longer be considered explicit. Such food porn may then escape the label of pornographic altogether. This is not hardcore pornography because, after all, it has a story with depth and complexity. The spectator's relationship with food is structured around romantic and attractive intensities: they should expect food to tease, beseech, and seduce them.

FRENZIED

Film scholars have contextualized "hardcore" as the outcome of a system of formal and informal prohibitions on sexuality.[44] Working from Michel Foucault, studies on pornography find that repression is the very mechanism that proliferates discourses of sexuality.[45] Efforts to censor pornography, for instance, required prohibitionists to speak those very deplorable acts that they wished to banish.[46] Censorship conveyed the importance of sex as a public problem, crafting an exploitable taboo or, at the very least, the impression that explicit and visible sex acts were the opposite of repression. Hardcore is characterized by visibility, or the capacity and desire to display the presumed truth of bodily interiority and the mysterious ineffability of bodily pleasure. Hardcore lays everything bare and demands that the body confess its hidden truths. What, then, is hardcore *food* pornography? Although it has not faced the same types of legal prohibitions, food is subject to cultural taboos—Conley and Eckstein's "dotted lines" signifying that which is "out of bounds"—including standards of cleanliness, appropriate portion size and calorie count, and dietary restrictions. As Helene Shugart argues, American food rhetoric is simultaneously preoccupied with dietary restrictions and fascinated with indulgent food.[47] America's cultural obsession with thinness is directly at odds with its ideology of mass consumption. Thus, hardcore food pornography—explicit and graphic depictions of massive overconsumption—has similarly emerged as an unintended but unsurprising response to discourses of repression. Hardcore food pornography mediates the tension between prohibition and liberation, defending itself as a form of release, even liberation, in a body conscious culture. Ultimately, hardcore food porn is a form of cultural bulimia, inviting the spectator to binge before they purge. It cloaks indulgence as a form of liberation; yet, as Foucault reminds us, liberation cannot escape the machinations of power.

Hardcore food porn purports to represent unbridled or raw expressions of desire. That is, it proposes yet fails to avail us of the mysteries of jouissance. It offers the fantasy of unlimited indulgence without consequence, promising to liberate the spectator from taboos against overconsumption through a vicarious release. Hardcore, thus, tends to be frenzied and even sexualized, at points almost primitive and transgressive. This type of food pornography then is concerned with speed: privileging the rapid overconsumption of both food and images. One prime example is the popular YouTube channel *Epic Meal Time*, a platform that features low-budget viral episodes in which a group of self-stylized degenerates seeks to create dishes with extraordinary calorie counts, absurd portions of bacon and fat, and large quantities of alcohol, often using ingredients from fast food restaurants, such as Big Mac Lasagna or Arby's Sushi.[48] The show features over-testosteroned men, who frequently make lurid and sexist remarks about women while launching into gonzo-style missions of excessive consumption—a kind of taboo consumption that might even be considered too extreme for hardcore. In each episode, the group cooks and then ravenously consumes meals that far exceed the limits of acceptable consumption, dishes that stretch into the tens of thousands of calories. Their unrestricted use of butter and bacon is gratuitous yet playful. While always with an ironic wink, men yell and aggressively curse at the audience in defense of their unrestricted cuisine. In Shugart's words, I suggest that *Epic Meal Time* is not about decadence but "defiant decadence."[49] The web series is a culinary snuff film, a kind of low-budget, grind house–style exploitation film or a Mondo documentary, where the pleasure of the text is an explicitly perverse substitution: acts so extreme that spectators are left to ask, did that really happen? This must be fake! Did they really eat that??[50] In other words, *Epic Meal Time* is "foodsploitation."

In one of their most popular episodes, titled "TurBacon Epic Thanksgiving," host Harley Morenstein starts by going to a local butcher and demanding a whole pig. The episode wastes little time with narrative, immediately cutting to extreme close-up shots of whole animal butchery, including a turkey, chicken, quail, duck, and Cornish hen. Captions report the calorie counts of each animal, along with a running tally of the total calories of the dish. Even at this early stage, the meal is 33,920 calories (eventually it reaches over 70,000). Next, Morenstein excitedly narrates the construction of "bacon-crescent stuffing" and what he calls "meal glue," a mysterious mixture of fat designed to hold the meal together. Close-ups record the frenzied motion of knives slicing raw meat and hands sloppily mixing slippery mounds of raw chopped bacon. Then, anonymous hands compile layers of deboned birds and pile them with bacon strips before stuffing them inside the pig. When the pig is sewn shut it is placed in a smoker and basted with a Dr. Pepper and butter glaze, and of course, wrapped in more bacon. Morenstein sits at the head of table surrounded by seated guests, quietly awaiting the stuffed pig. When it arrives, the cook cuts the concoction open. Morenstein turns to the chef and asks, "Do you want to fuck this or what?" The guests begin haphazardly grabbing enormous portions with their hands. The table is covered in plastic wrap and eating utensils are nowhere in sight. The camera shows individuals stuffing messy portions of the meal into their mouths with reckless abandon (fig. 3.2).

As this example demonstrates, *Epic Meal Time* transgresses the boundaries of socially acceptable consumption. This is hardcore par excellence: a

Figure 3.2. *Epic Meal Time*'s "TurBacon Epic Thanksgiving." Screen capture by author.

graphic display of frenzied desire. The show mirrors the id's affective urges without the restraint of the ego, the psyche's uninhibited pursuit and maximization of the pleasure principle.[51] The program presents consumption that is wild, feverish, and even violent and sadistic; the kind of consumption that reflects a less civilized and less repressed version of the psyche. Culturally speaking, the show presents a fantasy of limitless consumption without consequence, throwing off the strictures of dietary regimens, public health guidelines, and even the rules of decorum that govern eating. Moreover, the show presents extreme situations that would be difficult if not undesirable for the spectator to imitate. Indeed, viewers of pornography may take scopic pleasure from images of cruelty, sadism, and taboo expressions of desire and yet at the same time disavow such behaviors. This particular example presents acts so extreme and situations so outlandish that the spectator can experience enjoyment while maintaining their distance. Viewers of *Epic Meal Time* are unlikely to imitate such frenzied consumption. Thus, food pornography may reflect the somatic desires of the id but does little to challenge social and psychic repression. It is a text that presents itself as playful liberation from the seemingly Victorian conventions of bodily restraint. Yet, while it produces visibility, food pornography reveals no hidden truths; instead, it constructs knowledge/power and regulates bodily pleasures through the proliferation of sex/food talk. In accordance with the ideological apparatus of food production, food pornography prepares audiences to participate in the culture of bodily restraint and regulation by giving them an outlet to binge without violating the taboos governing overconsumption.[52] A culture fraught with tension between bodily restraint and mass consumerism requires a fantasy of consumption without consequence in the popular imaginary to help mediate these contradictory demands. Food porn gives audiences the impression that both objectives are attainable, that they need not question the tension between the body image and the culture of overconsumption.

THE SAFETY WORD IS . . .

The pornographic gaze has transformed the public's relationship with food as much as its relationship with sex. With its emphasis on excess and visual spectacle, pornography is the preferred genre of industry. The ubiquity of the form is concomitant with the decline in home cooking and the corporate takeover of our food and agricultural systems. It is in the interest of advertisers to make food "dirty," not merely to give food products a sexual life of their own but to create a distanced relationship with food in which consumers needs industry to construct and then satisfy their elaborate fantasies. In all its varied incarnations, food porn builds affinity and courts affective investments in consumer fetishism and constructing products and consumption as a surrogate form of both pleasure and social relations. As a hybrid body genre, food pornography excites an almost involuntary mimicry in the spectator, or desire to imitate the type of consumption it represents or infers. Where pornography invites masturbation, food pornography invites consumption. Consumerism, however, is a vexing form of enjoyment because it, too, is a vicarious and visual pleasure. The enjoyment of a commodity is temporary and fleeting; its use-value is always a disappointment when contrasted against its fetishistic qualities. The only solution is perpetual and unending consumption, a process that reflects how advanced industrial society functions on the continual cultivation and satisfaction of false needs.[53] Food pornography cultivates desire for the visually pleasing spectacle of corporate food even at the expense of physical enjoyment, particularly of meals at home. Often, spectators are the most enthusiastic participants in this process. Meanwhile everything between the home-cooked meal and delicious but visually imperfect meals at the local dive are constructed as a letdown. The form, then, dictates what counts as acceptable desire and consumption in the public imaginary. DIY, softcore, hardcore: all valorize excessive and spectacular modes of conspicuous consumption; modes of consumption that, ironically, are the most disappointing.

This analysis illustrates how an emerging genre of visual discourse aggregates and directs felt bodily intensities in ways that intervene into the public's conception of taste. The purpose of this chapter is to map the rhetorical genre of food pornography over the influence architecture of the industrial food system. That is to say, food pornography is a rhetorical form that prepares bodies to accept what counts as desire and satisfaction within the industrial food system. Ideally, the consumer who is addled by the advertising image will perform immaterial labor on the behalf of industry by demanding the ersatz version of the home-cooked meal or sharing pictures that circulate the polished aesthetic. Either way, circulating affective attachments to the polished product of industry nurtures consumer dependence and thus obviates the need for cooking at home. As Pollan has argued, separating people from the practice of cooking is the end goal of the food industry. The less we cook at home the more reliant we become on restaurants and frozen pre-prepared meals endorsed by celebrity chefs. The implications of the decline of cooking should concern those interested in both public health and the health of the public sphere. In terms of the former, home-cooked meals are by-and-large healthier and more nourishing. According to a study conducted at Johns Hopkins University, people who frequently cook at home eat healthier diets and consume less calories than those who do not.[54] Indeed, this decline in cooking should be concerning, as two thirds of Americans are considered overweight or obese.[55] Yet, the food industry has successfully manipulated the public's craving for unhealthy food, not only through products that are comprised of an addictive combination of salt, fat, and sugar but by circulating an accompanying aesthetic that whets our appetites for more.

In terms of the health of the public, the home-cooked meal cultivates modes of civic engagement that enrich public culture. As Justin Eckstein and Anna M. Young argue, "If we cook together, then turn taking, sharing, invitational speaking, and arguing linger as habits for future encounters. That is, the practice of coming together shapes potential interactions with others—the dinner table offers a democratic lure."[56] The packaged meal, designed for individual consumption, discourages forms of social bonding centered around a shared dinner table. Diners are encouraged to see themselves as atomized individuals who should prefer the time saved by using the microwave to the conviviality of the common plate. In other words, conversations over cooking and shared meals constitute a kind of proto-public sphere wherein the norms of participation in civic culture are nurtured and tested.[57] Cooking and sharing meals are constructive and political acts that together cultivate social bonds among a democratic polity. "Cooking," Eckstein and Young write, "is an inherently political topos because it is a practice of citizenship."[58] Where the food industry does the work of cooking for us, it replaces forms of democratic sociality that connect disparate communities at a local and intimate level. Food pornography not only cultivates a divestment from cooking imperfect meals that do not meet the industry's unattainable aesthetic but also encourages a distant form of sociality in which consumers relate to each other through a reified visual commodity. Put differently, our social relations are captured and repurposed to do immaterial labor on the behalf of industry. No longer producers of food, consumers are alienated from their own living labor. Food pornography is a genre that directs the body of the consumer—not the mind of the citizen—to desire ersatz pleasures and invest in her or his own subjugation.

NOTES

1. Linda Williams, *Hard Core: Power, Pleasure, and the "Frenzy of the Visible"* (Berkeley: University of California Press, 1989), 100–101.

2. Joshua Gunn, "Maranatha," *Quarterly Journal of Speech* 98, no. 4 (2012): 372. For more on the concept of *jouissance* see Jacques Lacan, *The Seminar of Jacques Lacan, Book XVII: The Other Side of Psychoanalysis*, trans. Russell Grigg (New York: W. W. Norton, 2007), 46.

3. Fetish genres are not explicitly pornographic, they depend solely on context for stimuli and arousal. Thus, they evade clear definition. For instance, in clothed porn or object porn, it is not explicit acts but the explicit displacement or concealment of explicit material that is the source of arousal. David Andrews writes that "these forms have been situated as pornography by circumstances of their production, distribution, or reception." Something similar could be said of "softcore" or "erotica" where the most graphic or explicit elements of sex are not disclosed to the audience. For more on the definition and history of "softcore" and fetishism see David Andrews, "Toward a More Valid Definition of 'Pornography,'" *Journal of Popular Culture* 45, no. 3 (2012): 460.

4. See Casey Ryan Kelly, *Abstinence Cinema: Virginity and the Rhetoric of Sexual Purity in Contemporary Film* (New Brunswick: Rutgers University Press, 2016); and Richard Dyer, *White: Essays on Race and Culture* (London, New York: Routledge, 1997), 191. The term "frenzied" is borrowed from Williams, *Hard Core*.

5. See Frederick Kaufman, "Debbie Does Salad," *Harper's Magazine*, October 2005, http://harpers.org/archive/2005/10/debbie-does-salad/.

6. Andrews argues against efforts to create an objective definition of pornography in favor of one dependent on the context of production, consumption, and reception. He writes that "though in its infancy as a recognized form, pornography has proved textually diverse and contextually polysemic. This heterogeneity has been explosively expansionary, coming unmoored from artistic basics with stunning alacrity." See Andrews, "Toward a More Valid Definition," 465.

7. According to Marx, commodity fetishism describes how producers and consumers come to see the relationships of production not as between people but as relationships of economic exchange between money and commodities in a marketplace. Products or commodities take on a life of their own that exceeds their use-value, and thus, the real producers are rendered invisible. See Karl Marx, *Capital: A Critique of Political Economy* (New York: Penguin, 2004).

8. See Michael Pollan, *The Omnivore's Dilemma: A Natural History of Four Meals* (New York: Penguin, 2007).

9. See Eckstein and Young, "Cooking, Celebrity Chefs, and Public Chef Intellectuals" (chapter 2, n. 4).

10. See Guy Debord, *Society of the Spectacle* (Detroit: Black & Red, 2000); Slavoj

Zizek, *Welcome to the Desert of the Real: Five Essays on September 11 and Related Dates* (New York: Verso, 2013).

11. Brian Massumi, *Parables for the Virtual: Movement, Affect, Sensation* (Durham: Duke University Press Books, 2002).

12. Jenny Rice, "The New 'New': Making a Case for Critical Affect Studies," *Quarterly Journal of Speech* 94, no. 2 (2008): 201.

13. See Michael Pollan, *In Defense of Food: An Eater's Manifesto* (New York: Penguin, 2008).

14. Karlyn Kohrs Campbell and Kathleen Hall Jamieson, *Form and Genre: Shaping Rhetorical Action* (Falls Church, VA: The Speech Communication Association, 1978), 21.

15. See Linda Williams, "Film Bodies: Gender, Genre, and Excess," *Film Quarterly* 44, no. 4 (1991): 2–13.

16. See Kenneth Burke, *Counter-Statement*, rev. ed. (Berkeley: University of California Press, 1968); Hawhee, *Moving Bodies*; Robert L. Heath, "Kenneth Burke on Form," *Quarterly Journal of Speech* 65, no. 4 (1979): 392–404.

17. See Gunn, "Maranatha," 369; see also Joshua Gunn, "The Rhetoric of Exorcism: George W. Bush and the Return of Political Demonology," *Western Journal of Communication* 68, no. 1 (2004): 1–23.

18. See Sara Ahmed, *Cultural Politics of Emotion* (Edinburgh: Edinburgh University Press, 2014); and Erin J. Rand, "'What One Voice Can Do': Civic Pedagogy and Choric Collectivity at Camp Courage," *Text and Performance Quarterly* 34, no. 1 (2014): 28–51.

19. Erin J. Rand, *Reclaiming Queer: Activist and Academic Rhetorics of Resistance* (Tuscaloosa: University of Alabama Press, 2014), 132.

20. Valerie J. Smith, "Aristotle's Classical Enthymeme and the Visual Argumentation of the Twenty-First Century," *Argumentation & Advocacy* 43, no. 3/4 (2007): 114–23.

21. See Cara A. Finnegan, "The Naturalistic Enthymeme and Visual Argument: Photographic Representation in the 'Skull Controversy,'" *Argumentation & Advocacy* 37, no. 3 (2001): 133; and Stephanie L. Young, "Running Like a Man, Sitting Like a Girl: Visual Enthymeme and the Case of Caster Semenya," *Women's Studies in Communication* 38, no. 3 (2015): 331–50.

22. David S. Birdsell and Leo Groarke, "Toward a Theory of Visual Argument," *Argumentation & Advocacy* 33, no. 1 (1996): 7.

23. See David S. Birdsell and Leo Groarke, "Outlines of a Theory of Visual Argument," *Argumentation & Advocacy* 43, no. 3/4 (2007): 103–13; Kevin Michael DeLuca and Jennifer Peeples, "From Public Sphere to Public Screen: Democracy, Activism, and the 'Violence' of Seattle," *Critical Studies in Media Communication* 19, no. 2 (2002): 125–51; Janis L. Edwards and Carol K. Winkler, "Representative Form and the Visual Ideograph: The Iwo Jima Image in Editorial Cartoons," *Quarterly Journal of Speech* 83, no. 3 (1997): 289–310; Robert Hariman and John Louis Lucaites, *No Caption Needed: Iconic Photographs, Public Culture, and Liberal Democracy* (Chicago: University of Chicago Press, 2011); Lester C. Olson, "Benjamin Franklin's Pictorial Representations of the British Colonies in America: A Study in Rhetorical Iconology," *Quarterly Journal of Speech* 73, no. 1 (1987): 18–42; and Jennifer Peeples, "Toxic Sublime: Imaging Contaminated Landscapes," *Environmental Communication* 5, no. 4 (2011): 373–92.

24. Michel Foucault, *The History of Sexuality: Volume 1* (New York: Random House,

1978); *Discipline and Punish: The Birth of the Prison* (New York: Vintage Books, 1977); and *The Birth of Biopolitics: Lectures at the Collège de France, 1978—1979* (New York: Picador, 2010).

25. See Eric S. Jenkins, "The Affections of the American Pickers: Commodity Fetishism in Control Society," *Communication and Critical/Cultural Studies* 12, no. 4 (2015): 347–66.

26. "Film Bodies," 4.

27. Gunn, "Maranatha," 369.

28. See Susan Sontag, *Regarding the Pain of Others* (New York: Picador, 2004).

29. Laura Mulvey, "Visual Pleasure and Narrative Cinema," *Screen* 16, no. 3 (1975): 6–18.

30. Sut Jhally, *The Codes of Advertising: Fetishism and the Political Economy of Meaning in the Consumer Society* (New York: Routledge, 1987).

31. Carolyn R. Miller, "Genre as Social Action," *Quarterly Journal of Speech* 70, no. 2 (1984): 151.

32. Hollie Shaw, "The Food Porn Trend: How Restaurants Are Catering to Instagram-Hungry Patrons," *Financial Post*, January 3, 2015, http://business.financialpost.com/news/retail-marketing/the-food-porn-trend-how-restaurants-are-catering-to-instagram-hungry-patrons.

33. Bolthouse Farms, "URWHATUPOST, Food Porn Index," accessed December 12, 2016 at http://www.urwhatupost.com.

34. Herbert Marcuse, *Eros and Civilization: A Philosophical Inquiry into Freud* (Boston: Beacon Press, 1974).

35. Marcuse, quoted in Douglas Kellner and Clayton Pierce, *Philosophy, Psychoanalysis, and Emancipation: Collected Papers of Herbert Marcuse, Volume Five: Herbert Marcuse Collected Papers* (New York: Routledge, 2010), 56.

36. Greg Dickinson observes that corporate chains such as the Olive Garden and the Macaroni Grill sell suburban fantasies to consumers by modeling the aesthetics of their restaurants after the mythic small-town community. Moreover, such restaurants cultivate identification with consumers through the key topoi of the American Dream: abundance and choice. The chain restaurant industry not only offers to do the cooking for Americans but to stand as an ersatz version of community space. Food pornography is but another version of the aesthetic: a perfectly crafted but shallow simulation of real enjoyment. See Dickinson, *Suburban Dreams* (chapter 2, n. 17).

37. Jonathan Blake, "Instagram Now Bigger than Twitter," BBC, December 10, 2014, http://www.bbc.co.uk/newsbeat/article/30410973/instagram-now-bigger-than-twitter.

38. See "#foodpornography," at https://www.instagram.com/explore/tags/foodpornography/.

39. Mark Prigg, "Study Reveals #Foodporn 500 Years before Instagram," *Daily Mail*, July 22, 2016, http://www.dailymail.co.uk/sciencetech/article-3703679/Foodporn-500-years-Instagram-Study-reveals-artist-s-obsessions-documenting-great-meals-bear-no-resemblance-people-really-eat.html.

40. Beth Kowitt, "How Restaurants Use Instagram and OpenTable to Gather Data on Diners," *Fortune*, June 22, 2016, http://fortune.com/2016/06/22/restaurants-instagram-opentable/.

41. Jeff Kauflin, "How a New York Restaurant Uses Instagram Influencers to Drive Sales," *Forbes*, September 26, 2016, http://www.forbes.com/sites/jeffkauflin/2016/09/28/how-a-new-york-restaurant-uses-instagram-influencers-to-drive-sales/.

42. As participatory media and user-generated content are supported by profit-driven platforms, vernacular websites and applications can be thought of as hybrid to the extent that they never fully escape the political economy of contemporary mass media. See Robert Glenn Howard, "The Vernacular Web of Participatory Media," *Critical Studies in Media Communication* 25, no. 5 (2008): 490–513.

43. See Kelly, *Food Television and Otherness* (introduction, n. 17).

44. Helen Hester, *Beyond Explicit: Pornography and the Displacement of Sex* (Albany: SUNY Press, 2014); Walter M. Kendrick, *The Secret Museum: Pornography in Modern Culture* (Berkeley: University of California Press, 1996); and Alan Soble, *Pornography: Marxism, Feminism, and the Future of Sexuality* (New Haven: Yale University Press, 1986).

45. See Foucault, *The History of Sexuality: Volume 1*; and *Discipline and Punish*.

46. See also Judith Butler, *Excitable Speech: A Politics of the Performative* (New York: Routledge, 1997).

47. Helene A. Shugart, *Heavy: The Obesity Crisis in Cultural Context* (London: Oxford University Press, 2016).

48. *Epic Meal Time* is a Canadian YouTube channel created in 2010 by Harley Morenstein and Sterling Toth. The channel has produced 341 episodes and spawned a 2012 spin-off titled *Epic Chef* that borrows from the format of the *Food Network*'s show *Chopped* but replaces the secret ingredient challenge with bacon and an alcoholic beverage. The YouTube Channel has over seven million subscribers (see https://www.youtube.com/user/EpicMealTime). See Rachel Tepper, "'Epic Chef,' Food Competition Show from Epic Meal Time, Features Talented Chefs and Gross Challenges (VIDEO)," *Huffington Post*, December 14, 2012, http://www.huffingtonpost.com/2012/12/14/epic-chef-epic-meal-time_n_2300815.html.

49. Shugart, *Heavy*, 6.

50. For more on snuff pornography see Clarissa Smith, "Breathing New Life into Old Fears: Extreme Pornography and the Wider Politics of Snuff," in *Snuff: Real Death and Screen Media*, ed. Neil Jackson et al. (New York: Bloomsbury Academic, 2016), 81–104.

51. See Sigmund Freud, *The Ego and the Id*, ed. and trans. James Strachey (New York: Norton, 1961).

52. For more on the rhetoric of gluttony see Carlnita P. Greene, *Gourmands and Gluttons: The Rhetoric of Food Excess* (New York: Peter Lang, 2015).

53. See Herbert Marcuse, *One-Dimensional Man: Studies in the Ideology of Advanced Industrial Society* (Boston: Beacon Press, 1964).

54. Mike Smith and the Johns Hopkins Bloomberg School of Public Health, "Study Suggests Home Cooking Is a Main Ingredient in Healthier Diet," *Johns Hopkins Bloomberg School of Public Health*, accessed April 16, 2017, http://www.jhsph.edu/research/centers-and-institutes/johns-hopkins-center-for-a-livable-future/news-room/News-Releases/2014/Study-Suggests-Home-Cooking-Main-Ingredient-in-Healthier-Diet.html.

55. National Institute of Diabetes and Digestive and Kidney Diseases, "Overweight

and Obesity Statistics," 2012, https://www.niddk.nih.gov/health-information/health-statistics/Pages/overweight-obesity-statistics.aspx.

56. Eckstein and Young, "Public Chef Intellectuals," 206.

57. The concept of "proto-publics" is borrowed from Rosa A. Eberly, *Citizen Critics: Literary Public Spheres* (Urbana: University of Illinois Press, 2000).

58. Eckstein and Young, "Public Chef Intellectuals," 208.

4

Rhetorically Strange Foods

JEFF RICE

EPISODE 1 OF MICHAEL POLLAN'S Netflix show *Cooked* begins with Australian aboriginals pulling monitor lizards out of burrows, slapping the animals' heads against the ground to kill them, and then throwing the lizards into a fire to cook. This food act, no doubt practiced for hundreds, if not thousands, of years in the Australian outback, poses discomfort for an American audience. The imagery of killing and eating lizards appears strange, foreign, and unpalatable to the average American viewer used to beef, pork, and chicken as dietary meat staples that arrive precut and not slammed on the ground. Our initial reaction to eating lizard, as well, might be one of immediate repulsion. "The choice of what we put in our mouths for substance," as Andrew Chase proclaims, "seems to elicit primitive reactions; it is, after all, the most basic of human actions."[1] As we watched the show's initial scene, my wife immediately turned her head away in disgust. "Tell me when it's done," she said. Why, I asked myself, did this scene, an otherwise daily encounter with food captured on film, seem so strange as to repulse?

I could call our television moment an example of "othering" aboriginal food practices. Fredric Jameson argues that "culture must thus always be seen as a vehicle or a medium whereby the relationship between groups is transacted. If it is not always vigilantly unmasked as an idea of the Other (even when I reassume it for myself), it perpetuates the optical illusions and false objectivism of this complex historical relationship."[2] Othering the aboriginal moment allows those encountering strange eating practices to avoid Jameson's "false objectivism," to revel in the assumption that my food practices are "normal" by comparison. Dana Goodyear writes, "Most people hold back some species or another from consideration as food, and the reasons can seem arbitrary."[3] False objectivism can lead us to form an image of abnormality, which in turn prevents alternative understandings of food practices and the language we use to describe such practices. Pollan adds that food attitudes are manipulated into the tropes of either the strange or the normal by forces we consider habitual or commercial: "We Americans are amazed to learn that some of the cultures that set their culinary course by the lights of habit and pleasure rather than nutritional science and marketing are actually healthier than we are."[4]

Such food bias politicizes eating so that, as Casey Kelly argues, a "neocolonial discourse" fashions "the superiority of Western values and the imperative to extend its civilizing mission to the non-Western world."[5] Kelly's project analyzes food narratives' effect on readers/viewers who, via othering, "vicariously participate in consumptive excursions to exotic regions while erasing the power lines of iniquity that divide the globe."[6] For Kelly, televised food narratives—some of which I will write about in this chapter—reinforce "the difference between self and Other; an Other permitted to exist according to what suits the Western palate."[7] This critique is familiar to rhetorical studies; it is one in which the "strange" is made exotic by a Western readership in racist or, at least, problematic ways. This approach would be one way to politicize eating monitor lizards as colonial or racist. Kelly's method, however, is limiting in that it delivers what it already expects or knows. Its reading may not be based on the language or imagery of the discourse but instead on an already established belief that centralizes one type of political stance—in this case, Othering—above all others.

In this chapter, I propose a different political reading, one which does not repeat traditional critical tropes, such as imperial or neocolonial, but instead studies how so called "dirty" food rhetorics work against our expectations of the exotic or difference and instead emphasize the everyday and the banal. In my reading, the politics of strange food is not about how readers romanticize supposedly exotic or non-Western cultures. Rather, my project shows how strange food is often not strange at all; the rhetoric of food narratives often borrows familiar language and tropes that, when traced out, demonstrate typical, not imperial, eating practices. The implications of such a reading extend beyond the specific foods I focus on; they suggest that familiarity—either as critique or as discourse—is a complex political gesture whose rhetoric must be dislodged, at times, in order for us to fully grasp the power of narrative.

RHETORICAL DIFFERENCE

Pollan's "habit and pleasure" politicizes a common rhetorical gesture that contrasts one narrative of apprehension against another narrative of difference.[8] The contrast restores normalcy to the perception of abnormal food events. I see this narrative in my own close circle where, in addition to the above-described episode with my wife, friends and family members have been known to express shock at what I feed my daughter (and that she enjoys): beef hearts, lamb tongue, cow tongue, and lamb fries. To these people, we are engaging with a strange food; we are creating a culture clash that pits American, traditional eating habits (steak, chicken breast, ground beef) against a supposedly foreign practice. In their eyes, we are no better than the aboriginals who eat monitor lizards. This rhetorical stance can reach an extreme state at times, such as when my father refused to eat the Indian food catered at my wedding because of its exotic position in his cultural vocabulary and his "primitive reaction" to, or "othering" of, that vocabulary. He brought a cheese sandwich with him to eat instead.

The issue of cultural difference, though real and prominent, ignores the larger rhetorical constructions of strange that dominate food rhetorics in basic, yet powerful, ways. To be shocked at the consumption of foods eaten the world over is not so much an act of power—as we often frame such moments—as it is a matter of rhetorical difference. In other words, without our attempting to project a specific act as strange, familiarity in taste or expectation may still generate a strange meaning. Nothing, for instance, in Pollan's opening scene claims eating monitor lizards is strange; the rhetorical framing of the Australian outback as a wild space, the presence of a roaring fire, and the image of people eating outside under the stars, however, may re-enforce tropes regarding strange practices since none of this ambiance constitutes a familiar set of images (dining table, plates, silverware) that communicate food to a typical American audience. Food is a "system of communication," Roland Barthes wrote, "a body of images, a protocol of usages, situations, and behavior."[9] Food "constitutes an information, it signifies."[10] Strange is one system of signification. Strange, media often demonstrate, is a rhetorical transformation of the everyday—what we eat—into the unique and the novel. Strange marks a space where we believe that what we are witnessing, or eating, is not common. Strange is a narrative reaction against the banal.

Michel de Certeau documented the everyday as banal and often did so via narrative, and at times food narratives. His canonical "Walking the City" promotes narrative as the focus of a spatial analysis that avoids grand gestures—the large, sweeping generalizations of culture, such as "colonial" or "Othering"—in favor of the supposedly minor or banal. To approach the banal, de Certeau argued, one tells stories. These stories, in turn, familiarize readers/audiences with what were previously unfamiliar activities—such as de Certeau's example of Manhattan's grandness masking the unfamiliar streets below. Introducing the second volume of the coauthored *Practice of*

Everyday Life, de Certeau remarks that objects of study—such as food—are not just for cultural analysis but rather are performative; they are the objects of stories that tell "the relationship that their strangeness has with familiarity."[11] Food stories demarcate how the familiar, such as eating, is always connected to what is not familiar, such as what one eats. His coauthor Luce Giard adds to de Certeau's observation by noting that culturally we tell stories about food that are neither rational nor representational. They are based on shifting variables of perception, whether the focus is a monitor lizard or Indian food. "Nothing is more variable from one human group to another than the notion of what is edible: one has only to think about the dog, spurned in Europe but appreciated in Hong Kong; or grasshoppers, considered disgusting here, yet highly prized in the Maghreb; or the worms savored in New Guinea."[12] Giard's examples of dog and grasshopper foreground two variables that I, too, will focus on for their rhetorical shaping of strange food. These variables do not other, as traditional or "grand" cultural critiques (the other, the colonial) claim, but instead perform.

In rhetorical studies, Gregory Ulmer has championed the variables that perform narratives (the personal, school practices, theory, disciplinary issues) as a means of communicating one's place in the world. These variables, Ulmer argues, make the familiar—traditional argumentation about a subject, such as whether a culture's food is strange or not, or whether a culture is othered—unfamiliar by allowing rhetors to trace out connections among them. Relying on a food metaphor, Ulmer connects this process to what he calls the *unheimlich maneuver*, based on an inversion of the well-known method of saving an individual choking on food lodged in the throat. Playing off the circumstance that Freud equated *unheimlich* with the uncanny, or unfamiliar, Ulmer uses the term as a pun for the process of dislodging the unfamiliar from the familiar. In this rhetorical construction, the familiar is unwanted because it is an obstacle, like food lodged in a throat, to invention. Ulmer's analogy begins with a typical Heimlich instruction: "Attempt to chew a large chunk of unchewed flank steak in a public place. Begin to choke to death. Wait for someone present to come forward and perform the HEIMLICH MANEUVER."[13]

Ulmer's focus here is rhetorical invention. The familiar blocks invention practices by treating the everyday *as is*. "The most common expression of creative insight," Ulmer writes, "—to put together two ideas that previously seemed unrelated—explains this effect: the unfamiliar is suddenly recognized as familiar. Such is also the experience of learning."[14] By practicing unheimlich maneuvers, Ulmer argues, one overcomes obstacles that familiar thinking poses. In this chapter, I will apply the unheimlich maneuver to specific rhetorical constructions of strange food in order to dislodge the blockage of unfamiliarity. Instead of reading the strange through the traditional (heimlich or familiar) lenses Kelly and others argue for, I dislodge these familiar readings so that another reading of strange food emerges. I explore several supposedly unfamiliar food practices to ask how their rhetorical construction might allow for an unheimlich intervention on my part, a de-familiarizing gesture that contrasts to traditional approaches such as exoticism or critiquing otherness.

That Ulmer chooses food as a metaphor for the creative/invention process is important in the way that Barth claims food as communicative. Food, in its most familiar forms, blocks meaning when eaters react in predictable ways, such as a gag reflex that follows disgust. As I appropriate unheimlich gestures among written, digital, and television food projections, I relieve the gag of the unfamiliar. In any given food informational moment, possible meanings blocked by the gag reflex might involve the supposed importance of consuming dog or grasshopper, as Giard suggests, or the aboriginal practices of eating monitor lizards, as my initial anecdote describes.

Communicative blockages politicize food. Framing food practices as strange or other displaces what is often banal rhetoric. With food, strangeness is not so much an uncanny experience—such as eating grasshopper—but a familiar rhetorical rejection. The familiar is posed as an ideal communicative moment one lives up to (familiar food). Yet, in a rhetoric of the strange, there is no, as Brad Vivian writes, "affirmation of an ideal subject."[15] An "ideal" suggests a state of accepted being (the individual in Vivian's study; food in this chapter). The unheimlich (uncanny) suggests that accepted being cannot be affirmed.

A rhetoric of strange food suggests a false affirmation of the food interactions many of us engage with. In print, digital, and video projections that tend to focus on the pivotal rhetorical objects of dog, grasshopper, penis, and other food items we can identify how this rhetoric generates binaries such as the civilized vs. the uncivilized or the exotic vs. the mainstream. These narratives are often disseminated so that, in the end, the strange becomes the familiar, and not vice versa—as we would expect when we look away from a TV broadcast or refuse to eat a specific ethnic food. Instead of telling that type of narrative, I *trace*, as Bruno Latour might call it, a few key food objects, exploring how exotic stories are in fact rhetorically banal. Tracing, Latour notes, allows us to follow strands of thought, connections, and associations without resorting only to the tropes of critique or analysis.[16] Tracing is a methodology of presentation, *showing* how texts and ideas connect. In the following, I examine the rhetorical framing of strange food as the opposite of what we anticipate. My method is not critical analysis but rather a tracing of the rhetorical markers that construct strange as normal. This tracing allows me to move through language usage and media projection, following usage form point to point, and allowing these points to connect. Strange food rhetorics are, we see, not very strange at all. Our intervention through this tracing will either alert us to their sudden strangeness, or more likely, allow for a rethinking of what constitutes the strange in food.

EATING HUMANS

In food communication, there may be nothing stranger than eating human flesh. Yet, many descriptions of eating humans often rely upon "tradition" and "banality" as a tropes to justify such a practice. Without writing a wide-ranging overview of the practice of cannibalism, I map some descriptions that provide banal readings of what should be posed as the most barbaric of all civilized cultures. "There seems to be a great deal of speculation about the flavor of human flesh," Gary Allen writes.[17] "What we need," he advises as antidote to this unruly speculation, "is a modern individual, preferably someone like us (to avoid possible cultural confusion), a sane, intelligent person who just happens to have eaten human flesh."[18] Eating human is no different, in this case, from any other accepted behavior we recognize in ourselves. The unknown author of the 1840 *Cabinet of Curiosities, Or Wonders of the World Displayed* understood human flesh as a traditional food item, historically consumed by notable thinkers, even if he himself would not necessarily engage in such a practice. He speculated, "The philosophers Diogenes, Chrysippus, and Zeon, followed by the whole sect of Stoics, maintain that there is nothing unnatural in the eating of human flesh; and that it is very reasonable to use dead bodies for food."[19] Continuing with tradition as a trope, Brian S. Hook theorizes Plato's description of cannibalism as based on fairly common and accepted artistic expression, for the language Plato uses here is "taken from the tragic stage."[20] With Diogenes, Hook postulates that the rhetorician used tragedy as well, in this case to "sanction cannibalism" and the "belief that a human element pervades all things, as all things pervade the human element."[21] The topos of "traditional" is one way that historical reflection tames the exotic. Reflection on the past makes the strange—such as eating human—familiar and part of common experiences.

In addition to tradition, the rhetoric of eating flesh is also framed as a daily encounter, such as we see in Hook's comment that eating flesh can "pervade all things." In *Eating Right in the Renaissance*, Ken Albala notes that "the idea of eating human flesh was, in fact, a perennial obsession for dietary writers" of the Renaissance period who negotiated this binary in their writing.[22] Nineteenth-century ethnographies of colonialism in Africa and Asia, even as they were saturated with colonialist rhetoric, generate a narrative of cannibalism as quotidian. One example, the tales of explorer Captain J. S. Erskine, are documented in the *Journal of the Ethnological Society of London*. Erskine's experiences in nineteenth-century Kenya included watching tribesmen carry off a slaughtered enemy and eating him as if it were nothing more than a typical meal where meat is broiled: "They took all the flesh of the body, leaving only the big bones, and carried it to their boats, and we all saw them broil (panggang), and afterwards eat it. They ate it with great relish."[23] No exotic adjectives. No critique. No variable interference. One eats with great energy via a basic cooking method, broiling.

The rhetorical banality of eating humans may also be traced in descriptions of eating body parts associated with humans: notably hearts and brains (i.e., offal). Language and method dislodge strangeness. In *Unmentionable Cuisine*, Calvin Schwabe's descriptions could apply to any meat: "Brain is a delectable meat of good texture and a mild flavor to which few who give it a fair trial could honestly object."[24] Regarding sheep's brains, Schwabe writes, "Prejudice against the idea of brains must assuredly be overcome for this one: there is no disguising the origin of this attractive dish with its fine combination of flavors."[25] Early American cookbooks, such as *The Dixie Cook-Book*, likely influenced by Western settler culture, express no prejudice in recipes for body parts. The recipes' language treats such items as everyday fare. "Take a beef's or sheep's or veal's heart," one begins, and "make a stuffing of breadcrumbs same as for roast turkey, fill the cavity," and bake for two hours. But do not discard the valves, "which must be cut off after washing, into a saucepan, with a pint of cold water and a sliced onion. Let simmer slowly one hour."[26] The *Mohawk Valley Cookbook*, too, offers heart recipes: "The hearts, livers, gizzards of roast fowls should be boiled in salted water until tender, chopped very fine, and stirred with the water in which they have been cooked, into the dripping pan, after the fowl has been removed."[27] Shoved into the final miscellaneous section of the 1881 *Housekeeping in the Bluegrass* is a recipe for hog brains. "Take the brains from two heads; wash and soak overnight in salt water; wash in fresh water and put in a frying pan with salt and pepper; cover with hot water and stew till done. Just before serving stir in two eggs well beaten, and a tablespoonful each of butter and cream. Serve hot."[28] The 1839 *Good Housekeeper* advises cooks preparing pigs: "Cut off the head and part it down the middle, take out the brains, chop them fine with some boiled sage leaves, and mix these with veal or beef gravy."[29]

Similar to the authors of these early cookbooks, food writer M. F. K. Fisher familiarizes offal via language and method. The language of Fisher's recipes makes heart as familiar as any meat one might stuff or roast: "Another vital part of a beef is the heart, which is not well enough known as a meat unusually rich in vitamins and minerals too. A larger heart should be stuffed with a regular poultry dressing, aromatic with fresh or dried herbs, and based often with fat of rich stock in a slow oven until it is tender."[30] Fisher also offers a recipe for cooking brains. In doing so, she engages in a familiar rhetorical gesture of equation, describing the supposedly strange (brains) as similar to something familiar (eggs): "Brains are, to my mind, unfortunately coupled with scrambled eggs on most menus. The combination is an unpleasant one, because of the similar textures of the two things. Instead, I think brains should be cooked so that they are crisp, and should be served with crisp things, to offset the custard-like quality of their interiors."[31] Equation, as these examples demonstrate, nullifies the supposed "otherness" of the strange. With bodily consumption, equation is a gesture that nullifies strangeness.

EATING PENIS

The initial tracing above demonstrates the rhetorical banality of eating a human or a body part associated with humans. Food communicates supposed barbarian practices as civilized. Andrew Zimmern has made a career out of promoting the "bizarre," or supposedly barbarian, through televised performances that communicate global food practices as fascinatingly other. Fermented foods, yak blood, horse, spoiled food, insects, and rodents have all been the focus of Zimmern's *Bizarre Foods* show on the Travel Channel.

A great deal of *Bizarre Foods* plays off the rhetorical constructions I identify in texts about eating human, particularly the trope of tradition. One traditional food Zimmern eats is penis. For example, in season 6 episode 4 he documented local men in Madagascar eating the foreskin of newly circumcised babies, describing the moment as traditional: "At the end of the ceremony, someone has to eat the foreskin," Zimmern calmly narrates as two maternal grandfathers share the honor. Penis, this example suggests, is *traditional*. Traditions are not strange; they reflect heritage, practice, and commonality. In episode 12 of season 1, Zimmern ate bull penis in Vietnam; in episode 15 of season 2, he visited the "world's first penis restaurant" and ate snake, deer, and yak penis; in episode 19 of season 2 he travelled to Bolivia to eat bull penis again; and in episode 68 of season 6 he consumed penis soup in Indonesia.

For all this penis consumption, one might think of Zimmern as an advocate of the unexpected, with penis functioning as a rhetorical marker of an edible object guaranteed to shock an audience because of its sexual connotations. Yet, the repetition of penis consumption in *Bizarre Foods* suggests the opposite. That Zimmern is able to eat penis so often and in so many countries suggests the food's consumption—its traditional placement in a variety of cultures—as anything but bizarre. If penis were strange and untraditional, its exceptional status could not be located across continents.

When Jerry Hopkins published *Strange Foods* in 1999, he pre-empted Zimmern's show in displacing the culinary "other" with the traditional. In the book, Hopkins acknowledged that, historically speaking, people have commonly eaten blood, spiders, rats, and genitalia. Like the examples I've given, Hopkins's prose shapes the strange as banal and everyday: "Cat meat—generally not so greasy as dog."[32] "Horse may be substituted for beef in many recipes,"[33] and "Because most bats available for eating are small, and they are generally grilled or deep-fried, the entire creature may be cooked and consumed."[34] Hopkins also focuses on penis eating, recalling a bowl of penis soup he ate in Singapore as "nothing special." He provides a recipe for "double-boiled penis soup," a traditional dish one can make at home.[35]

Other writers describe penis much as Hopkins does. Writing in *Vice Magazine*'s Munchies section in 2015, Micah Spangler tells a story of La Paz, Bolivia's, national hangover cure: bull penis soup. Spangler switches the focus from the traditional—as Hopkins describes the soup—to ingredient familiarity: "The cardan—local slang for the way a bull penis mimics the shape of a car's drive shaft—is thinly sliced and stewed, leaving it with a not-too-chewy texture. Given its density, the penis meat sinks to the bottom of the bowl, leaving the more hearty ingredients to occupy the top of the dish."[36] Jacob Weaver also relies on ingredient familiarity to describe the penis soup he enjoyed at Beijing's Guolizhuang restaurant: "The food is cooked at the table in a pot of simmering broth. The organs arrived variously filleted, scalloped, or sliced, though their original shape was usually still recognizable."[37] Filleted. Scalloped. Sliced. This is the everyday language of food preparation. Food preparation, whether in the cutting of meat or its cooking, offers communal experience. Los Angeles food critic Jonathan Gold, for example, describes eating bull penis at Feng Mao Korean barbecue by drawing attention to the familiar "bubbling" and "hissing" sounds meat makes when cooked. Readers should recognize these sounds—much as they would recognize filleting and slicing—as everyday: "A sharp, glistening steel skewer stabbed through thin coins of meat sliced from a bull penis, which bubble and hiss when they encounter the heat of the fire, sizzling from proud quarters to wizened, chewy dimes. It doesn't taste like much, this bull penis, pretty much just cartilage and char, but the spectacle is as emasculating as a Jonas Brothers CD."[38] In this case, communal awareness is a rhetorical trope used to normalize consumption. Simmering broth, filleted, scalloped, sliced, sizzling heat: all of these terms act as keyword culinary terms. Many meats or vegetables are sliced or filleted; penis is no different. It sizzles. It is chewy. It doesn't taste like much, and neither do many other foods.

EATING GRASSHOPPER

Penis foregrounds commonality through its accessibility (as common as soup; prepared like any meat) as well as the language used to describe its taste. Grasshopper is treated in similar fashion: the insect's status among various cultures is traditional, based on familiar ingredients, and prepared in familiar ways. In season 1 episode 8 of *Bizarre Food* Zimmern visits Oaxaca. In addition to his survey of the stomachs, hearts, and lungs he discovers at the local market, Zimmern eats grasshopper tacos and informs us, "folks from Oaxaca have been harvesting them for centuries." And in the factory where grasshoppers are processed, Zimmern narrates the event as conventional and natural, posing, again, the "traditional" aspect of this food: "Every technique here draws inspiration from centuries of Oaxacan chapuline tradition," he tells the audience. In season 3 episode 1, Zimmern eats grasshopper once more in Phuket, Thailand. In episode 28 of the same season, he eats grasshopper in Los Angles and in episode 34 of the same season he will eat the insect in Uganda, calling it "a staple" that tastes like "lobster or crab roe," categories that normalize the experience as luxurious but not exceptional. Three times in one season, grasshopper was consumed even though it is not unique to one place or one people, and as Zimmern noted, has been eaten for "centuries" in various individual "traditions."

In the same vein, Hopkins demystifies the supposed otherness of food in the opening pages of *Strange Foods* with a nod to eating grasshoppers and other insects: "Over a period of twenty-five years, I have rejected my meat-and-potatoes upbringing in the United States frequently to try a wide variety of regional specialties, from steamed water beetles, fried grasshoppers and ants, to sparrow, bison and crocodile, the latter three served en casserole, grilled, and in a curry, respectively."[39] Writing specifically about grasshoppers, Hopkins offers the same historical and cultural tropes Zimmern does in order to persuade readers of the insect's banality. He regards Western disgust of grasshopper as a curiosity since they are "traditional," associated with ancient wisdom: "Why modern Euro-Americans don't include the locust in their diet remains a mystery. Grasshoppers sure seemed fit to eat in other eras and in other parts of the world," he notes. "Pliny the Elder, Rome's greatest naturalist, said that they were much eaten by the Parthians. Herodotus, the Greek historian, described the method adopted by the Nasamones of powdering locusts, then baking them into cakes."[40]

Tradition, whether one is talking about either penis or grasshopper, performs a gesture of familiarity. "Insect consumption is in our cultural heritage," Dana Goodyear indicates.[41] Similarly, Emma Bryce introduces a TED-Ed talk with the words, "For centuries, people have consumed bugs." She then offers a historical contextualization of the insect, surveying its centuries-old role as food and ending by exhorting the audience to "savor the crunch."[42] Food writer Calvin Trillin turns to flavor profiles to conjure up tradition. Like Zimmern, he describes eating grasshoppers in Oaxaca, using language an audience will identify with. In this case, tradition is evoked by traditional Mexican flavor descriptors: chili, lime, and salt. These items normalize the eating experience for readers who may already appreciate Mexican cuisine: "I picked up a grasshopper, pulled the big legs off, and popped it into my mouth. It tasted like crunch that had been sautéed in oil flavored with chilies and garlic and lime and salt. I have no idea what the big legs would taste like."[43] Ordering dinner in a Philadelphia Mexican restaurant, food writer Robert Sietsema orders chapulines and reports back to his readership in a nonchalant manner; the insects are served in traditional tortillas: "Then the second snack arrived, a pair of tacos made with soft fresh corn tortillas, flopping open to reveal a dozen nearly intact insect bodies—heads, antennae, and all."[44]

The "novelty" of eating grasshoppers can also be mitigated by appeal to traditional methods not primarily associated with the critters. In an interview with Munchies, bug expert David George Gordon describes a traditional cooking method (skewers/fondue) appropriated for grasshopper: "All I do in my cookbook is put them on skewers and dip them in chocolate fondue. Now you have chocolate and a little bit of spicy chili seasoning with salt and then it kind of tastes like salted caramel."[45] In his *Eat-A-Bug Cookbook*, Gordon's grasshopper recipes for shish kebabs and grasshopper Hoppin' John are based on traditional foods.

"Why not eat insects?" Vincent Holt asked as far back as 1885.[46] One answer he gives is tradition: "Beginning with the earliest times, one can produce examples of insect eating at every period down to our own age."[47] "We have seen that, from the time of Moses down to the present day, various members of the insect family of *Orthopiera*, which includes the locusts, crickets, and grasshoppers, have been and are eaten and appreciated in many parts of the world."[48] Why not eat insects when so many food seekers before us have? Tradition, equation, foregrounds the strange as normal and expected. Tradition counters a Why not? question with the banality of normalcy.

EATING DOG

I began with human flesh and conclude with dog, whose consumption should pose the most disgust since dogs have become the ultimate human companion animal. The rhetoric of dog eating, however, follows all the patterns I have traced until now. It begins with normalization; "normal" people like "us," writers note, eat dog. "Many are surprised," Robert Ji-Song Ku writes, "to discover that contemporary Europeans, such as Belgians and people of various Alpine nations, are known to favor dog-meat."[49] Many, as well, might be surprised to hear of traditional dog eating, another normalizing gesture, as we have seen. In the 1859 *Curiosities of Food*, Peter Lund

Simmons quotes an anonymous traveler in Hawaii as commenting on native food practices that prefer dog to human: "I felt as if dog-eating were only a low grade form of cannibalism."[50] The perception of dog eating is likely shaped by public declarations of disgust over the "other's" barbarian practices. As Frank Wu states, "Dog eating becomes an excuse . . . to disrespect complete cultures as primitive."[51] Thus, we might recall Mike Huckabee's 2015 tweet during a Democratic presidential debate, "I trust @BernieSanders with my tax dollars like I trust a North Korean chef with my labrador!"[52] Or we might notice Dutch DJ Tiësto's 2013 tweet, "What Korean dishes should we have for dinner tonight? Any suggestions? Heard dog is really good here." In the 2014 satire about North Korea, *The Interview*, James Franco's character Dave Skylark tells a puppy, "Guess who's going to America, where they don't eat doggies." An April 19, 2012, *New York Post* cartoon depicted President Obama eating the family dog while Michelle Obama asks from another room, "Has anyone seen Bo?"[53]

As these public pronouncements demonstrate, dog should be the most difficult meat to rhetorically treat as banal. Dog, however, is framed as traditional by such temporally distinct moments such as *The Curiosities of Food* and Barack Obama's memoir of growing up in Indonesia. In *Dreams from My Father*, Obama reflects on indigenous foods he ate: "I was introduced to dog meat (tough), snake meat (tougher), and roasted grasshopper (crunchy)."[54] For his part, Hopkins treats dog not as a fond memory but as traditional sustenance: "Dog is an affordable protein source not only in Korea but in most of southern China (including Hong Kong) and much of Southeast Asia, as well as in parts of Latin America."[55] He also notes that "dog has been a welcome dish across much of the world's history and geography."[56]

Overall, to treat dog as something not other, the meat must either be described as no different than other consumed meats (drawing on the ingredient or food preparation gesture) or in comparison to other meats (drawing on the equivalence gesture). "But unlike all farmed meat, which requires the creation and maintenance of animals, dogs are practically begging to be eaten," writes Jonathan Safran Foer.[57] Juliana Liu tells the story of the pet dog turned into dinner by interjecting into the narrative Chinese food expert Fuschia Dunlop's description of the animal's taste as resembling pork or lamb: "In the course of many years of studying Chinese cuisine, I've only eaten dog meat on a handful of occasions. The first time, it reminded me of pork; the second, in a fiendishly spicy Hunanese stew, it recalled the taste of lamb."[58] One Korean food website declares that dog meat "has a taste and texture close to that of goat meat."[59] Like tradition or sustenance food gestures, comparisons minimize strangeness by identifying commonality among disparate eating acts. Comparisons don't situate an "other" to be compared with but instead familiarize eating via spices or taste tropes. Familiar food preparation techniques, too, allow for comparisons to communicate normalcy. Note this description, similar to Calvin Trillin's depiction of eating grasshoppers, which relies on the mentioning of recognizable Asian spices in order to pose an equivalence or normalizing framing: "On the night in question, Phong cared most about the dog restaurants that offered delicious, testosterone-soaked nights off from girlfriends, wives, and mothers. Behind their bamboo curtains, guys like him could spend a night in a haze of rice wine and dark, gamey meat dressed up in fresh herbs, a spicy rhizome called *galangal*, and deeply-funky fermented shrimp paste."[60]

Taste generates comparisons that establish familiarity. We familiarize experience by associating one taste with another, recognizable one. Taste, Raymond Williams wrote, is metaphoric.[61] To say that dog tastes like goat or lamb is to create a metaphoric communicative moment where the variables—as Giard argues—can anchor the reader of a strange food experience in unnecessary exoticism or—as Ulmer argues—can dislodge the reader from the familiar reliance on exoticism or otherness. For Melanie Joy, a hypothetical dog-eating situation—wherein one is told first that a meal is dog and then that it isn't—acts as a metaphor for taste perception comparisons: "Indeed, why is it that we have such radically different reactions to beef and dog meat? The answer to this question can be summed up by a single word: *perception*. Perception forms a comparison—or equivalence—with goat or dog, and in that perception, the strange is familiarized for a reader or viewer of a TV episode. We react differently to different types of meat not because there is a physical difference between them, but because our perception of them is different."[62] Rhetorical exchanges shape perception, particularly when definitional variables such as disgust and pleasure are used, or when food communication projects what Edward Schiappa calls a "fact of essence": "Anytime someone posits a question of the form 'What is X' or attempts to offer a definition based on what he or she believes X really or truly is, the result is an effort toward a fact of essence, or what also is called a 'real' definition."[63] The perception regarding the eating of monitor lizards, penis, or dog meat is a kind of "what is X" question (what is a meat that is acceptable to eat; what is strange) often based on a "real" meaning of disgust shaped by word choice, heritage, tradition, ingredients, familiarity, and the other examples I trace out here.

With this final example of dog, I shift the comparison to cruelty, an area where equivalence allows the animal's strangeness to be dislodged further. Objecting to cruelty is treated as a fact of essence depending on the animal in question or the definition of what kind of animal in what kind of situation is being treated cruelly. With dog, if one animal is raised in humane conditions for food, why can't another be, writers ask; or, if one animal is subject to inhumane practices, eating that animal can alleviate suffering. But this same logic does not hold for dogs, because of how terms like cruelty or civilized are used. "Many young people don't eat dog because they think it's uncivilized," Elizabeth Rosen adds, quoting Vietnam resident Ngyuen Hang, "especially in cities, where we have a lot of options that are tastier than dog. They're also influenced by Western media."[64] In this rhetorical approach, dogs are treated humanely in urban areas, so why would we eat them? Animal rights—the question of eating an animal vs. far worse animal practices—become a focal point for the normalization of dog. Cruelty issues incorporate the sustenance argument at times; at others, they offer comparison rhetoric. One such comparison, like other examples I trace, is the civilized vs. the barbaric.

For instance, even while investigating the cruelty of the Vietnamese dog-eating industry (what should be strange), *Guardian* writer Kate Holden paints a complementary picture of the social and health benefits of eating the animal (the familiar). In this instance, barbaric practices such as eating dog are made civilized by contextualizing them as sustenance: "Dog is the go-to dish for drinking parties, family reunions and special occasions. It is said to increase a man's virility, warm the blood on cold winter nights, and help provide medicinal cures and is considered a widely available, protein-rich, healthy alternative to the pork, chicken, and beef that the Vietnamese consume every day."[65] For its part, Safran Foer's overall argument regarding eating dog establishes a comparison between euthanizing unwanted animals and food availability. Thus, Safran Foer's position is to familiarize dog eating through these two circulated narratives, even if done with a bit of humor: "Three to four million dogs and cats are euthanized annually. The simple disposal of these euthanized dogs is an enormous ecological and economic problem. But eating those strays, those runaways, those not-quite-cute-enough-to-take and not-quite-well-behaved-enough-to-keep dogs would be killing a flock of birds with one stone and eating it, too."[66] John Sutter repeats the same rhetorical framing, pitting animal treatment against acceptable (and possibly traditional) eating practices: "The cruelty of this trade—the fact that dogs are smashed into cages; suffocated; 'skinned alive, strung up, and beaten,' according to a CNN report—is what should shock and sadden you. The fact that people are eating dog meat? That shouldn't."[67] We see this gesture elsewhere as well. If killing dogs for meat is barbaric, Ji-Song Ku reflects, so too should be the butchering of all the other animals we eat: "Here in the United States, some 45 million turkeys are killed each year for Thanksgiving, and workers in a hog factory can cut as many as a thousand porcine throats per hour."[68] Perspective, therefore, creates definitions of acceptability through a comparison with other eating habits we likely identify with. Perspective, rather than colonializing or othering, flattens difference into sameness, into banal recognition. If the death of millions of turkeys for consumption is banal and unremarkable, why wouldn't the death of a few dogs be as well?

Dog consumption, more so than penis or grasshopper consumption, represents the dividing point between the broader tropes of strange food, such as civilized (familiar) and barbarian (strange) cultures, which have often prompted the traditional "other" critique I began this chapter by citing. The writings I conclude with depend on the substance/cruelty tropes, but they also use them to demonstrate contradictions in perspective. Definitions of otherness, barbarism, or civilized eating all fluctuate between various contradictory practices regarding which animal is defined as food, which as pet, and which as the object of cruel treatment. William Saletan admonishes accordingly, "If you refuse to eat only the meat of 'companion' animals—chewing bacon, for example, while telling Koreans that they can't stew Dalmatians—you're saying that the morality of killing depends on habit or even whim."[69] The whim, I note, is where I began this chapter, the turning of the head to an otherwise banal depiction of Australian aboriginals eating besides a fire.

CONCLUSION

Ulmer's unheimlich maneuver dislodges the familiar—whether we are discussing food or some other topic—as it metaphorically sticks in our throats and causes us to choke. The strange chokes. It gags. It causes us to look away. Yet, as my tracing demonstrates, most of what chokes us is not that strange at all. What my tracing here suggests is an unheimlich repetition across writings that dislodges *the strangeness* of certain eating habits, even if we are often not paying attention to that dislodging. Rhetorical writings (in print, video, social media) have done the dislodging for us. My act of invention involves tracing out the patterns in these writings so that an alternative reading may emerge, one that does not depend on traditional notions of the other or the colonial when addressing different eating practices. This act of rhetorical invention recognizes that the politics of reading often defaults to traditional meanings and that we must dislodge these, at times, in order to not assume that every situation—related to food or otherwise—automatically follows a prescribed route.

While our perception may be otherwise, it is difficult to pose eating animal penis or grasshopper or dog as strange when so many people write about their fairly common moments eating these items or when people write about other common instances that are no worse nor any better than our treatment of these animals. It is difficult to pose any of these foods as strange when so many people eat them. Just as my father cannot reasonably call the eating habits of a billion people strange (favoring a cheese sandwich to aloo gobi), neither does it make sense to call common food consumption strange when a television personality can easily eat penis across the globe. While Ulmer's unheimlich is an intentional intervention with the familiar, as in making the familiar strange, the repetition of banality I point to in this chapter operates in the opposite direction: it dislodges strangeness by demonstrating food practices as familiar across rhetorical expression.

Repetition alleviates strangeness. In this way, we can understand the strange food rhetoric as one of *contagions,* Tony Sampson's term for repetitive discourse (as opposed to the more popular, digital terms *virus* or *meme*). The contagion, Sampson argues, involves "the microrelational forces of imitative encounters."[70] He posits that imitation's agency is not with a person or figure (such as an animal's penis or a dog's eaten flesh) but with the imitation itself, that which "makes the agent part of an assemblage of relationality."[71] Repetition easily familiarizes any number of objects or texts via circulation and generates relational connections (in this case, among strange food writings). Circulation, such as with commonplaces or topoi, makes the unfamiliar familiar, even when perception might suggest otherwise (i.e., we still think grasshopper is strange).

The tension, as I'm trying to tease out briefly here, is between repeating familiar patterns as unfamiliar (unheimlich) and allowing the unfamiliar to become familiar (strange food). Further, I claim that the larger implications of this observation are political in nature, as they challenge "facts of essence" against the discourse used to describe such definitional moments. The specific discursive example I contrasted this tracing with is otherness. Otherness is a political rhetorical gesture dependent on facts of essence, but its lack of attention to banality might deserve a rethinking, as I have tried to show here. We may continue to be disgusted or repulsed by specific food suggestions, but it would be beneficial, as well, to recognize the constructedness of our food perceptions; for those perceptions can deny the commonality that underrides even the most seemingly "bizarre" of foods, and of Others.

NOTES

1. Andrew Chase, "Strange Foods," *Gastronomica: The Journal of Critical Food Studies* 2, no. 2 (Spring 2002): 94.

2. Fredric Jameson, "On 'Cultural Studies,'" *Social Text,* no. 34 (1993): 34.

3. Dana Goodyear, *Anything that Moves: Renegade Chefs, Fearless Eaters, and the Making of a New American Food Culture* (New York: Riverhead, 2013), 222.

4. Pollan, *Omnivore's Dilemma,* 300. See chapter 4, n. 8.

5. Casey Kelley, *Food Television and Otherness,* 11. See introduction, n. 17.

6. Kelley, *Food Television and Otherness,* 17.

7. *Food Television and Otherness,* 25.

8. I.e., the gesture of the "colonial" or "other" as opposed to other possible circulating gestures.

9. Roland Barthes, "Toward a Psychosociology of Contemporary Food Consumption," in *Food and Culture: A Reader,* ed. Carole Counihan and Penny Van Esterik (New York: Routledge, 1997), 24.

10. Barthes, "Psychosociology of Food Consumption," 21.

11. de Certeau et al., *Practice of Everyday Life,* vol. 2, 3. See introduction, n. 19.

12. *Practice of Everyday Life,* vol. 2, 168.

13. Gregory Ulmer, "The Unheimlich Maneuver," *Lusitania—A Journal of Reflection and Oceanography* 8 (Spring 1996): 138.

14. Ulmer, "The Unheimlich Maneuver," 141.

15. Bradford Vivian, *Being Made Strange: Rhetoric beyond Representation* (Albany: State University of New York Press, 2004), 15.

16. Bruno Latour, *Reassembling the Social: An Introduction to Actor-Network Theory* (New York: Oxford University Press, 2007), 1–17.

17. Gary Allen, "What is the Flavor of Human Flesh?" in *Cultural and Historical Aspects of Foods: Yesterday, Today, and Tomorrow,* ed. M. W. Kelsey and Z-A Holmes (Corvallis: Oregon State University, 1999), 29.

18. Allen, "Flavor of Human Flesh?", 31.

19. Unknown author, *The Cabinet of Curiosities, Or Wonders of the World Displayed: Forming a Repository of Whatever is Remarkable in the Regions of Nature and Art Extraordinary Events, and Eccentric Biography,* vol. 1 (New York: Piercy and Reed, 1840), 14.

20. Brian S. Hook, "Oedipus and Thyestes among the Philosophers: Incest and Cannibalism in Plato, Diogenes, and Zeno," *Classical Philology* 100, no. 1 (January 2005): 21.

21. Hook, "Oedipus and Thyestes," 28.

22. Ken Albala, *Eating Right in the Renaissance* (Berkeley: University of California Press, 2002), 68.

23. Sir Charles Malcolm, "Anniversary Address, 1851," *Journal of the Ethnological Society of London* 3 (1854): 101.

24. Calvin Schwabe, *Unmentionable Cuisine* (Charlottesville: University Press of Virginia, 1979), 24.

25. Schwabe, *Unmentionable Cuisine,* 132.

26. Estelle Woods Wilcox, *The Dixie-Cookbook* (Atlanta: L. A. Clarkson & Company, 1885), 209.

27. The Ladies Society of St. Mark's Lutheran Church, Canajoharie, NY, *Mohawk Valley Cookbook* (Utica, NY: Childs & Son, 1889), 21.

28. Ladies of the Presbyterian Church, Paris, KY, *Housekeeping in the Bluegrass: A New and Practical Cookbook* (Cincinnati: Robert Clarke & Co., 1881), 170.

29. Sara Josepha Buell Hale, *The Good Housekeeper or the Way to Live Well and to be Well while We Live Containing Directions for Choosing and Preparing Food, in Regard to Health, Economy, and Taste* (Boston: Weeks, Jordan, and Company, 1839), 35–36.

30. M. F. K. Fisher, *How to Cook a Wolf* (New York: Farrar, Straus, and Giroux, 1988), 105.

31. Fisher, *How to Cook a Wolf*, 104.

32. Jerry Hopkins, *Strange Foods: Bush Meat, Bats, and Butterflies: An Epicurean Adventure around the World* (Hong Kong: Periplus Editions, 1999), 8.

33. Hopkins, *Strange Foods*, 12.

34. *Strange Foods*, 23.

35. *Strange Foods*, 58–59.

36. Micah Spangler, "Bull Penis Soup is the National Hangover Cure of Bolivia," *Munchies*, October 21, 2015, https://munchies.vice.com/en_us/article/8qkvqg/bull-penis-soup-is-the-national-hangover-cure-of-bolivia.

37. Jacob Weaver, "Strength in the Pot," *Gastronomica* 6, no. 4 (2006): 5–6.

38. Jonathan Gold, "Of Cumin Bondage: Korean at Feng Mao," *LA Weekly*, August 12, 2009, http://www.laweekly.com/restaurants/of-cumin-bondage-korean-at-feng-mao-2161060.

39. Hopkins, *Strange Foods*, x.

40. *Strange Foods*, 145.

41. Goodyear, *Anything that Moves*, 59.

42. Emma Bryce, "Should We Eat Bugs?" TEDed, January 2, 2014, https://ed.ted.com/lessons/should-we-eat-bugs-emma-bryce.

43. Calvin Trillin, "Land of the Seven Moles: Adapting to Life's Changes at the Table," *New Yorker*, December 3, 2012, https://www.newyorker.com/magazine/2012/12/03/land-of-the-seven-moles.

44. Robert Sietsema, "Crunching on Grasshopper Tacos," Gourmet.com, December 22, 2008, http://www.gourmet.com.s3-website-us-east-1.amazonaws.com/restaurants/2008/12/grasshopper-tacos.html.

45. David George Gordon, "How to Cooks Bugs: Grasshoppers and Crickets," *Munchies*, May 14, 2015, https://munchies.vice.com/en/articles/how-to-cook-bugs-grasshoppers-and-crickets.

46. Vincent Holt, *Why Not Eat Insects?* (London: Field & Tuer, the Leadenhall Press, 1884), 9.

47. Holt, *Why Not Eat Insects?*, 34.

48. *Why Not Eat Insects?*, 48.

49. Robert Ji-Song Ku, *Dubious Gastronomy: The Cultural Politics of Eating Asian in the USA* (Honolulu: University of Hawai'i Press, 2014), 139.

50. Peter Lund Simmons, *The Curiosities of Food: Or Dainties and Delicacies of Different Nations Obtained from the Animal Kingdom* (London: Richard Bentley, New Burlington Street, 1859), 56.

51. Frank H. Wu, "The Best 'Chink' Food: Eating and Dilemma of Diversity," *Gastronomica* 2, no. 2 (Spring 2002): 43.

52. Mike Huckabee (@GovMikeHuckabee), "I trust @BernieSanders with my tax dollars like I trust a North Korean chef with my labrador! #DemDebate," tweet, October 13, 2015, https://twitter.com/GovMikeHuckabee/status/654114071336189952?ref_src=twsrc%5EtfE.

53. Geoff Earle, "Dog Eat Dog Fight," *New York Post*, April 19, 2012.

54. Barack Obama, *Dreams from My Father: A Story of Race and Inheritance* (New York: Crown Publishers, 2004), 37.

55. Hopkins, *Strange Foods*, 4.

56. *Strange Foods*, 5.

57. Jonathan Safran Foer, "Let Them Eat Dog: A Modest Proposal for Tossing Fido in the Oven," *Wall Street Journal*, October 31, 2009, https://www.wsj.com/articles/SB10001424052748703574604574499880131341174.

58. Juliana Liu, "The Day My Dog Was Cooked for Dinner," BBC News, June 28, 2015, https://www.bbc.com/news/magazine-33283694.

59. "Bosintang: Dog Meat Stew," Eatinkorea.com, November 28, 2014, http://www.eatinkorea.com/en/food/bosintang-dog-meat-stew.

60. Calvin Godfrey, "The Dog Thief Killings," *Roads & Kingdoms*, February 25, 2016, http://roadsandkingdoms.com/2016/the-dog-thief-killings/.

61. Raymond Williams, *Keywords: A Vocabulary of Culture and Society* (New York: Oxford University Press, 1983), 314.

62. Melanie Joy, *Why We Love Dogs, Eat Pigs, and Wear Cows: An Introduction to Carnism* (San Francisco: Conari Press, 2010), 12.

63. Edward Schiappa, *Defining Reality: Definitions and the Politics of Meaning* (Carbondale: Southern Illinois University Press, 2003), 6.

64. Elizabeth Rosen, "To Eat Dog, or Not to Eat Dog," *The Atlantic*, December 30, 2014, https://www.theatlantic.com/international/archive/2014/12/to-eat-dog-or-not-to-eat-dog/384107/.

65. Kate Holden, "How Eating Dog Became Big Business in Vietnam," *The Guardian*, September 27, 2013, https://www.theguardian.com/world/2013/sep/27/eating-dog-vietnam-thailand-kate-hodal.

66. Safran Foer, "Let Them Eat Dog."

67. John D. Sutter, "The Argument for Eating Dog," CNN, July 24, 2014, http://www.cnn.com/2014/07/23/opinion/sutter-dog-meat-ethics/index.html.

68. Ji-Song Ku, *Dubious Gastronomy*, 149.

69. William Saletan, "Wok the Dog: What's Wrong with Eating Man's Best Friend," *Slate*, January 16, 2002, http://www.slate.com/articles/news_and_politics/frame_game/2002/01/wok_the_dog.html.

70. Tony Sampson, *Virality: Contagion Theory in the Age of Networks* (Minneapolis: University of Minnesota Press, 2012), 19.

71. Sampson, *Virality*, 29.

5
More Than a Membrane

Donovan Conley

Hermetia illucens, a.k.a. the black soldier fly, is a nonbiting critter found throughout the southern United States resembling a stingerless black hornet. This unassuming little creature, which does nothing but mate and lay eggs as an adult, is a marvel of ecological efficiency. In its larval phase, the black soldier grub will eat twice its weight in organic waste material over the course of a day. Indeed, the grubs have a ravenous appetite for virtually any organic waste—fish and animal carcasses, used brewer's barley, human and animal feces, all food scraps—and are rivaled only by the earthworm in their ability to transform waste into reusable nutrients. The potential range of uses for this little composting machine is staggering. As Dan Charles writes, "Think of slaughterhouses, for instance. Americans only eat 50 percent of a cow or a hog. The rest of the animal goes to industrial rendering plants, which turn that waste into a variety of products, including 'processed animal protein' that's fed, in turn, to animals."[1] It is hard to ignore the perversity inherent in this roundabout method of forced cannibalism. By contrast, one could happily imagine farmers renting crates of black soldier grubs to not only meat processing plants but grocery stores, restaurants, cafeterias, hospitals, prisons, stadiums, airports, casinos, hotels, and so on. What makes better sense than maximizing the ecological magic of a tiny recycling factory, transforming yesterday's waste into tomorrow's nutrition?

What's more, by consuming organic waste the black soldier larva itself becomes a valuable source of protein and fat. This means the grubs can be harvested as a source of food through a basic curing process. The culinary possibilities for these astonishing creatures abound, from tacos to salads to stir fries to bar snacks, and so on. It is not terribly difficult to imagine this little snack becoming a staple food, and sure enough some two billion of earth's inhabitants already consume insects as an acutely efficient source of daily protein.[2] Dana Goodyear puts the matter into focus: "From an ecological perspective, insects have a lot to recommend them. They are renowned for their small 'foodprint'; being cold blooded, they are about four times as efficient at converting feed to meat as are cattle, which waste energy keeping themselves warm. Ounce for ounce, many have the same amount of protein as beef—fried grasshoppers have three times as much—and are rich in micronutrients like iron and zinc. . . . They are natural recyclers, capable of eating old cardboard, manure, and by-products from food manufacturing. And insect husbandry is humane: bugs like teeming and thrive in filthy crowded conditions."[3] The black soldier fly, in other words, is about the closest thing we have to a perfect agent of sustainable coexistence. Transforming waste into food with minimal energy lost in the process: few other creatures offer so many pure ecological benefits with so few costs. It is a no brainer; we should be cultivating these insects on a massive scale to confront our waste problem while generating cheap protein for an ever-growing human population.[4]

We should be doing this, but we are not, and are not likely to, principally because garbage-consuming grubs are disgusting. Despite the work of "dislodging" that Jeff Rice performs in his chapter, bugs are felt to be dirty with a singular intensity; never mind that crab and shrimp are bugs of the water and yet widely regarded as luxuries. Louisiana folk take pride in sucking the juices from the head of boiled crawfish, also known as "mudbugs," before tearing open their shells, and the bottom feeding catfish is a beloved staple of the southern table; yet land insects pose a culinary existential threat to most Americans. Looy, Dunkel, and Wood get to the heart of the matter when they observe, "Insect cuisine is, for Westerners, emblematic of the alien, a threat to our psychological and cultural identity."[5] This assertion is undoubtedly accurate, but it fails to capture the internal tensions—the oddities, ironies, and outright hypocrisies—that such perceived threats are built upon.[6] The Western palate may repulse at the notion of eating land critters yet still cherishes lobster, the roach of the ocean, as one of its most prized delicacies. Taste can be a fickle and self-contradictory thing, yet the contours of taste form real grooves in market trends and public policies—taste shapes history. We should hope to see black soldier fly taco trucks on the social scene, as a wise effort in ecological planning, and yet today this scenario is virtually unfathomable.

We are faced, then, with the conundrum of perfectly sound reasons on the one hand and capricious desires on the other. Rhetoric traditionally finds itself tugged in both directions, shuttling back and forth between rational judgment and nonrational sensation. The burden of this chapter will be to etch out and defend a middle position, suggesting that the question of the political in an eco-rhetorical mode involves the aesthetic practice of dis/articulating qualitative distinctions. Whereas syllogistic forms of reason are too rigid for differential application, bottom-up micropolitics suffer from vague relations to the social itself. Yet the latter, "molecular" approach has become attractive to both critical theorists and social entrepreneurs alike, and so I focus primarily on that side of the dialectic. Following a section detailing a social crisis called the "hunger-obesity paradox," my analysis works through a set of cases that, I argue, confuse the reigning logic of social production (postmodern capitalism) with a rhetorical politics of invisibility. The set piece of this analysis is called Locol, a politically progressive eco-friendly "fast food" joint founded by California wunderchefs Roy Choi and Daniel Patterson. Their original mission was to embrace a rhetorical strategy of culinary camouflage. Choi and Patterson aimed to cloak their political intentions and go "toe to toe" with the fast food giants, attempting to surreptitiously swap an unhealthy addiction with a healthy one. As a paradigm of rhetorical action, I argue that this venture stands as a cautionary tale in the embrace of invisible influence. A conception of social production grounded in the "atomization of influence" quickly finds itself rudderless, bogged down by ambivalence and indeterminacy. My position, instead, is that an eco-rhetorical mode of political engagement requires a firm grounding in the concept of antagonism, without which no robust account of the political can be hazarded.

THE WANT-EXCESS HOMOLOGY

> *"If you define 'hunger' as malnutrition, and you accept that overweight and obesity are forms of malnutrition as well, then almost half the world is malnourished."*
>
> —Mark Bittman

By almost any measure, today's Western eater represents a disaster of consumption wrought by the tentacles of modern industrial agriculture. One of our greatest social dilemmas is the articulation between "at risk" communities (poor, undereducated) and "risky" food (hyper-processed, nutritionally weak, perversely cheap).[7] We live in an unprecedented historical moment in which many of our poorest citizens are also many of our most obese. As Lauren Berlant puts it, "For the first time in the history of the world there are as many overfed as underfed people, and for the first time in the history of the world the overfed are no longer the wealthiest compared to the poor and starving. All Americans, the absolute and relatively well off and the poor, are getting fatter. But it is specifically the bodies of US working-class and subproletarian populations that fray slowly from the pressure of obesity on their organs and skeletons. . . . *Mass emaciation and obesity are mirror symptoms of the malnourishment of the poor throughout the contemporary world.*"[8] Today, to be poor in the US is to have a greater than average likelihood of being undereducated, and to be undereducated and poor is to have a greater than average likelihood of being obese.[9] These cruel probabilities inflect with race and gender as well. Scheier adds, "Lower-income women of all ethnic groups are more likely to be obese. . . . For women, food insecurity/insufficiency, body weight, and poverty all come together."[10] This conclusion affirms the interplay between culture and ecology, with political economy mediating the two. Through this interplay we see that to exist on the bottom rungs of the socio-economic ladder, in terms of gender and ethnicity and cultural capital and social mobility, is equally to endure the fate of physiological and environmental indignity.[11]

This unique state of affairs has become known as the *Hunger-Obesity Paradox*. Today in the United States the crisis of obesity is homologous to the crisis of starvation in less developed parts of the world.[12] The two are, to re-borrow Berlant's language, "mirror symptoms of the malnourishment of the poor throughout the contemporary world." A group of nutritional scientists characterized this homology in a 2007 report:

> Historically, use of the term *malnourished* or reference to *malnutrition* has been associated with a state of undernutrition. *Malnutrition* is usually associated with poverty and food insecurity, and *malnourished* is defined as poorly or wrongly fed and having a poor or inadequate diet. However, a newly appreciated paradox has been described that links poverty, food insecurity, and malnutrition to obesity, or the state of *overnutrition*. . . . As a result, we need to expand the construct of malnutrition to include two subcategories, specifically *undernutrition* and *overnutrition*, and recognize that both conditions can emerge from living in poverty or having an inadequate food supply.[13]

Poverty and obesity are two great abjections of American culture. To be both poor and overweight is to live a doubly outcast existence and thus to suffer the compounded embarrassments of a lifestyle rooted in a state of both want *and* excess.

This socioeconomic homology is typified in a *New York Times* piece on the spending breakdown of households using the Supplemental Nutrition Assistance Program (SNAP), a.k.a. "food stamps." Drawing on a report by The United States Department of Agriculture, *Times* reporter O'Connor writes, "The findings show that the No. 1 purchases by SNAP households are soft drinks, which accounted for 5 percent of the dollars they spent on food. The category of 'sweetened beverages,' which includes soft drinks, fruit juices, energy drinks, and sweetened teas, accounted for almost 10 percent of the dollars they spent on food. 'In this sense, SNAP is a multibillion-dollar taxpayer subsidy to the soda industry,' said Marion Nestle, a professor of nutrition, food studies and public health at New York University. 'It's pretty shocking.'"[14] The fact that these two social phenomena—want and excess—are now braided in the bodies of the over-*and*-underfed marks a distinct revolution in human history. The "victor" in this upheaval is transnational capitalism, specifically industrial fast food conglomerates like McDonalds, Coca Cola, Kraft, General Mills, and Unilever and their vast networks in research, marketing, distribution, and congressional lobbying.[15]

If these claims seems hyperbolic, consider the perspective on the hunger-obesity paradox of a United Nations "Special Rapporteur on Right to Food," Hilal Elver, who has declared the global prevalence of junk food a human rights emergency. As she puts it, "The rise of industrial food production combined with trade liberalization has allowed large corporations to flood the global market with cheap, nutrient poor foods that force poor people to choose between economic viability and nutrition, effectively violating the right to adequate food."[16] The key part of this statement is the phenomenon of forced choice. Here, impoverished consumers are faced with a "choice" between wholesome food and cheap food, but the cheap food involves scientifically engineered levels of sugar and fat designed to achieve maximum craveability. Indeed, the consumer's "bliss point"—a state of chemically induced euphoria associated with irresistibility—has become the white whale of processed food conglomerates.[17] We have to question seriously what counts as consumer choice when the cheaper option has been lab tested for addictiveness while the more expensive option has a comparatively muted flavor and takes far longer to prepare. The absurdity of forced choice further accentuates the paradox of hunger and obesity lurking at the intersection of various social challenges today (health, income, education, mobility, violence, teenage births, etc.), and—as Casey Kelly aptly demonstrates in his chapter on "food porn"—the underlying historical tale is one of increasing aesthetic subterfuge on the part of food conglomerates (with endorsement by the state).

What's more, the dynamics of influence at work in the hunger-obesity paradox are part of what David Howes calls the "sensorial subconscious," an endemic feature of late capitalism. As he puts it, "It is in the domain of taste that capitalist sensualism (forget realism) has enjoyed some of its greatest successes with respect to the commodification of 'subjective human sensibility' (Marx). No business is more shrouded in secrecy than that of the artificial flavor industry, where the great 'Flavor Houses' of the New Jersey industrial corridor, and elsewhere, compete with each other, and with Nature, to divine and develop new tastes to gratify the ever-changing palates of consumers."[18] Indeed, marching under the banner of convenience and chanting slogans like "You deserve a break today" (McDonalds), "Have it your way" (Burger King), "Because I'm worth it" (L'Oreal), "Once you pop, you can't stop" (Pringles), "Betcha can't eat just one" (Lays), "Obey Your Thirst" (Sprite), and "I can't believe I ate the whole thing" (Alka Seltzer), postmodern capitalism arrests consumers' entire selves, bypassing traditional markers of reluctance like cost, proximity, time, seasonality, assembly, cultural capital, indigestion, and so on. The foodscapes of late capitalism are designed to squash any remaining daylight between the "healthy" choices we "ought" to make and the resplendent trash glittering within arm's reach of our next (engineered) craving. Erasing "dotted lines" of distinction between the slightly better and slightly worse choice is one of contemporary capitalism's greatest feats. Smooth, frictionless, unencumbered, uninterrupted cheap bliss is what it wants for us.

And yet, as Raj Patel and Jason W. Moore point out, "Here we come to an important point about cheap food regimes: they guarantee neither that people are fed nor that they are fed well—as the global persistence of diet-related ill health and malnutrition can attest. Indeed, capitalism's cheap food regimes are, as Farshad Araghi quips, *hunger* regimes."[19] Andrew Fisher doubles down on this insight when he refers to the Western hunger regime as the "hunger industrial complex." This phrase captures the full range of institutional buy-in on hunger as a social problem, from food processing conglomerates flooding markets with cheap pseudo food to charitable organizations in fact perpetuating the paradox through the redistribution of captured excess. As Fisher framed it in a 2017 interview with *Civil Eats*, "The anti-hunger field is arguably the most politically and morally powerful force of civil society when we consider the millions of people who donate food or volunteer, or the 40 million-plus people who go to food pantries or receive food stamps. Over the last few decades, economic inequality driven by stagnating wages has surged. At the same time, the charitable food sector has become ever more institutionalized and complicit with neoliberalism. By failing to organize around wages and jobs, and perpetuating dependency on free food and food stamps, the anti-hunger community contributes to economic insecurity."[20] Both the production of, and response to, the social problem of hunger have become big business; yet food insecurity itself continues to worsen. As Fisher elaborates in his book, *Big Hunger: The Unholy Alliance between Corporate America and Anti-Hunger Groups*, "Charitable food receives a billion dollars or more in government support through tax credits to donors, cash, and USDA commodities. Companies large and small donate billions of dollars' worth of food and cash to the effort as well, while encouraging their employees to volunteer by packing boxes and sorting food."[21] Funneling excess production toward the gaps of insecurity is a superficial fix to the deeper structural quandary known as poverty. As Mark Bittman puts it, "We should not be asking, 'How will we feed the world?' but 'How can we help end poverty?' Claiming that increasing yield would feed the poor is like saying that producing more cars or private jets would guarantee that everyone had one."[22] Fisher echoes this point when he declares, "The solution to hunger is justice, not food."[23]

These statements bring us back to the hunger-obesity paradox, where both poverty and obesity are hastened in the pursuit of cheap bliss. With this seemingly intractable historical paradox we find ourselves at the center of a story about food that is equally a cautionary tale about the fraught relations between the social and the political. As we shall see next, the hunger-obesity paradox is precisely the conundrum that Roy Choi and Daniel Paterson sought to confront as they conceived their fast food venture, Locol. The premise of Locol's original mission was, *if you're forced to choose junk food anyway, our version at least won't kill you.* Yet, as we have seen, invisible influence has already degraded much of the consuming public's ability to discern between the slightly better and the slightly worse. As I shall proceed to argue, caution should be emphasized with social justice movements relying on the something-for-nothing logic of covert rhetorical operations. An ecocritical mode of political rhetoric would seek, rather, to render qualitative distinctions apparent.

CULINARY PASSING

Superstar California chefs Roy Choi and Daniel Patterson first announced the concept for Locol at the 2014 "MAD" Symposium in Copenhagen (MAD is Danish for "Food"). Together Choi and Patterson represent pinnacles of success in both "low" and "high" culinary registers. Choi is the godfather of our national food truck sensation, which he singlehandedly popularized in 2008 in Los Angeles, with a Korean BBQ taco truck called Kogi. He has since turned the truck into a small army of casual outposts (plus catering) and has added a collection of low-key restaurants along the way (Hawaiian, Asian, vegetarian "greenhouse"). Most recently, Choi hit the Las Vegas jackpot and opened a Korean-inspired restaurant in one of the Strip's new hot spots, MGM's "The Park," where visitors can enjoy public art and hip cuisine before strolling to the T-Mobile arena for a concert or hockey game. Yet despite his pedigreed education and increasing celebrity status, Choi steadfastly defends his reputation as a street chef: casual, relevant, youthful, and on the move. Patterson, meanwhile, earned his fame at the helm of Coi, a high concept, chef-centric, seafood-and-tweezers, single nightly-tasting menu San Francisco establishment. Choi is the populist and Patterson the elitist, dynamics that come through in the MAD presentation with Choi emphasizing social justice and Patterson hailing "the Chef" as a revolutionary hero.

Choi begins the MAD talk by declaring abruptly, "I'll just say it: we're gonna tackle the fast food industry."[24] In a twenty-minute talk, Choi and Patterson (at roughly ten minutes each) offer a series of provocative statements detailing their vision for Locol. Most of these come in the first eight-minute segment by Choi. He declares at the outset, "We're gonna build a concept that has the heart and ideology and the science of a chef, but that has the relevance of a McDonalds or a Burger King, out there in the neighborhoods and in the streets." He then adds, "We're gonna go toe-to-toe. Not in a confrontational way, but to see how we can challenge the status quo." A few key insights stand out in these comments, particularly "the relevance of a McDonalds" and "not in a confrontational way." Adding these together we see that Locol's plan is specifically not to oppose or even challenge the basic code of the fast food experience—cheap, convenient, familiar, and stimulating—but rather to offer consumers a clean, eco-friendly simulacrum of that exact experience.

To be sure, Choi and Patterson are clear-headed in their disgust with the current state of industrial fast food. Choi names the enemy directly in the MAD talk: "Fast food, junk food, institutional food, commodities, corporations, GMOs, school food, cheap cheap cheap cheap cheap cheap—nasty food, but addicting." Indeed, these two chefs have spent their careers fashioning dining experiences at the highest levels: sourcing the freshest, most seasonally appropriate ingredients; handling and preparing them with utmost rigor and care; and transforming them into dishes that surprise, provoke, inspire, and edify. It would be foolish to assume that Choi and Patterson misrecognize the profound gulf separating their food from the kind they are attempting to supplant with Locol. Instead, through an abundance of cheffy confidence—Choi says at one point, "Let's get the chefs, us, to make the food, and the moral choices, for the people"—they have elected to shroud their political vision in the clothing of the enemy. *Let us make the moral choices, and then hide those moral choices in good food camouflaged as bad food*: This is a strategy of culinary "passing," where invisibility of purpose constitutes the rhetorical logic of influence.

Locol's mission was to exploit the combination of convenience and craveability that has already forced choices away from healthy but slow food to hyper-processed fast food. In order to disarticulate the hunger-obesity paradox, Choi and Patterson wagered, you cannot rely on good reasons, publicized grievances, or articulatory aesthetics; you need to go deeper, hitting people's hedonic sweet spot where so much of their daily lives already plays out. Choi reiterated this core vision, and business strategy, in a 2014 Reddit "Ask Me Anything" session. The goal is to open shops, he said, "right next to any other fast food joint. This is not just inner cities, this is everywhere. We eat some of the worst food in our suburbs . . . So I would love it if Locol sat next to McDonalds, a Burger King, a KFC, a Taco Bell, a Del Taco. So anyone who doesn't know about who we are, will just see another fast food restaurant."[25] This point affirms Locol's core strategy of invisibility. Choi and Patterson did not want their progressive, eco-friendly intentions known. They wanted to be able to compete with the mega chains in a blind taste test, passing healthy food off as its "nasty but addictive" evil twin. This is a political strategy built on the rhetorical power of camouflage. Choi and Patterson were attempting to slide imperceptibly into the increasingly stubborn habit loops of an unhealthy eating public, to coax better choices on a level that falls below cognition or even aesthetic discernment. The rhetorical trick is to not bother persuading consumers away from eating hamburgers, French fries, and chicken nuggets, since they are already, presumably, hopelessly locked into those loops. The trick for Choi and Patterson was to deploy their full culinary powers to develop an addictive burger substitute—theirs is called the "Burg"—made partially with whole grains, seaweed, beef garum, and tofu. The fundamental challenge was to stealthily replace an unhealthy compulsion with a healthy one.

This endeavor, it ought to be stressed, is not unique to Choi and Patterson, nor is it unique to fast food. The emerging alt-protein phenomenon, including the recent "bleeding veggie burger" concept, is an ally in this expanding frontier of social production founded on the logic of invisible influence. A handful of companies, including Beyond Meat and Impossible Foods, are developing vegetable-based hamburger simulacrums that are designed to mimic their animal referents down to the most granular level of sight, taste, smell, and texture. When Baudrillard theorized simulacra he had in mind the visual surfaces of postmodern media culture, but now the same loss of distinction increasingly holds true in the realm of edible matter (a.k.a. food). These companies have moved a quantum leap beyond the likes of "Tofurkey" and Morning Star's cartoonish homages to sausage and bacon. Those old vegetarian products were vague analogs of their animal counterparts. By comparison the new high-tech, Silicon Valley based companies are manipulating components like coconut oil ("fat"), beet juice ("blood"), and heme ("iron") to produce ultra-high-definition digital meat copies that yield an uncannily familiar taste effect.[26] The audience for these new products is not vegetarians but carnivores—today they are sold in the meat section of grocery stores rather than in the health food section—and the goal is precisely not to persuade them into reducing their lust for animal-based comfort foods. Instead the goal is to Trojan horse a more ecologically friendly version into their established habit loops, to swap an unhealthy compulsion for a healthy one. As Lindsey Hoshaw reports, "'The demand for meat is going through the roof, and the world is not going to be able to satisfy that using animals—there's just not enough space, not enough water,' says [Patrick] Brown, Impossible Foods' founder and CEO . . . 'If people are going to be eating burgers in 50 years, they're not going to be made from cows,' said Brown. 'We're saving the burger.'"[27] Worldwide meat consumption has tripled over the past four decades and jumped 20 percent in just the last ten years—thanks largely to the explosive growth in China's middle class—bringing with it dramatic environmental and public health implications, so that the "bleeding veggie burger" is seen as a way to roll back this tidal wave through the transformative potential of unperceived influence.[28]

For Locol, Beyond Meat, and Impossible Foods, the global enemy of industrialized fast food looms as a colossal foe. As we have seen, the wager of Locol was whether two highly inventive chefs could "go toe to toe" against the fast food behemoths and their enormous research and marketing budgets. The wager was whether cheffly ingenuity—advancing values of wholesomeness, dignity, community, integrity, sustainability, *and* deliciousness—could tackle a global empire that has become an addiction-producing delivery system for sugar-salt-fat.[29] It is by no means a fair fight, as massive structural differences stand behind these separate ventures. Choi hit on this fact when he stated, "Really the core of the idea is how do we get the food to be ninety-nine cents and sit right next to a Popeye's, sit right next to a Church's or a KFC, be in the neighborhood." A separate economic analysis would be needed to adequately track the dynamics that shape the fragile balance between flavor, nutrition, and cost in a ninety-nine cent burger. Choi gives a sense of these dynamics when he describes their efforts to save on costs while improving the nutritional quality of the hamburger patties. He notes, with perhaps an excess of confidence, "We cut the meat with grains but you never get the feel of the fact that the burger is not a hundred percent meat," then a moment later offers a more blunt explanation: "we're not big enough to buy futures in meat."

With this off-handed remark Choi unwittingly problematizes the relations between taste, cost, and scale that constitute the ultimate distinction between a Locol and a KFC. It matters greatly that the mega chains, with their meat futures, are able to purchase patties for a fraction of what Choi and Patterson were forced to pay; and it matters greatly what kinds of "cuts" the chefs were compelled to make in order to achieve cost-flavor invisibility.[30] Indeed, these core structural dynamics are the most important yet most elusive aspect of Locol's ability to exert the kind of social influence it hoped to achieve. To get a quick sense of how these dynamics played out, let us recall the tremors that hit the culinary world when Pete Wells, the *New York Times* premiere restaurant critic, published a zero-star review of the second Locol in Oakland. Wells had this to say: "The neighborhoods Locol is targeting have serious nutritional problems, from hunger to obesity, but the solution isn't to charge people for stuff that tastes like hospital food. If Locol were a nonprofit, then institutional-quality cooking might be unavoidable. It is a restaurant, though, and it is run by two chefs who are famous for cooking food that people really, really want to eat. I had a hard time remembering that as I worked my way through Locol's menu, where appeals to your appetite are about as scarce as chicken in the no-noodle soup."[31] That the most high profile restaurant critic in the country would travel to California from New York in order to review a fast food venture says much about the evolving relations between food and online media as forms of social production. The most salient issue, however, was rarely mentioned directly: how the institutional dynamics of taste, cost, and scale translate (or do not) into Choi and Patterson's rhetorical strategy of invisibility. The reason Wells's review struck such a chord is because he disregarded Choi and Patterson's intentions—their sincerity, pride, integrity, and compassion—and focused on the food itself. Wells had done exactly what Choi wanted, approaching the food as though he didn't know the difference between Locol and any other fast food joint, and in doing so discovered a jarring lack of balance between the dynamics of taste, cost, and scale. A more sympathetic response came a few days later from LA's sage of lowbrow ethnic food, the late Jonathan Gold, who responded to Wells's review by noting, "The question wasn't how Locol's $5 Fried Chicken Burg might compare to the vastly better $9 fried chicken sandwiches at Night + Market or Oakland's own Bakesale Betty. It was why the *New York Times* was using its main restaurant column to gripe about bland turkey chili in an Oakland burger stand whose mandate was to feed a community with limited access to good, nutritious food. . . . In my opinion, Wells may not have been wrong, but he was ungenerous."[32] The disconnect between Wells's and Gold's readings of Locol comes down to a matter of deliberativeness of purpose and/vs. actual influence as a matter of performance. Choi and Patterson envisioned Locol as a "toe to toe" simulacrum of the generic fast food experience, yet their supporters felt betrayed when Wells refused to add bonus points for their lofty moral aspirations.

One lesson to be drawn from this study is that to live by the invisibility of influence is also potentially to die by the invisibility of influence. In the years since Locol was first conceived, only two stores opened—one in the LA neighborhood of Watts, the other in Oakland, CA—and both were closed, ostensibly for "retooling," in late 2017 (never to be reopened). Masking Locol's noble intentions in hopes of franchising globally on a wave of social transformation did not prove a winning business model. Locol subsequently partnered with the industrial organic behemoth Whole Foods (now owned by the world's second largest retailer, Amazon). They briefly operated a streamlined version of the original concept inside the San Jose Whole Foods store, but that iteration shuttered as well. Before that final closing Choi conducted a lengthy interview with Giant Robot Media, where he stated, "I hope this thing makes millions and billions of dollars. I hope the money is flowing, but that money's going back to the community. It's not going to go to us as owners. Hopefully as Locol grows, we'll have other stores that serve as revenue centers for us as owners of the business. But the stores that are in the inner cities, that are built within communities that need us the most at this point of life, those will be built as community centers."[33] With the Whole Foods/Amazon partnership, Choi and Patterson briefly went "toe-to-toe" with the major fast food conglomerates, but not as originally envisioned. Gone was the rhetorical strategy of culinary subterfuge, and in its place was a clear distinction between social goods (revenue centers) and political goods (community centers).

Locol's parable of well-intentioned rhetorical camouflage thus reveals the political significance of "dotting lines." Choi and Patterson originally attempted to *erase* the lines between "their" food and the "other" food, all while smoothing over qualitative distinctions between political grievances and the reigning logic of social production. Antagonisms invariably arise where the assurances of a discourse clash with actually existing conditions; where for instance the economic trope of "convenience," which undergirds virtually every claim associated with industrial fast food, clashes with the lived realities of the hunger-obesity paradox. An embrace of invisible influence requires cloaking such distinctions and, thus, avoiding the antagonistic cry of the political; yet the cry remains, even if unheard or ignored.

DISOBEY YOUR THIRST (THE ATOMIZATION OF INFLUENCE)

> *"I came out to Silicon Valley because we were gonna change the world. 3D printing to me was that exact same feeling. We're gonna change the world again, except this time, I think if the last revolution was about bits, this one is about atoms."*
>
> —Print the Legend

In one of the philosophical ur-texts of contemporary critical theory, *Anti-Oedipus*, Gilles Deleuze and Felix Guattari disperse the question of the political throughout the entirety of the social. They do so by weaving both social and political energies around the concept of libidinal production, grounded in the monistic pulsations of desire. In the first chapter on "Desiring Machines," for instance, they assert, "There is no such thing as the social production of reality on the one hand, and a desiring production that is mere fantasy on the other. . . . The truth of the matter is that social production is purely and simply desiring production itself under determinate conditions. We maintain that the social field is immediately invested by desire, and that libido has no need of any mediation or sublimation, any psychic operation, any transformation, in order to invade and invest the productive forces and the relations of production. *There is only desire and the social, and nothing else.*"[34] No mention is made of the political as such, and in fact Deleuze and Guattari rarely theorize the concept head-on. Instead, the category of the political becomes molecularized through the immanent forces of desiring-production. In their work the political can be found potentially anywhere, since desire shimmers across the entire social terrain. In a more explicit declaration of this view, they add, "The truth is that sexuality is everywhere: the way a bureaucrat fondles his records, a judge administers justice, a businessman causes money to circulate; the way the bourgeoisie fucks the proletariat; and so on. And there is no need to resort to metaphors, any more than for the libido to go by way of metamorphoses. Hitler got the fascists sexually aroused. Flags, nations, armies, banks get a lot of people aroused. A revolutionary machine is nothing if it does not acquire at least as much force as these coercive machines have for producing breaks and mobilizing flows."[35] The mention of a revolutionary machine brings us back to Locol, for this is how Choi and Patterson originally viewed their mission: to acquire the same force as the crushing rhetorical machinery of the fast food giants. On the plane of libidinal urges, they wanted to sneak a healthy compulsion inside an unhealthy one.

This is the alluring prospect of invisible influence one finds baked into a Deleuzian ontology of social production. Choi and Patterson originally embraced Deleuze and Guattari's major premise—*there is only desire and the social, and nothing else*—that sees political formations flattened and absorbed within the plane of social production writ large. Indeed, there are compelling reasons for social influencers to head in this very direction, at least conceptually. When corporations have "colonized" the life-world down to the patenting and editing of genetic sequences, of life itself, we may legitimately question whether any uncompromised social space remains to forge alliances, gather, compose, and push back.[36] Jane Bennett adds, "One might today avoid voting and overt political activity, but not taxes, roads, electricity, tap water, sewers, or the pressures of normalization . . . the welfare state, the corporatized and internationalized economy, and globalized pollution leave the individual nowhere to hide."[37] Indeed, if the social totality is always-already infested by corporate and/or state influence, it follows that what qualifies as political will always-already manifest as social in nature. It certainly *feels* this way much of the time, as when some of our gravest social problems are packaged as commodities and then sold back to consumers as tidy moral sentiments. When Starbucks offers its customers plastic bottles of water, with a portion of the proceeds going to help solve the problems of water shortage in less-developed parts of the world, we find ourselves caught in an uncanny loop where the social production of libidinal urges (the urge to care) cannibalizes the political energy it would take to address the real problems of structurally generated resource scarcity at home and abroad. Here we are back in Howes's "sensorial subconscious," the social space where raw desire is captured by corporate marketers wielding the dark arts of invisible influence.

This analysis seems to echo Matthew May's assertion that "the same surplus that capital strives to subsume is also constitutive of the potential for the affirmation of the living and active forces of mutual aid and cooperation to create a world beyond capitalism."[38] Invoking Spinoza's premise that all bodies/objects are extensions of a singular substance, May is referring to the surplus of desire and affectability that traverses all bodily composition—including, inevitably, the composition of edible matter—as the latent hope of a cooperative world beyond capital. But May is quick to ground this statement in the *uncollaborative* organizing power of labor as at least provisionally distinct from capital, for what distinguishes labor from capital more visibly than the strike? So what might a Spinozist-Deleuzian approach to class struggle look like for May? He answers: "*intentionally acting* through practices that organize the surplus of struggle into more widespread and powerful compositions," to which he adds by way of conclusion, "I have further argued that such a Spinozism [of class struggle] begins—or more precisely happens—with *the refusal* to transform the power of our living labor into capital."[39] Tension continues to lurk here between conscious/unconscious and active/passive forms of noncollaboration—are they begun or do they merely happen—but May offers a welcome opening on how we might envision the political arising from within the fluidities of the social. It begins in refusal, and refusal begins when we make distinctions between "goods" and "bads."

What the case of Locol reveals, then, are the pitfalls accompanying the uncanny loop that collapses the political into the social, bypassing qualitative lines of distinction between that which enriches and that which poisons. We might say that Locol offers a preview of how the political implodes when qualitative distinctions are atomized through the pursuit of invisible influence. Thus, while a Deleuzian ontology of social production offers a powerfully *descriptive* lens for tracking the surface gloss of postmodern capitalism, its political prospects remain tenuous and vague. As Frederic Jameson puts it, "The Deleuzian notion of schizophrenia is therefore certainly a prophetic one, but it is prophetic of tendencies latent within capitalism itself and not the stirrings of a radically different order capable of replacing it. Indeed, it is questionable whether Deleuze was ever interested in theorizing any alternative social order as such."[40] This embrace of capitalism's latent tendencies is the cruel hope that nourishes the logic of invisible influence, this notion that eddies of transformative potential are waiting to surge through the cracks in the sensorial subconscious. As we have seen with Locol, however, waiting for that irruption apart from the organizing power of antagonisms can prove a fickle and costly gambit.[41]

Still, the hoping and the waiting continue. Today's post-industrial food producers increasingly court consumers in realms of unawareness and invisibility. Companies like Just Meat, Memphis Meats, and Finless Foods are developing eggs without chickens through cell cultivation, beginning with a single feather, not to mention lab-grown "beef," even fish "meat" and "foie gras." And as previously discussed, companies like Impossible Foods and Beyond Meat are concocting plant-based "bleeding" burger patties using soy roots, yeast, and beet juice to mimic the crucial role that heme (iron) plays in a regular burger patty. Meanwhile, say hello to Chefjet, the first commercial 3D food printer. In a *New York Times* article, "Dinner is Printed," A. J. Jacobs writes, "In his book *Fabricated*, Mr. Lipson dreams of digitally driven dinners, where the printer uses your body's up-to-the-minute data to create the perfect lasagna for your nutritional needs, with, say, extra protein or vitamin A."[42] As all this takes shape previous distinctions between different kinds of things, like plants and animals or meals and book chapters, continue to dissolve.

Meanwhile two more companies, Tellspec and SCIO, are developing handheld "molecular food scanners" that use "spectroscopic" sensors to detect the genetic composition of any food item down to the level of photons. A SCIO promotional video tickles the fancy when it states, "Imagine if there was a way to know the chemical makeup of everything you come in contact with." Gluten, pesticides and other chemicals, artificial additives, and so on—the point of these little gadgets is to demystify the murky origins and composition of our everyday food. This astonishing development bears repeating: tech companies have created electromagnetic scanners to help consumers identify the unknown provenance and genetic structure of any morsel of food they happen to come in contact with on a daily basis. With these recent technological advances our food system has tumbled into the uncanny valley, where it is becoming vanishingly difficult to determine the origins and makeup of a given ingredient. There is much talk lately about "post truth," but there is almost no talk about the emergence of "post-food." At stake is the question of value—social, political, moral, economic, and their distinctions—yet we cannot hazard even an approximate notion of value when it is no longer possible to distinguish between parts and wholes or even parts and parts.

As a culminating example, and stepping back from the consideration of food proper, consider a project coming out of Erin Manning and Brian Massumi's SenseLab called "A Cryptoeconomy of Affect." According to an interview Massumi gave to *The New Inquiry*'s Uriah Todoroff, "Erin Manning and Brian Massumi were given a challenge by the Economic Space Agency—a global collective working to create a network of noncapitalist, blockchain-based economies—to reconsider value in financial terms."[43] The goal of the Cryptoeconomy project is to drill down on the shared libidinal energies that slosh back and forth between collaborative emergence driven by social experimentation and market-based utilities in determining the question of social value. Whereas Locol aspired to flatten the political into the socioeconomic, the Cryptoeconomy project wants to flatten the aesthetic into the socioeconomic:

> We want to foster emergence and process, but at the same time find ways of making it sustainable. That means that the strategic duplicity has to extend to the economy as we currently know it. We have to be parasitical to the capitalist economy, while operating according to a logic that is totally alien to it. What we're thinking of is making the collaborative process moving through the platform function according to the radically anti-capitalist principles we were just talking about, centering on the collective production of surplus values of life, and separating that from the dominant economy by a membrane. A membrane creates a separation, but at the same time allows for movements across. It has a certain porosity. The idea is that we would find ways, associated with the affect-o-meter we were describing earlier, to register qualitative shifts in the creative process as it moves over its formative thresholds, and moves back and forth between online operations and online events. What would be registered is the affective intensity of the production of surplus value of life, its ebbs and flows. The membrane would consist in a translation of those qualitative flows into a numerical expression, which would feed into a cryptocurrency.[44]

The key concepts Massumi invokes here are "parasitical" and, most especially, "membrane." A membrane is a line of separation and distinction, but a porous and often imperceptible line of distinction. A membrane is a mesh pretending to be a barrier and/or a barrier pretending to be a mesh. Membranes leak. A very great deal will ride on this skin of meshwork when it comes time to sort through the distinctions between "the collective production of surplus values of life" (art cooperatives) and "the dominant economy" (postindustrial capitalism). How is it possible to remain simultaneously parasitical on *and* alien to the same host body? This would seem to be a logical contradiction. Leakage will become inevitable, engendering the "bloodletting" of creative agency on one side and the "infection" of extractive impulses on the other. We are in hazy territory with the membrane, and so it would seem that yet another paradox dwells in the bosom of a social project founded on the hope of invisible, porous, and mutually indeterminate influence without loss or cost.

These various forms of social production, from Locol to bleeding vegetables to plant-based foie gras to cryptoeconomics, miss the prerogative of the political, which is *to enact critical judgment by drawing qualitative distinctions and aestheticizing grievances as bids on alternative futures.* Missing from a Deleuze-inspired logic of social production is the ineradicable character of antagonisms, which retain their historicity despite either the ingenious seductions of the sensorial subconscious or the noblest aims of covert social justice efforts. Politically speaking, an antagonism does not exist until it receives some form of aggrieved expression, and thus the refusing "shout" becomes the elemental expression of political utterance. Dewey said it best when he observed, "The man who wears the shoe knows best that it pinches and where it pinches, even if the expert shoemaker is the best judge of how the trouble is to be remedied."[45] Antagonisms are the pinches that give rise to aestheticized shouting as forms of refusal grounded in qualitative distinctions between things as they actually are and things as they might otherwise become. While grounded in critical judgment, political shouting also requires an embrace of aesthetics precisely for the reason Bennett states: "For if reason alone is incapable of moving us to enact the ethical and political injunctions it devises, then a political ethics must include an aesthetic dimension."[46] But antagonisms will exist, objectively, apart from the aesthetic forms through which grievances are mobilized. The toxic water in Flint, Michigan, will poison bodies even if no one shouts or listens; but the matter *becomes* political when signs and slogans are developed, narratives crafted, arguments marshaled, menus written, and/or when the powerful machinery of Hollywood snaps into action—shouting aesthetics, all. This point accords with Rancière's assertion that "the real must be fictionalized in order to be thought."[47]

The lesson that Locol offers, then, is the need for an eco-minded rhetorical politics to embrace the ineluctable presence of antagonisms, without which the social lacks a sufficiently political dimension. Expanding on Dewey's pinch, Kevin DeLuca describes antagonism (drawing on the seminal work of Laclau and Mouffe) this way: "Antagonisms point to the limit of a discourse. An antagonism occurs at the point of the relation of the discourse to the surrounding life world and shows the impossibility of the discourse constituting a permanently closed or sutured totality. . . . Today, antagonisms such as global warming, ozone depletion, toxic waste, and pesticides in food and water provide the opportunity to question and disarticulate Industrialism."[48] The simplest way to think of the limit of a discourse is as a lie. When assurances of public health run up against the contradicting evidence of toxic water, we encounter the limit of that discourse to cover its constituents. In the presence of this lie we discover a rupture within the social, a contradiction—between discourse and the life world—around which new articulatory practices become necessary. Indeed, the political labor of an eco-critical rhetoric entails the distinction-making practices of articulation (bringing elements together) and disarticulation (breaking elements apart).[49] Further, these articulatory and disarticulatory practices perform the rhetorical operations of agrilogistical line dotting, and line erasing, as discussed in the introduction to this volume. The aesthetics of "shouting"—from silently taking a knee or raising a fist to smashing shop windows or screaming through a bullhorn—are grounded in the ability of social actors to enact critical judgment and forge qualitative distinctions as the basis of noncollaboration.

Hunger and obesity have become articulated phenomenon under the industrial discourse of "convenience." Roy Choi and Daniel Patterson have attempted to cloak their aesthetic practices under this same regime of signs, seduced by the allure of invisible influence but as we have seen, the limits of that discourse cannot be so easily erased. With its Whole Foods/Amazon partnership, and the newly wrought distinction between revenue centers and community centers, Locol's original grievances against the industrial food system have been rendered usefully transparent. Disarticulating the element of "affordable" from the element of "yummy" is one of the great political challenges we face today. The crushing dynamics of scale and cost mean that Locol's food will never look or taste like the generic fast food they are hoping to replace. They have come to embrace this fact and appear to have abandoned the rhetorical strategy of culinary camouflage. Chantal Mouffe adds some helpful thoughts when she writes, "I am convinced that artistic and cultural practices can offer spaces for resistance that undermine the social imaginary necessary for capitalist reproduction. But I think that to apprehend their political potential, we should visualize forms of artistic resistance as agonistic interventions within the context of counter-hegemonic struggles."[50] When it comes to "artistic resistance," let us take some liberty and include the gastronomic. Mouffe's comment suggests that one should not conceal one's efforts in food justice, nor should one disguise one's politically formative grievances. Rather than attempting to become a slightly healthier version of "that" food, better (following Rancière) to make the distinctions apparent, sensible, visible, and legible.

CONCLUSION: DELIVERING THE GOODS

The prospect of eating insects would seem to mark the outer limit of rhetoric's achievable civic progress. It would be eminently wise for many reasons, and ecologically beneficial on multiple fronts, if Western eaters took up this particular culinary practice. Again, Looy, Dunkel, and Wood put it well: "Embracing entomography is a concrete way of literally becoming the stranger, and in so doing, embracing them as our neighbor—fully authentic, fully human, and fully acceptable. It is a deeply hospitable act that welcomes without obliterating the other. Not until people of Western culture can freely do this will we know, in a deeply embodied way, how to help one another find ways to live and nourish ourselves sustainably on this planet."[51] This is an eloquent and compelling argument. It is an expression of *phronesis*, or good judgment, that offers sensible reasons and appeals to humane values. Sloop and McDaniel offer this take on phronesis: "Crudely put, judgment connects subject and object in an appropriate manner, rendering a state of affairs intelligible to a consciousness that then, in an informed manner, may proceed to make decisions about how to act."[52] Connecting subjects and objects in an "appropriate manner" by rendering conditions intelligible—this is the work of dis/articulating qualitative distinctions and aestheticizing grievances. The point here is not that engaging in articulatory practices in response to antagonisms will dramatically close the gap between Western palates and garbage-consuming grubs. The point is that we get steadily nearer to that goal, inch by inch, through the repetition of just such efforts.

Take junk food as another example. As we know, the term *junk* is a specific cultural designation for the outworn, discarded, cast aside, inferior, and lacking worth or significance. In other words, junk is that which has been drained of social value. But as our dumpster diving and garage sale "junkie" friends will remind us, one person's trash is another's treasure. Junk is at least partly in the eye of the beholder. Indeed, that additional term, *junkie*, takes us into tricky waters. Is a junkie not one who gets hooked on objects drained of value? We have reality show junkies, red bull junkies, professional wrestling junkies, soap opera junkies, etc.—connoisseurs of trash. "Addiction" and "compulsion" are terms we use to situate this ruinous attachment to valuelessness. Although fraught, these terms usefully shine a light on the repetitious looping back to the same vacant space of sensation. These terms are markers of distinctions; they carry the assumption that we should not want to consume *that*, should know better; should be able to exercise sounder judgment, wise up, or seek help. Slippery though it may be, the term *addiction* carves out a zone of danger in the highly charged terrain of production and consumption. It allows us to point and say, "there be dragons."

So while the distinctions between "trash" and "treasure" may be culturally fluid, I have attempted to argue that it is becoming increasingly important to maintain our distinction-making rhetorical sensibilities (as formative agrilogistical labor). Social value may be impermanent and tricky to pin down, it may be contingent, arbitrary, and hypocritical, it may even be an exercise in political contestation and the expression of power imbalances—still, we must not lose our rhetorical powers of distinction and the articulatory/dotting practices they engender. The examples of Locol, bleeding plants, and crypto membranes provide a portrait of the social becoming a vast ocean of affective sloshing, where the market and the atelier are interwoven at the level of photons. Given this increasing tendency, it becomes difficult to advocate for the radical democratization of junk, food or otherwise (which is not the same as opposing junk itself). Rather, what needs opposing is the flattening or erasure of any wavering line—*even a membrane*—between, for instance, food and trash or animals and plants or life and non-life or delicious and stimulating or even healthy and sick. Politically speaking, we are better served through the rhetorical pursuit of contingent solidities rather than permanent porosities.

NOTES

1. Dan Charles, "Making Food from Flies (It's Not That Icky)," NPR, September 19, 2013.

2. Anonymous, "Where's the Beef? The Market for Alternative-Protein Products," *Economist*, February 2, 2017.

3. Dana Goodyear, "Grub," *New Yorker*, August 15, 2011.

4. The research supporting this claim is overwhelming. See Aaron T. Dossey, "Why Insects Should be in Your Diet," *The Scientist*, February 1, 2013; M. Premalatha, Tasneem Abbasi, Tabassum Abbasi, and S. A. Abassi, "Energy-Efficient Food Production to Reduce Global Warming and Ecodegradation: The Use of Edible Insects," *Renewable and Sustainable Energy Reviews* 15, no. 9 (2011): 4357–60; Julieta Ramos-Elorduy, "Insects: A Sustainable Source of Food?" *Ecology of Food and Nutrition* 36, nos. 2–4 (1997): 247–76; Aaron T. Dossey, Juan A. Morales-Ramos, and M. Guadalupe Rojas, eds., *Insects as Sustainable Food Ingredients: Production, Processing, and Food Applications* (Elsevier, San Diego: 2016); and Dana Gunders, "Wasted: How America is Losing Up to 40 Percent of Its Food from Farm to Fork to Landfill," *NRDC Issue Paper*, August 21, 2012.

5. Heather Looy et al., "How Then Shall We Eat? Insect-Eating Attitudes and Sustainable Foodways," *Agriculture and Human Values* 31, no. 1 (2014): 131.

6. For a sampling of the range of associated issues here, see Brian Wansink and Jeffery Sobal, "Mindless Eating: The 200 Daily Food Decisions We Overlook," *Environment and Behavior* 39, no. 1 (2007): 106–23.

7. I use the term "articulation" here deliberately to reference the historical coming together of nonessential elements; in this case "poverty" and "obesity." The Hunger-Obesity Paradox is a unique historical configuration, one that is contingent (non-necessary) yet produced through concrete material and discursive forces.

8. Lauren Berlant, "Slow Death (Sovereignty, Obesity, Lateral Agency)," *Critical Inquiry* 33, no. 4 (Summer 2007): 766–67. Italics added.

9. On the articulation of (low) income and (lack of) education, Alana Semuels writes in "America's Great Divergence" for *The Atlantic*, "People with a college degree or more now earn 50 percent of aggregate US household income, up from 37 percent in 1991, while people with less than a high school degree now earn 5 percent, down from 12 percent in 1991." For more on this "divergence" see Robert Putnam, *Our Kids: The American Dream in Crisis* (New York: Simon and Schuster, 2015), especially pages 183–90. Putnam writes, "So when I speak of kids from 'upper-class' homes, I simply mean that at least one of their parents (usually both) graduated from college, and when I speak of kids from 'lower class' homes, I simply mean that neither of their parents went beyond high school" (45).

10. Lee M. Scheier, "What is the Hunger-Obesity Paradox?" *Journal of the American Dietetic Association* 105, no. 6 (2005): 884.

11. Further support for these articulations can be found in Cynthia L. Ogden et al., "Obesity and Socioeconomic Status in Adults: United States, 2005–2008," *NCHS Data Brief* 50 (2010): 1–7; R. Huang et al., "The Spatial Clustering of Obesity: Does the Built Environment Matter?" *Journal of Human Nutrition and Dietetics* 28, no. 6 (2014): 1–9; and V. Inglis et al., "Why Do Women of Low Socioeconomic Status Have Poorer Dietary Behaviors than Women of Higher Socioeconomic Status? A Qualitative Exploration," *Appetite* 45, no. 3 (2005): 334–43.

12. By "homology" I refer to the shared formal dynamics of *want* that undergird both "undernutrition" and "overnutrition." For more on homologies see Barry Brummett, *Rhetorical Homologies: Form, Culture, Experience* (Tuscaloosa: University of Alabama Press, 2004).

13. Sherry A. Tanumihardjo et al., "Poverty, Obesity, and Malnutrition: An International Perspective Recognizing the Paradox," *Journal of the American Dietetics Association* 107, no. 11 (2007): 1966.

14. Anahad O'Connor, "In the Shopping Cart of a Food Stamp Household: Lots of Soda," *New York Times*, January 13, 2017.

15. On the powerful role of lobbying in this corporate configuration, O'Connor writes, "PepsiCo lobbied the federal government to prevent restrictions on food stamp purchases in 2011, 2012 and 2013, according to the Center for Responsive Politics, a nonprofit that tracks money in politics. Coca-Cola, Kraft Foods and the sugar industry lobbied against a bill in 2012 that would have banned using food stamps to buy soda and junk food. And in 2011, the Snack Food Association teamed up with beverage

industry lobbyists and the National Confectioners Association, which represents candy companies, to defeat New York City's proposed ban on using food stamps to buy sugar-sweetened beverages."

16. Michael Astor, "UN Expert: Junk Food is a Human Rights Concern," *Associated Press*, Oct. 25, 2016.

17. The engineering of cheap foods for maximum pleasure has been researched at length in recent years. Some of the key texts include Eric Schlosser, *Fast Food Nation: The Dark Side of the All-American Meal* (New York: Harpers Perennial, 2004), David A. Kessler, *The End of Overeating: Taking Control of the Insatiable American Appetite* (New York: Rodale Books, 2009), Michael Moss, *Salt Sugar Fat: How the Food Giants Hooked Us* (New York: Random House, 2013), and Gary Taubes, *The Case against Sugar* (Toronto: Alfred A. Knopf, 2016).

18. David Howes, "Hyperesthesia, or, the Sensual Logic of Late Capitalism," in *Empire of the Senses: The Sensual Cultural Reader*, ed. David Howes (Oxford: Berg, 2005), 289. For more on the "flavor houses" he mentions, see Raffi Khatchadourian, "The Taste Makers: The Secret World of the Flavor Factory," *New Yorker*, November 23, 2009.

19. Raj Patel and Jason W. Moore, *A History of the World in Seven Cheap Things: A Guide to Capitalism, Nature, and the Future of the Planet* (Oakland: University of California Press, 2017), 158.

20. Mark Winne, "To Solve Hunger First Solve Poverty," Civil Eats, April 20, 2017, https://civileats.com/2017/04/20/to-solve-hunger-first-solve-poverty/.

21. Andrew Fisher, *Big Hunger: The Unholy Alliance between Corporate America and Anti-Hunger Groups* (Cambridge, MA: MIT Press, 2017), 3.

22. Mark Bittman, "Don't Ask How to Feed the 9 Billion," *New York Times*, November 11, 2014.

23. A. Fisher, *Big Hunger*, 238.

24. All quotes are taken from an online video, found at: https://vimeo.com/114680357.

25. As reported in Erin DeJesus, "Roy Choi Reveals His Fast-Food Concept Loco'l is Heading to Detroit," *Eater*, October 21, 2014, https://www.eater.com/2014/10/21/7031275/roy-choi-reveals-his-fast-food-concept-locol-is-heading-to-detroit.

26. For more on the science and marketing behind these "burgers" see Lindsey Hoshaw, "Silicon Valley's Blood Plant Burger Smells, Tastes, and Sizzles Like Meat," NPR, June 21, 2016; and Nick Pachelli, "I Love Meat. But These New 'Bleeding' Veggie Burgers Convinced Me to Give it Up for Good," *Vox*, December 8, 2016.

27. Hoshaw, "Blood Plant Burger," 7.

28. Hanna Ritchie and Max Roser, "Meat and Seafood Production and Consumption," *Our World in Data*, August 2017, https://ourworldindata.org/meat-and-seafood-production-consumption. Robert Paarlberg adds, "Globally, meat consumption has been increasing at a rapid rate, tripling over the past 50 years. To sustain this higher consumption, herders and livestock producers around the world are now managing more than 26 billion animals at any one time, triple the 1970 number. The earth, in other words, is now supporting four times as many agricultural animals as people." In *Food Politics: What Everyone Needs to Know*, 2nd ed. (New York: Oxford University Press, 2013), 138.

29. Pete Wells offers a nice summary of their ambitions: "To start, they intend to

build a network of small restaurants that people in some of the country's poorest, most neglected urban neighborhoods can afford. Beyond that, though, the chefs hope that their example of progressive labor practices, interior design attuned to the pulse of the city, and cooking that shows responsibility for the health of both customers and the environment will spark a reformation of the fast food industry." From his review, "Fast Food for Needy Neighborhoods, at Locol in California," *New York Times*, January 3, 2017.

30. Frederick Kaufman explores the dynamics of scale and cost, tracing the financialization of a slice of pizza, in his book *Bet the Farm: How Food Stopped Being Food* (Hoboken: John Wiley & Sons, 2012).

31. Wells, "Needy Neighborhoods."

32. Jonathan Gold, "After NYT Pans Locol, Jonathan Gold Wonders if Some Restaurants are Unreviewable," *LA Times*, January 7, 2017.

33. Eric Nakamura, "Going Locol from the Inside Out," *Giant Robot Media*, September 28, 2017, https://giantrobotmedia.squarespace.com/stories/2017/9/28/locol.

34. Gilles Deleuze and Felix Guattari, *Anti-Oedipus: Capitalism and Schizophrenia* (Minneapolis: University of Minnesota Press, 1983), 29.

35. Deleuze and Guattari, *Anti-Oedipus*, 293.

36. On "corporate colonization" see Carl Boggs, *The End of Politics: Corporate Power and the Decline of the Public Sphere* (New York: Guilford Press, 2000); on the "biopolitical" aspects of genetics, see Vindana Shiva and Ingunn Moser, eds., *Biopolitics: A Feminist and Ecological Reader on Biotechnology* (London: Zed Books, 1995).

37. Jane Bennett, *Thoreau's Nature: Ethics, Politics, and the Wild* (Boulder, CO: Roman and Littlefield, 2002), 86.

38. Matthew S. May, "Spinoza and Class Struggle," *Communication and Critical /Cultural Studies*, 6, no. 2, 204–8.

39. May, "Spinoza and Class Struggle," 206–7. Italics added.

40. Frederic Jameson, "The End of Temporality," *Critical Inquiry* 29, no. 4 (2003), 711.

41. A separate essay is needed to fully elaborate the point, but what tends to hobble many Deleuze-inspired political projects is an excess of confidence in pure, frictionless becoming. The best response to this lack in the literature I've yet encountered is Levi Bryant's discussion of "entropy" in the fourth chapter of his terrific book, *Onto-Cartography* (see introduction, n. 43).

42. A. J. Jacobs, "Dinner is Printed," *New York Times* September 21, 2013. https://www.nytimes.com/2013/09/22/opinion/sunday/dinner-is-printed.html.

43. Uriah Marc Todoroff, "A Cryptoeconomy of Affect," *The New Inquiry*, May 14, 2018, https://thenewinquiry.com/a-cryptoeconomy-of-affect/.

44. Todoroff, "Cryptoeconomy," 6–7.

45. John Dewey, *The Public and Its Problems* (Athens, OH: Ohio University Press, 1954), 207.

46. Bennett, *Thoreau's Nature*, 99.

47. Jacques Rancière, *The Politics of Aesthetics: The Distribution of the Sensible*, trans. Gabriel Rockhill (New York: Continuum, 2004), 38.

48. Kevin DeLuca, "Articulation Theory: A Discursive Grounding for Rhetorical Practice," *Philosophy & Rhetoric* 32, no. 4 (1999), 336.

49. Further reading on articulation should include Ernesto Laclau and Chantal

Mouffe, *Hegemony and Socialist Strategy towards a Radical Democratic Politics* (New York: Verso, 2014); Nathan Stormer, "Articulation: A Working Paper on Rhetoric and Taxis," *Quarterly Journal of Speech*, 90, no. 3 (2004): 257–84; and Lawrence Grossberg, "On Postmodernism and Articulation: An Interview with Stuart Hall," in *Stuart Hall: Critical Dialogues in Cultural Studies*, ed. David Morley and Kuan-Hsing Chen (New York: Routledge, 1996), 131–50.

50. Chantal Mouffe, *Agonistics: Thinking the World Politically* (New York: Verso, 2013), 88.

51. Looy et al., "Insect Eating Attitudes," 139.

52. John M. Sloop and James P. McDaniel, eds., *Judgment Calls: Rhetoric, Politics, and Indeterminacy* (Boulder, CO: Westview Press, 1998), 9.

Afterword

Rhetoric and Cookery

Greg Dickinson

Food is good for eating. And so is rhetoric, it turns out.

Food and rhetoric alike are practical and cultural, material and symbolic. Good food must delight us aesthetically and affectively and yet, in the end, it must also nourish us. Likewise, good rhetoric must delight us aesthetically and affectively and yet, in the end, it must also nourish us. Similarly, bad food is like bad rhetoric. Both can be empty, destructive, community damaging, and—potentially anyway—world destroying. And, as Donovan Conley and Justin Eckstein point out in this volume's introduction, the rhetorical tradition has long engaged food and a wide range of attendant issues like cookery, art, skill, craft, and practice.

Conley and Eckstein begin the book with a meditation on the famous passages from Plato's *Gorgias* where Plato has Socrates compare the false art of rhetoric to cookery. Rhetoric and cookery pretend to offer real solutions to real problems—injustice and ill-health respectively. Neither can do so, however, because they are based on common knowledge, belief, and everyday wisdom untethered from fundamental truths that can heal soul and body. This, anyway, is the argument Plato puts in Socrates' mouth.

As I read these passages in Conley and Eckstein's essay, I remembered the setting for this dialogue. Socrates, the story goes, appeared at Callicles's home just as a fine banquet was ending and Gorgias—the older, wise, and well-known foreign teacher of sophistry—was providing the after-dinner entertainment. Food—cookery—as a rhetorical slander about rhetoric arrives partway through this after-dinner entertainment, and I imagine Plato imagining Socrates not only making a claim about the nature of knowledge and justice but also being a bit of a scold, telling the dinner's participants that maybe, just maybe, they had over-indulged. And so, the setting and the argument weave together, material bodies sated and well-prepared for the sparring that was entertainment in ancient Greece, with participants feeling the jab of Socrates's ascetic claims.

I am also struck by how the body returns again and again, not only in the *Gorgias* (Callicles and Socrates engage in an extended argument about the pleasures of scratching an itch near the end of the dialogue and, in the final mythic story Socrates tells, the guardians at the River Styx demand to see beyond the material bodies and clothing of the passersby) but in the much later dialogue of the *Phaedrus*. Here again, Plato has Socrates express deep misgivings about bodily desires. But this distinction is, in Conley and Eckstein's language, leaky. For even as the body's desires are offered as a sure sign of perdition, at the exact same time the body's mad desire for beauty is, according to Socrates, the royal road to knowledge.

The speech, you will remember, begins with a definition of love as a mad desire for beauty wherein the madness is conferred by the gods for love, Socrates asserts, is a god. Midway through his exhortation, Socrates has the hero of the speech encounter a beautiful man. This beauty powerfully—madly—moves both body and soul. "They come," Plato writes, "to the beloved and behold his radiant face. At this sight the charioteer's memory is borne back to the form of real beauty."[1] What is at stake in the *Phaedrus* and the *Gorgias* before it and in rhetoric more broadly are the rhetorical, social, embodied, material weavings and imbrication of our daily lives.

What is at stake in this book are these very same spinnings. The book knits four important issues beyond the obvious food/rhetoric entanglement: 1) bodies, 2) everyday practices, 3) porosity, and 4) sociability:

1. To write food and rhetoric is to write bodies and rhetoric. Food addresses bodies. A thing only becomes food in very particular interactions with a desiring, eating, digesting body. As this book makes clear, however, there is not a natural, inherent, or purely biological relationship between food and bodies. Instead, both food and bodies are wound together such that they produce each other, and this coproduction is always social, always political, always ethical, and thus always rhetorical. What is particularly clever about this book is its shift in attention from food to cookery. Cooking gives us a strong sense of the relations of bodies that create what I want to signify as food/bodies. The acting human body manipulates material and immaterial things to create dishes. Knives and spoons and stoves and pots and pans and flour and all the other things of cooking come together to produce the meals. Of course, our (human) bodies are also tempered by these tools, objects, and

practices, all of which are overseen or underwritten by rhetoric. Rhetorics of health and disease, deliciousness and abhorrence, gender and race, place and space, sexuality and desire all weave together in seemingly mundane practices of getting dinner on the table. These essays enrich my understanding of these relationships.

2. As this discussion of bodies, rhetoric, food, and cookery suggests, it is nearly impossible to write food/body/rhetoric without also writing the everyday. Sure, in some times and in some places, practices of food and cooking engage us in the extraordinary. Most of the time and in most places these food/body/rhetoric practices are performed at the interstices of everyday life. Rice's discussion of strange eating may seem to be the antithesis of this, and yet in important ways cooked and raw foods' strangeness depends on and produces the distinction between the everyday and the extraordinary. A food is strange because it is *not* part of the everyday. To not be part of the everyday of a person or a culture is also a signaling of—as Pierre Bourdieu and many others point out—cultural distinctions.[2] These everyday cultural distinctions are also, always, distinctions of power and privilege, as nearly all the essays here detail.

3. As should already be clear, everydayness and body-ness are porously related, as everyday embodied practices produce food even as the food produces and enables the body. But porosities abound. Food practices render the human body porous. We eagerly invite foodstuffs to penetrate the body through the mouth. Food also penetrates us aurally, olfactorily, visually, and through the skin. A candy shop pumps out the smell of browning sugar, which in turn penetrates the body and urges it to veer into the store. The heat blasting from the wood-fired pizza oven or the burr of the grinding coffee or the rhythms of noodles slapping a work-table in a Monterey Park noodle shop all cross over the outside of our bodies to the inside. It is not surprising, then, that food and cooking are sites of deep, overwhelming, unconscious desires. Nor is it a surprise that surprising food is also the site of revulsion. In this porosity resides affect; in this porosity resides desire. This porosity is one of the powerful ways in which rhetoric moves from outside in, inside out, and even more fundamentally that rhetoric is a mode of performing these very boundaries. Again, I learned much about these complexities from the essays here.

4. And then, sociality. I come back, here, to the book's opening gambit and my playing with that narrative. In the *Gorgias*, diners gathered for a feast—a feast of food and words—listen to an argument about cookery and scratching. What parts (the banquet, the argument, the metaphors) of this are the

most important if we want to grapple with food and rhetoric? Does Socrates's denigration apply to both cooking and rhetoric? Is it the odd discussion of the pleasure in relieving the itch (which, by the way, is so similar to the pleasure of a cold cup of water on a hot summer's day: scratching and drinking slack desire)? Considering the essays here, my attention turns to the stitching of food and rhetoric into individual bodies and social bodies. I am newly alive to the ways specific bodies (of all sorts) are sewn into the corporate body, the ways the corporate body is always corporeal, and the ways we can only know the individual in light of the social while the social only performs itself through individual, radically local actions.

I think everything I have said so far is only said better in the pages that come before this afterword. You will find there careful consideration of these four themes (and much else). I want to end here, however, using these themes to reflect on why this work matters so much.

Some time ago, near the end of a graduate seminar I was teaching called Rhetoric of Everyday Life, I pondered the work we had done together. We had read work on food and place, everyday practices, and rhetoric. I was struck by a realization that had been rattling around in my soul for some time, but I hadn't found a way to express. I remember saying something like there are few decisions more politically important than the decisions we make about where we live and what we eat. I said that then and I say it now from my own powerfully privileged position: white, male, well educated, well fed, tall, cis-gendered. I have lots of access to the foods of my town and the world. I can live nearly anywhere I might want. Thinking hard and carefully about these choices deeply matters.

Think bodies. We can think of our current politics as being deeply about and performed on bodies. Black Lives Matter means, in part, that black bodies matter. Me Too is an effort to (re)claim women's bodies from men. We are constantly arguing about—both through material means and with material consequences—whose bodies count, under what conditions, and for what purposes. In mundane and powerful ways, we think and practice these relations in part through and with food. At times we use food practices to give ourselves excuses to *not* develop deeper, more caring connections with others. My love of grits and biscuits can substitute for my love of black Americans, for example. But we also deny food to bodies that don't count, we build neighborhoods without access to quality food options, we lace food with poisons to which farmworkers and food factory employees are exposed.[3] Just a few miles from my hometown, we recruit refuges from Africa to kill and butcher environmentally destructive meat, but we refuse to give them time for daily prayers.

Think porosity. As Josue David Cisneros, Karma Chávez, Rob DeChaine, and others have so eloquently argued over the years, borders are a rhetorical/material construction with rhetorical/material consequences.[4] Deep worries about the porosity of borders—which is barely veiled white racism—drives too much of the politics of the US. These porous borders are figured as sites of entry of illicit drugs, diseased bodies, and violent criminals, all of whom threaten—this figuration asserts—the sanctity of the white male body. The border of the individual body can map—though it clearly is not directly analogous to—the borders of nations. The desires and revulsions that attend to these porosities are figured and performed in food and cooking even as food and cooking stage the possibility of particular desires and revulsions.

But I think of porosity in another, more positive way as well. I think of the practices I can engage in that, rather than building the boundaries between me and those unlike me, can make my own self porous—vulnerable—to others. I can open myself to experiences that are not, in the first instance, comfortable. I am not suggesting I learn to eat a greater number of cuisines. That is the neoliberal, gourmand's easy way of doing diversity. Instead, I can begin to let my body understand the place, time, and culture from whence those—and so many other—practices come. I can open my body and soul to the values and ways of being these practices materially and rhetorically embody.

Think everydayness. We are struck, of course, by the dramatic moments when embodied porosity comes to the fore—the travel ban, or family separation spring to mind. But I think too of the daily strains and stresses of embodying the body that is imagined as out of place, the body that raises revulsions in dominant culture. I think of the everydayness of the violence committed in the name of these figurations, the exhaustion of living always with a protective guard in place. I think here of the remarkable National Memorial to Peace and Justice in Montgomery, Alabama. There is a box for each county in the south and counties and states across the rest of the nation where one or more of the four thousand-plus racial terrorism lynchings occurred. The boxes have the names of the lynching victim and date etched into them. As you walk through the memorial you slowly walk down into the space and the boxes rise above your head. Box after box after rusted box presses down. I found myself toggling between the individual stories of lynching victims and the systemic terror meted out on black bodies from Reconstruction to the 1940s. Everywhere I turned to escape, to find some relief, the memorial met me with another story, another etched box, another county where white folks murdered African Americans. Their crimes? Asking for fair wages. Trying to vote. Being acquitted—that's right, acquitted—of murdering a white person. Being in the vicinity of angry white people.

Being black. The memorial demanded of my white body a recognition that living in bodies always precariously situated on the porous border takes an everyday toll. But it is also in response to these everyday harms that the everyday practices of cooking and eating together can so deeply matter. To tarry together over bread and drink, to share a table and a conversation can be a balm to these everyday stresses.

Think sociability. In each of the above themes, I have reflected on the ways the terms raise important questions of ethics and politics in today's world. And in each I have pointed to the risks, harms, and opportunities to our public flourishing that thinking cookery and rhetoric together raises. It is in the ways that food is always social that makes our consideration of cookery important. To eat—even when we eat alone—is to eat (with) others. Bodies and everyday practices and porousness made our food possible. We always, *always* rely on others. We are imbricated in each other's lives. And so, the choices I make about my own food habits spins out into the world. My choices of whom to eat with and beside, whom to value and whom to discount as I eat and cook and procure and grow, all of these are powerful—if everyday—determinates of the impact I will have on my world. Eating high up on the food chain and doing so without demanding fundamental reforms of the meat and dairy industry inserts me right into the environmental destruction so many of us are worried about. Seeking out the cheapest food (at all costs) shifts the costs and burdens of cooking and eating from me to the least privileged among us (this is what Michael Carolan has called the real cost of cheap food).[5]

Conversely, eating with folks different from me, remaking my food habits away from the cheapest to the most sustainable, from high up on the food chain toward plants, will be small steps to making a more liveable world. So too will our concerted advocacy for agricultural reform, immigration reform, farm labor reform.[6] For food always, always, *always* weaves us into crucial social, economic, material, and rhetorical relations. What we eat, who we eat it with, and the places and spaces of our eating: these it seems to me are central to our nightmares and our hopes. The book in your hands deepens our understanding of this fundamental truth.

NOTES

1. Plato, *Phaedrus*, trans., W. C. Helmbold and W. G. Rabinowitz, (New York: Macmillian, 1956): 38.

2. Pierre Bourdieu, *Distinction: A Social Critique of the Judgement of Taste*, trans. Richard Nice (Cambridge, MA: Harvard University Press, 1984).

3. Lisa A. Flores, "Laboring to Belong: Differentiation, Spatial Relocation, and the

Ironic Presence of (Un)Documented Immigrants in the United Farm Workers 'Take Our Jobs' Campaign," *Rhetoric and Public Affairs*, 21, no. 3 (2018): 447–80.

4. Josue David Cisneros, *The Border Crossed Us: Rhetorics of Borders, Citizenship, and Latina/o Identity* (Tuscaloosa: University of Alabama Press, 2014); Karma R. Chávez, *Queer Migration Politics: Activist Rhetoric and Coalitional Politics* (Urbana: University of Illinois Press, 2013); D. Robert DeChaine, *Border Rhetorics: Citizenship and Identity on the US-Mexico Border* (Tuscaloosa: University of Alabama Press, 2012).

5. Michael Carolan, *The Real Cost of Cheap Food* (New York: Routledge, 2018).

6. Flores, "Laboring to Belong."

References

Ahmed, Sara. *Cultural Politics of Emotion.* Edinburgh: Edinburgh University Press, 2014.

Albala, Ken. *Eating Right in the Renaissance.* Berkeley: University of California Press, 2002.

Allen, Gary. "What is the Flavor of Human Flesh?" In *Cultural and Historical Aspects of Foods: Yesterday, Today, and Tomorrow,* edited by M. W. Kelsey and Z-A Holmes, 27–38. Corvallis: Nutrition and Food Management College of Home Economics and Education, Oregon State University, 1999.

Andrews, David. "Toward a More Valid Definition of 'Pornography.'" *Journal of Popular Culture* 45, no. 3 (June 2012): 457–77.

Anonymous. "Where's the Beef? The Market for Alternative-Protein Products." *Economist,* February 2, 2017.

Aristotle. *Rhetoric.* Translated by Edward P. J. Corbett. New York: Random House, 1984.

———. *Rhetoric.* Edited by Jonathan Barnes. Princeton: Princeton University Press, 2004.

———. *Topics.* Translated by W. A. Pickard-Cambridge. Stilwell, KY: Digigireads.com Publishing, 2006.

Astor, Michael. "UN Expert: Junk Food is a Human Rights Concern." *Associated Press,* October 25, 2016.

Barnett, Scot, and Casey Boyle, eds. *Rhetoric, through Everyday Things.* Tuscaloosa: University of Alabama Press, 2016.

Barthes, Roland. "Toward a Psychosociology of Contemporary Food Consumption." In *Food and Culture: A Reader,* edited by Carole Counihan and Penny Van Esterik, 20–27. New York: Routledge, 1997.

Bégin, Camille. *Taste of the Nation.* Champagne: University of Illinois, 2017.

Bennett, Jane. "Edible Matter." *New Left Review* 45 (May/June 2007): 133–45.

———. *Thoreau's Nature: Ethics, Politics, and the Wild.* Boulder, CO: Rowman and Littlefield, 2002.

———. *Vibrant Matter.* Durham, NC: Duke University Press, 2010.

Biesecker, Barbara A. "Rethinking the Rhetorical Situation from within the Thematic of Difference." *Philosophy and Rhetoric* 22, no. 2 (1989): 110–30.

Birdsell, David S., and Leo Groarke. "Outlines of a Theory of Visual Argument." *Argumentation & Advocacy* 43, nos. 3/4 (2007): 103–13.

———. "Toward a Theory of Visual Argument." *Argumentation & Advocacy* 33, no. 1 (1996): 1–10.

Bittman, Mark. "Don't Ask How to Feed the 9 Billion." *New York Times*, November 11, 2014.

Blake, Jonathan. "Instagram Now Bigger than Twitter." BBC, December 10, 2014. http://www.bbc.co.uk/newsbeat/article/30410973/instagram-now-bigger-than-twitter.

"Bosintang: Dog Meat Stew." Eat in Korea, November 28, 2014. http://www.eatinkorea.com/en/food/bosintang-dog-meat-stew.

Boggs, Carl. *The End of Politics: Corporate Power and the Decline of the Public Sphere*. New York: Guilford Press, 2000.

Bourdieu, Pierre. *Distinction: A Social Critique of the Judgement of Taste*. Translated by Richard Nice. Cambridge, MA: Harvard University Press, 1984.

"Brewing Process." *The Beer Temple*, accessed January 17, 2017, http://craftbeertemple.com/videoblog/brewing-process/.

Brock, Sean. *Heritage*. New York: Artisan, 2014.

Brooks, Rosa. "Uncle Sam Wants Who? The Real Reasons People Join the Military." *Foreign Policy*, July 31, 2013.

Brummett, Barry. *Rhetorical Homologies: Form, Culture, Experience*. Tuscaloosa: University of Alabama Press, 2004.

Bryant, Levi. *Onto-Cartography: An Ontology of Machines and Media*. Edinburgh: Edinburgh University Press, 2014.

Bryce, Emma. "Should We Eat Bugs?" TEDed, January 2, 2014. https://ed.ted.com/lessons/should-we-eat-bugs-emma-bryce.

Burke, Kenneth. *Counter-Statement*. Revised edition. Berkeley: University of California Press, 1968.

———. *Grammar of Motives*. Berkeley: University of California Press, 1969.

———. *Language as Symbolic Action: Essays on Life, Literature, and Method*. Berkeley: University of California Press, 1966.

Butler, Judith. *Excitable Speech: A Politics of the Performative*. New York: Routledge, 1997.

Campbell, Karlyn Kohrs, and Kathleen Hall Jamieson. *Form and Genre: Shaping Rhetorical Action*. Falls Church, VA: The Speech Communication Association, 1978.

Carolan, Michael. *The Real Cost of Cheap Food*. New York: Routledge, 2018.

Chase, Andrew. "Strange Foods." *Gastronomica* 2, no. 2 (Spring 2002): 94–96.

Charles, Dan. "Making Food from Flies (It's Not That Icky)." NPR. September 19, 2013.

Chávez, Karma R. *Queer Migration Politics: Activist Rhetoric and Coalitional Politics*. Urbana: University of Illinois Press, 2013.

Cisneros, Josue David. *The Border Crossed Us: Rhetorics of Borders, Citizenship, and Latina/o Identity*. Tuscaloosa: University of Alabama Press, 2014.

Conley, Donovan. "The Good Body, Skilled in Eating," *Pre/Text* 21, nos. 1–4 (Spring–Winter 2001): 9–34.

Consigny, Scott. "Rhetoric and Its Situations," *Philosophy and Rhetoric* 7, no. 3 (1974): 175–86.

Davis, Diane. *Inessential Solidarity: Rhetoric and Foreigner Relations*. Pittsburgh: University of Pittsburgh Press, 2010.

Debord, Guy. *Society of the Spectacle*. Detroit: Black & Red, 2000.

de Certeau, Michel, Luce Giard, and Pierre Mayol. *The Practice of Everyday Life. Volume 2: Living and Cooking.* Translated by Timothy J. Tomasik. Minneapolis: University of Minnesota Press, 1998.

DeChaine, D. Robert. *Border Rhetorics: Citizenship and Identity on the US-Mexico Border.* Tuscaloosa: University of Alabama Press, 2012.

DeJesus, Erin. "Roy Choi Reveals His Fast-Food Concept Loco'l is Heading to Detroit." Eater, October 21, 2014, https://www.eater.com/2014/10/21/7031275/roy-choi-reveals-his-fast-food-concept-locol-is-heading-to-detroit.

DeLanda, Manuel. "The Geology of Morals." Presentation at the Virtual Futures 95 Conference, Warwick University, UK, May 26, 1995.

Deleuze, Gilles, and Felix Guattari. *Anti-Oedipus: Capitalism and Schizophrenia.* Minneapolis: University of Minnesota Press, 1983.

DeLuca, Kevin. "Articulation Theory: A Discursive Grounding for Rhetorical Practice." *Philosophy & Rhetoric* 32, no. 4 (1999): 334–48.

DeLuca, Kevin, and Jennifer Peeples. "From Public Sphere to Public Screen: Democracy, Activism, and the 'Violence' of Seattle." *Critical Studies in Media Communication* 19, no. 2 (June 1, 2002): 125–51.

Depew, David. "Revisiting Richard McKeon's Architectonic Rhetoric: A Response to Richard McKeon's 'The Uses of Rhetoric in a Technological Age: Architectonic Productive Arts.'" In *Reengaging the Prospects of Rhetoric: Current Conversations and Contemporary Challenges,* edited by Mark J. Porrovecchio, 37–56. New York: Routledge, 2010.

Dewey, John. *The Public and Its Problems.* Athens, OH: Ohio University Press, 1954.

Dickinson, Greg. *Suburban Dreams: Imagining and Building the Good Life.* Tuscaloosa: University of Alabama Press, 2015.

Dossey, Aaron T. "Why Insects Should be in Your Diet." *The Scientist,* February 1, 2013.

Dossey, Aaron T., Juan A. Morales-Ramos, and M. Guadalupe Rojas, eds. *Insects as Sustainable Food Ingredients: Production, Processing and Food Applications.* San Diego: Elsevier 2016.

Dyer, Richard. *White: Essays on Race and Culture.* London, New York: Routledge, 1997.

Earle, Geoff. "Dog Eat Dog Fight," *New York Post,* April 19, 2012, https://nypost.com/2012/04/19/dog-eat-dog-fight/.

Eberly, Rosa A. *Citizen Critics: Literary Public Spheres.* Urbana: University of Illinois Press, 2000.

Eckstein, Justin, and Anna M. Young. "Cooking, Celebrity Chefs, and Public Chef Intellectuals." *Communication and Critical/Cultural Studies* 12, no. 2 (April 3, 2015): 205–8.

———. "wastED Rhetoric," *Communication & Critical/Cultural Studies* 15, no. 4 (2018): 274–91.

Edwards, Janis L., and Carol K. Winkler. "Representative Form and the Visual Ideograph: The Iwo Jima Image in Editorial Cartoons." *Quarterly Journal of Speech* 83, no. 3 (August 1997): 289–310.

Ehninger, Douglas. "Argument as Method: Its Nature, Its Limitations and Its Uses." *Speech Monographs* 37, no. 2 (1970): 101–10.

Elliott, Larry. "Globalisation Backlash Enters New Phase with Trump Win." *The Guardian,* November 9, 2016.

Finnegan, Cara A. "The Naturalistic Enthymeme and Visual Argument: Photographic Representation in the 'Skull Controversy.'" *Argumentation & Advocacy* 37, no. 3 (Winter 2001): 133–49.

Fisher, Andrew. *Big Hunger: The Unholy Alliance between Corporate America and Anti-Hunger Groups*. Cambridge, MA: MIT Press, 2017.

Fisher, M. F. K. *How to Cook a Wolf.* New York: Farrar, Straus, and Giroux, 1988.

Flores, Lisa A. "Laboring to Belong: Differentiation, Spatial Relocation, and the Ironic Presence of (Un)Documented Immigrants in the United Farm Workers 'Take Our Jobs' Campaign." *Rhetoric and Public Affairs,* 21, no. 3 (2018): 447–80.

Foss, Sonja, and Cindy Griffin, "Beyond Persuasion: A Proposal for an Invitational Rhetoric," *Communication Monographs* 62, no. 1 (1995): 2–18.

"The Food Porn Trend: How Restaurants Are Catering to Instagram-Hungry Patrons." *Financial Post* (blog). Accessed December 11, 2016. http://business.financialpost.com/news/retail-marketing/the-food-porn-trend-how-restaurants-are-catering-to-instagram-hungry-patrons.

Foucault, Michel. *The Birth of Biopolitics: Lectures at the Collège de France, 1978–1979*. Reprint edition. Basingstoke England; New York: Picador, 2010.

———. *Discipline and Punish: The Birth of the Prison*. New York: Vintage Books, 1977.

———. *The History of Sexuality: Volume 1*. New York: Random House, 1978.

Freud, Sigmund. *The Ego and the Id*. Edited and translated by James Strachey. New York: Norton, 1961.

Gladwell, Malcolm. "Drinking Games." *New Yorker*, February 15, 2010.

Godfrey, Calvin. "The Dog Thief Killings." *Roads & Kingdoms*, February 25, 2016. http://roadsandkingdoms.com/2016/the-dog-thief-killings/.

Gold, Jonathan. "After NYT Pans Locol, Jonathan Gold Wonders if Some Restaurants are Unreviewable," *LA Times*, January 7, 2017.

———. "Of Cumin Bondage: Korean at Feng Mao." *LA Weekly*, August 12, 2009. http://www.laweekly.com/restaurants/of-cumin-bondage-korean-at-feng-mao-2161060.

Goldthwaite, Melissa A. *Food, Feminisms, Rhetorics*. Carbondale: Southern Illinois University Press, 2017.

Goodyear, Dana. *Anything That Moves: Renegade Chefs, Fearless Eaters, and the Making of a New American Food Culture*. New York: Riverhead, 2013.

———. "Grub." *New Yorker*, August 15, 2011.

Gopnik, Adam. *The Table Comes First: Family, France, and the Meaning of Food*. New York: Vintage, 2011.

Gordon, David George. "How to Cooks Bugs: Grasshoppers and Crickets." *Munchies*, May 14, 2015. https://munchies.vice.com/en/articles/how-to-cook-bugs-grasshoppers-and-crickets.

GRACE Communications Foundation. "Impacts of Industrial Agriculture." *Sustainable Table*. http://www.sustainabletable.org/869/impacts-of-industrial-agriculture.

"Great American Writers and Their Cocktails." *NPR*, December 15, 2006. http://www.npr.org/2006/12/15/6624971/great-american-writers-and-their-cocktails.

Greene, Carlnita P. *Gourmands and Gluttons: The Rhetoric of Food Excess*. New York: Peter Lang Publishing Inc., 2015.

Greene, Carlnita P., and Lynn M. Walters. *Food as Communication/Communication as Food*. New York: Peter Lang, 2011.

Grossberg, Lawrence. "On Postmodernism and Articulation: An Interview with Stuart Hall." In *Stuart Hall: Critical Dialogues in Cultural Studies*, edited by David Morley and Kuan-Hsing Chen, 131–50. New York: Routledge, 1996.

Gunders, Dana. "Wasted: How America is Losing Up to 40 Percent of Its Food from Farm to Fork to Landfill." *NRDC Issue Paper*, August 21, 2012.

Gunn, Joshua. "Maranatha." *Quarterly Journal of Speech* 98, no. 4 (November 2012): 359–85.

———. "The Rhetoric of Exorcism: George W. Bush and the Return of Political Demonology." *Western Journal of Communication* 68, no. 1 (March 1, 2004): 1–23.

Hale, Sara Josepha Buell. *The Good Housekeeper or the Way to Live Well and to be Well While We Live Containing Directions for Choosing and Preparing Food, in Regard to Health, Economy and Taste*. Boston: Weeks, Jordan, and Company, 1839.

Hariman, Robert, and John Louis Lucaites. *No Caption Needed: Iconic Photographs, Public Culture, and Liberal Democracy*. Reprint, Chicago: University of Chicago Press, 2011.

Hawhee, Debra. *Moving Bodies: Kenneth Burke at the Edges of Language*. Columbia: University of South Carolina Press, 2009.

———. "Rhetoric's Sensorium." *Quarterly Journal of Speech* 101, no. 1 (2015): 2–17.

Heath, Robert L. "Kenneth Burke on Form." *Quarterly Journal of Speech* 65, no. 4 (December 1, 1979): 392–404.

Hester, Helen. *Beyond Explicit: Pornography and the Displacement of Sex*. Albany: SUNY Press, 2014.

Holden, Kate. "How Eating Dog Became Big Business in Vietnam." *The Guardian*, September 27, 2013. https://www.theguardian.com/world/2013/sep/27/eating-dog-vietnam-thailand-kate-hodal.

Holt, Vincent. *Why Not Eat Insects?* London: Field & Tuer, the Leadenhall Press, 1884.

Hook, Brian S. "Oedipus and Thyestes among the Philosophers: Incest and Cannibalism in Plato, Diogenes, and Zeno." *Classical Philology* 100, no. 1 (January 2005): 17–40.

Hopkins, Jerry. *Strange Foods: Bush Meat, Bats, and Butterflies: An Epicurean Adventure around the World*. Hong Kong: Periplus Editions, 1999.

Hoshaw, Lindsey. "Silicon Valley's Blood Plant Burger Smells, Tastes, and Sizzles Like Meat." NPR, June 21, 2016.

Howard, Robert Glenn. "The Vernacular Web of Participatory Media." *Critical Studies in Media Communication* 25, no. 5 (2008): 490–513.

Howes, David. "Hyperesthesia, or, the Sensual Logic of Late Capitalism." In *Empire of the Senses: The Sensual Cultural Reader*, edited by David Howes, 281–303. Oxford: Berg, 2005.

Huang, R., A. V. Moudon, A. J. Cook, and A. Drewnowski. "The Spatial Clustering of Obesity: Does the Built Environment Matter?" *Journal of Human Nutrition and Dietetics* 28, no. 6 (2014): 1–9.

Huckabee, Mike (@GovMikeHuckabee). "I trust @BernieSanders with my tax dollars like I trust a North Korean chef with my labrador! #DemDebate." Tweet, October 13, 2015. https://twitter.com/GovMikeHuckabee/status/654114071336189952?ref_src=twsrc%5EtfE.

Inglis, V., K. Ball, and D. Crawford. "Why Do Women of Low Socioeconomic Status

Have Poorer Dietary Behaviors than Women of Higher Socioeconomic Status? A Qualitative Exploration." *Appetite* 45, no. 3 (2005): 334–43.

Jackson, Neil. "Introduction: Shot, Cut, and Slaughtered: The Cultural Mythology of Snuff." In Jackson et al., eds. *Snuff*, 1–20.

Jackson, Neil, Johnny Walker, Shaun Kimber, and Thomas Joseph Watson, eds. *Snuff: Real Death and Screen Media*. New York: Bloomsbury Academic, 2016.

Jacobs, A. J. "Dinner is Printed." *New York Times*. September 21, 2013.

Jameson, Fredric. "The End of Temporality." *Critical Inquiry* 29, no. 4 (2003): 695–718.

———. "On 'Cultural Studies.'" *Social Text*, no. 34 (1993): 17–52.

Jenkins, Eric S. "The Affections of the American Pickers: Commodity Fetishism in Control Society." *Communication and Critical/Cultural Studies* 12, no. 4 (2015): 347–66.

Jhally, Sut. *The Codes of Advertising: Fetishism and the Political Economy of Meaning in the Consumer Society*. New York: Routledge, 1987.

Ji-Song Ku, Robert. *Dubious Gastronomy: The Cultural Politics of Eating Asian in the USA*. Honolulu: University of Hawai'i Press, 2014.

Joy, Melanie. *Why We Love Dogs, Eat Pigs, and Wear Cows: An Introduction to Carnism*. San Francisco: Conari Press, 2010.

Kastely, James L. *Rethinking the Rhetorical Tradition: From Plato to Postmodernism*. New Haven: Yale University Press, 1997.

Kauflin, Jeff. "How a New York Restaurant Uses Instagram Influencers to Drive Sales." *Forbes*, September 26, 2016. http://www.forbes.com/sites/jeffkauflin/2016/09/28/how-a-new-york-restaurant-uses-instagram-influencers-to-drive-sales/.

Kaufman, Frederick. *Bet the Farm: How Food Stopped Being Food*. Hoboken: John Wiley & Sons, 2012.

———. "Debbie Does Salad." *Harper's Magazine*, October 2005. http://harpers.org/archive/2005/10/debbie-does-salad/.

Kellner, Douglas, and Clayton Pierce. *Philosophy, Psychoanalysis, and Emancipation: Collected Papers of Herbert Marcuse, Volume Five: Herbert Marcuse Collected Papers*. New York: Routledge, 2010.

Kelly, Casey Ryan. *Abstinence Cinema: Virginity and the Rhetoric of Sexual Purity in Contemporary Film*. New Brunswick, New Jersey: Rutgers University Press, 2016.

———. "Bizarre Foods: White Privilege and the Neocolonial Palate." In *Race and Hegemonic Struggle in the United States: Pop Culture, Politics, and Protest*, edited by Michael G. Lacy & Mary Triece, 43–68. Lanham, MD: Rowman & Littlefield, 2014.

———. "Cooking without Women: The Rhetoric of the New Culinary Male." *Communication & Critical/Cultural Studies* 12, no. 2 (2015): 200–204.

———. *Food Television and Otherness in the Age of Globalization*. Lanham, MD: Lexington Books, 2017.

Kendrick, Walter M. *The Secret Museum: Pornography in Modern Culture*. Berkeley: University of California Press, 1996.

Kennedy, George. "A Hoot in the Dark." *Philosophy and Rhetoric* 25, no. 1 (1992): 1–21.

Kessler, David A. *The End of Overeating: Taking Control of the Insatiable American Appetite*. New York: Rodale Books, 2009.

Kowitt, Beth. "How Restaurants Use Instagram and OpenTable to Gather Data on

Diners." *Fortune* (blog), June 22, 2016. http://fortune.com/2016/06/22/restaurants-instagram-opentable/.

Lacan, Jacques. *The Seminar of Jacques Lacan, Book XVII: The Other Side of Psychoanalysis*. Translated by Russell Grigg. New York: W. W. Norton, 2007.

Laclau, Ernesto, and Chantal Mouffe. *Hegemony and Socialist Strategy towards a Radical Democratic Politics*. New York: Verso, 2014.

Ladies of the Presbyterian Church, Paris, KY. *Housekeeping in the Bluegrass: A New and Practical Cookbook*. Cincinnati: Robert Clarke & Co., 1881.

The Ladies Society of St. Mark's Lutheran Church, Canajoharie, NY. *Mohawk Valley Cookbook*. Utica, NY: Childs & Son, 1889.

Latour, Bruno. "The New Climate." *Harper's Magazine*, May 2017. http://harpers.org/archive/2017/05/the-new-climate.

———. *Reassembling the Social: An Introduction to Actor-Network Theory*. New York: Oxford University Press, 2007.

Liu, Juliana. "The Day My Dog Was Cooked for Dinner." BBC News, June 28, 2015. https://www.bbc.com/news/magazine-33283694.

Looy, Heather, Florence V. Dunkel, and John R. Wood. "How Then Shall We Eat? Insect-Eating Attitudes and Sustainable Foodways." *Agriculture and Human Values* 31, no. 1 (2014): 131–41.

Lowcountry Digital History Initiative. "African Passages, Lowcountry Adaptations." *Lowcountry Digital History Initiative*, March 18, 2017. http://ldhi.library.cofc.edu/exhibits/show/africanpassageslowcountryadapt/sectionii_introintrodu/ricelowcountry.

MacNeil, Karen. *The Wine Bible*. New York: Workman, 2000.

Malcolm, Sir Charles. "Anniversary Address, 1851." *Journal of the Ethnological Society of London* 3 (1854): 86–102.

Marcuse, Herbert. *Eros and Civilization: A Philosophical Inquiry into Freud*. Boston: Beacon Press, 1974.

———. *One-Dimensional Man: Studies in the Ideology of Advanced Industrial Society*. 2nd edition. Boston: Beacon Press, 1991.

Marx, Karl. *Capital: A Critique of Political Economy*. United Kingdom: Penguin, 2004.

Massumi, Brian. *Parables for the Virtual: Movement, Affect, Sensation*. Durham, NC: Duke University Press Books, 2002.

May, Matthew S. "Spinoza and Class Struggle." *Communication and Critical/Cultural Studies* 6, no. 2 (June 2009): 204–8.

McGee, Harold. *On Food and Cooking: The Science and Lore of the Kitchen*. New York: Collier Books, 1984.

McGreavy, Bridie, Justine Wells, George F. McHenry Jr., and Samantha Senda-Cook. *Tracing Rhetoric and Material Life: Ecological Approaches*. New York: Palgrave Macmillan, 2018.

McLaughlin, Seth. "Candidates' Disagreement on Drinking Shines Light on Presidential Temperance." *The Washington Times*, October 20, 2016. http://www.washingtontimes.com/news/2016/oct/20/hillary-clinton-donald-trump-disagreement-on-drink.

Meyer, Christian and Felix Girke. *The Rhetorical Emergence of Culture*. New York: Berghahn Books, 2011.

Miller, Carolyn R. "Aristotle's "Special Topics" in Rhetorical Practice and Pedagogy." *Rhetoric Society Quarterly* 17 (1987): 61–70.

———. "Genre as Social Action." *Quarterly Journal of Speech* 70, no. 2 (May 1984): 151–67.

Morton, Timothy. *Dark Ecology: For a Logic of Future Coexistence.* New York: Columbia University Press, 2016.

———. "She Stood in Tears Amid the Alien Corn: Thinking through Agrilogistics," *Diacritics* 41, no. 3 (2013): 90–113.

———. "Where the Wild Things Are." *LA+: An Interdisciplinary Journal of Landscape Architecture* 1 (Spring 2015): 60–65.

———. "Sublime Objects," *Speculations* 11 (May 2011): 208–9.

Moss, Jessica. "Pleasure and Illusion in Plato." *Philosophy and Phenomenological Research* 72, no. 3 (2006): 503–35.

Moss, Michael. *Salt Sugar Fat: How the Food Giants Hooked Us.* New York: Random House, 2013.

Mouffe, Chantal. *Agonistics: Thinking the World Politically.* New York: Verso, 2013.

Muckelbauer, John. *The Future of Invention: Rhetoric, Postmodernism, and the Problem of Change.* New York: SUNY Press, 2008.

Mulvey, Laura. "Visual Pleasure and Narrative Cinema." *Screen* 16, no. 3 (1975): 6–18.

Nakamura, Eric. "Going Locol from the Inside Out." *Giant Robot Media.* September 28, 2017.

National Institute of Diabetes and Digestive and Kidney Diseases. "Overweight and Obesity Statistics." 2012. https://www.niddk.nih.gov/health-information/health-statistics/Pages/overweight-obesity-statistics.aspx.

Obama, Barack. *Dreams from My Father: A Story of Race and Inheritance.* New York: Crown Publishers, 2004.

O'Connor, Anahad. "In the Shopping Cart of a Food Stamp Household: Lots of Soda." *New York Times,* January 13, 2017.

Ogden, Cynthia L., Molly M. Lamb, Margaret D. Carroll, and Katherine M. Flegal. "Obesity and Socioeconomic Status in Adults: United States, 2005–2008." *NCHS Data Brief* 50 (2010): 1–7.

O'Hair, Dan, Rob Stewart, and Hannah Rubenstein. *A Speaker's Guidebook: Text and Reference.* New York: MacMillan, 2012.

Olson, Lester C. "Benjamin Franklin's Pictorial Representations of the British Colonies in America: A Study in Rhetorical Iconology." *Quarterly Journal of Speech* 73, no. 1 (1987): 18–42.

Paarlberg, Robert. *Food Politics: What Everyone Needs to Know.* New York: Oxford University Press, 2013.

Pachelli, Nick. "I Love Meat. But These New 'Bleeding' Veggie Burgers Convinced Me to Give it Up for Good." *Vox,* December 8, 2016.

Patel, Raj, and Jason W. Moore. *A History of the World in Seven Cheap Things: A Guide to Capitalism, Nature, and the Future of the Planet.* Oakland: University of California Press, 2017.

Peeples, Jennifer. "Toxic Sublime: Imaging Contaminated Landscapes." *Environmental Communication* 5, no. 4 (December 2011): 373–92.

Pfister, Damien S. *Networked Media, Networked Rhetorics*. State College: Pennsylvania State University Press, 2014.

Pflugfelder, Ehren Helmut. "Rhetoric's New Materialism: From Micro-Rhetoric to Microbrew." *Rhetoric Society Quarterly* 45, no. 5 (2015): 441–61.

Plato. *Gorgias*. Translated by Walter Hamilton. New York: Penguin, 1960.

———. *Phaedrus*. Translated by W. C. Helmbold and W. G. Rabinowitz. New York: Macmillian, 1956.

Pollan, Michael. *In Defense of Food: An Eater's Manifesto*. New York: Penguin, 2008.

———. *The Omnivore's Dilemma: A Natural History of Four Meals*. New York: Penguin, 2007.

Pollock, Anne. "Queering Endocrine Disruption." In *Object-Oriented Feminism*, edited by Katherine Behar, 183–200. Minneapolis: University of Minnesota Press, 2016.

Premalatha, M., Tasneem Abbasi, Tabassum Abbasi, and S. A. Abassi. "Energy-Efficient Food Production to Reduce Global Warming and Ecodegradation: The Use of Edible Insects." *Renewable and Sustainable Energy Reviews* 15, no. 9 (2011): 4357–60.

Prigg, Mark. "Study Reveals #Foodporn 500 Years before Instagram." *Daily Mail Online*, July 22, 2016. http://www.dailymail.co.uk/sciencetech/article-3703679/Foodporn-500-years-Instagram-Study-reveals-artist-s-obsessions-documenting-great-meals-bear-no-resemblance-people-really-eat.html.

Putnam, Robert. *Our Kids: The American Dream in Crisis*. New York: Simon and Schuster, 2015.

Ramos-Elorduy, Julieta. "Insects: A Sustainable Source of Food?" *Ecology of Food and Nutrition* 36, nos. 2–4 (1997): 247–76.

Rancière, Jacques. *The Politics of Aesthetics: The Distribution of the Sensible*. Translated by Gabriel Rockhill. New York: Continuum, 2004.

Rand, Erin J. *Reclaiming Queer: Activist and Academic Rhetorics of Resistance* (Tuscaloosa: University of Alabama Press, 2014).

———. "'What One Voice Can Do': Civic Pedagogy and Choric Collectivity at Camp Courage." *Text and Performance Quarterly* 34, no. 1 (2014): 28–51.

Rice, Jeff. *Craft Obsession: The Social Rhetorics of Beer*. Carbondale: Southern Illinois University Press, 2016.

Rice, Jenny Edbauer. "The New 'New': Making a Case for Critical Affect Studies." *Quarterly Journal of Speech* 94, no. 2 (2008): 200–212.

———. "Pathologia." *Quarterly Journal of Speech* 101, no. 1 (2015): 34–45.

Rickert, Thomas. *Ambient Rhetoric: The Attunements of Rhetorical Being*. Pittsburgh: University of Pittsburgh, 2013.

———. "Rhetorical Prehistory and the Paleolithic." *Review of Communication* 16, no. 4 (2016): 352–73.

Ritchie, Hanna, and Max Roser. "Meat and Seafood Production and Consumption." *Our World in Data*. August 2017.

Robinson, Douglas. *The Deep Ecology of Rhetoric in Mencius and Aristotle: A Somatic Guide*. New York: SUNY Press, 2016.

Rosen, Elizabeth. "To Eat Dog, or Not to Eat Dog." *The Atlantic*, December 30, 2014. https://www.theatlantic.com/international/archive/2014/12/to-eat-dog-or-not-to-eat-dog/384107/.

Safran Foer, Jonathan. "Let Them Eat Dog: A Modest Proposal for Tossing Fido in the Oven." *Wall Street Journal*, October 31, 2009. https://www.wsj.com/articles/SB10001424052748703574604574499880131341174.

Saletan, William. "Wok the Dog: What's Wrong With Eating Man's Best Friend." *Slate*, January 16, 2002. http://www.slate.com/articles/news_and_politics/frame_game/2002/01/wok_the_dog.html.

Sampson, Tony D. *Virality: Contagion Theory in the Age of Networks*. Minneapolis: University of Minnesota Press, 2012.

Schiappa, Edward. *Defining Reality: Definitions and the Politics of Meaning*. Carbondale: Southern Illinois University Press, 2003.

———. "Second Thoughts on the Critiques of Big Rhetoric." *Philosophy and Rhetoric* 34, no. 3 (2001): 260–74.

Scheier, Lee M. "What is the Hunger-Obesity Paradox?" *Journal of the American Dietetic Association* 105, no. 6 (2005): 883–85.

Schlosser, Eric. *Fast Food Nation: The Dark Side of the All-American Meal*. New York: Harpers Perennial, 2004.

Schwabe, Calvin. *Unmentionable Cuisine*. Charlottesville: University Press of Virginia, 1979.

Semuels, Alana. "America's Great Divergence." *The Atlantic*, January 30, 2017. https://www.theatlantic.com/business/archive/2017/01/americas-great-divergence/514784/.

Shaw, Hollie. "The Food Porn Trend: How Restaurants Are Catering to Instagram-Hungry Patrons." *Financial Post*, January 3, 2015. http://business.financialpost.com/news/retail-marketing/the-food-porn-trend-how-restaurants-are-catering-to-instagram-hungry-patrons.

Shiva, Vindana, and Ingunn Moser, editors. *Biopolitics: A Feminist and Ecological Reader on Biotechnology*. New Jersey: Zed Books, 1995.

Shotwell, Alexis. *Against Purity: Living Ethically in Compromised Times*. Minneapolis: University of Minnesota Press, 2016.

Shugart, Helene A. *Heavy: The Obesity Crisis in Cultural Context*. Oxford: Oxford University Press, 2016.

Robert Sietsema, "Crunching on Grasshopper Tacos," Gourmet.com, December 22, 2008, http://www.gourmet.com.s3-website-us-east-1.amazonaws.com/restaurants/2008/12/grasshopper-tacos.html.

Simmons, Peter Lund. *The Curiosities of Food: Or Dainties and Delicacies of Different Nations Obtained from the Animal Kingdom*. London: Richard Bentley, New Burlington Street, 1859.

Sloop, John M., and James P. McDaniel, eds. *Judgment Calls: Rhetoric, Politics, and Indeterminacy*. Boulder, CO: Westview Press, 1998.

Smith, Clarissa. "Breathing New Life into Old Fears: Extreme Pornography and the Wider Politics of Snuff." In Jackson et al., *Snuff*, 81–104.

Smith, Mike, and JH Bloomberg School of Public Health. "Study Suggests Home Cooking Is a Main Ingredient in Healthier Diet." *Johns Hopkins Bloomberg School of Public Health*. Accessed April 16, 2017. http://www.jhsph.edu/research/centers-and-institutes/johns-hopkins-center-for-a-livable-future/news-room/News-Releases/2014/Study-Suggests-Home-Cooking-Main-Ingredient-in-Healthier-Diet.html.

Smith, Valerie J. "Aristotle's Classical Enthymeme and the Visual Argumentation of the Twenty-First Century." *Argumentation & Advocacy* 43, no. 3/4 (Winter/Spring 2007): 114–23.

Soble, Alan. *Pornography: Marxism, Feminism, and the Future of Sexuality*. New Haven: Yale University Press, 1986.

Sontag, Susan. *Regarding the Pain of Others*. New York: Picador, 2004.

Spangler, Micah. "Bull Penis Soup is the National Hangover Cure of Bolivia." *Munchies*, October 21, 2015. https://munchies.vice.com/en_us/article/8qkvqg/bull-penis-soup-is-the-national-hangover-cure-of-bolivia.

Stokes, Ashli Quesinberry, and Wendy Atkins-Sayre. *Consuming Identity: The Role of Food in Redefining the South*. Jackson: University Press of Mississippi, 2016.

Stormer, Nathan. An Appetite for Rhetoric," *Philosophy and Rhetoric* 48, no. 1 (2015): 99–106.

———. "Articulation: A Working Paper on Rhetoric and Taxis." *Quarterly Journal of Speech* 90, no. 3 (2004): 257–84.

———. "Rhetoric's Diverse Materiality: Polythetic Ontology and Genealogy," *Review of Communication* 16, no. 4 (2016): 299–316.

Stormer, Nathan, and Bridie McGreavy. "Thinking Ecologically About Rhetoric's Ontology." *Philosophy and Rhetoric* 50, no. 1 (2017): 1–25.

Sutter, John D. "The Argument for Eating Dog." CNN, July 24, 2014. http://www.cnn.com/2014/07/23/opinion/sutter-dog-meat-ethics/index.html.

Tanumihardjo, Sherry A., Cheryl Anderson, Martha Kaufer-Horwitz, Bars Bode, Nancy J. Emenaker, Andrea M. Haqq, Jessie A. Satia, Heidi J. Silver, and Diane D. Stadler. "Poverty, Obesity, and Malnutrition: An International Perspective Recognizing the Paradox." *Journal of the American Dietetics Association* 107, no. 11 (2007): 1966–72.

Taubes, Gary. *The Case against Sugar*. Toronto: Alfred A. Knopf, 2016.

Tepper, Rachel. "'Epic Chef,' Food Competition Show from Epic Meal Time, Features Talented Chefs and Gross Challenges (VIDEO)." *Huffington Post*, December 14, 2012. http://www.huffingtonpost.com/2012/12/14/epic-chef-epic-meal-time_n_2300815.html.

Todoroff, Uriah Marc. "A Cryptoeconomy of Affect." *The New Inquiry* (May 14, 2018).

Trillin, Calvin. "Land of the Seven Moles: Adapting to Life's Changes at the Table." *New Yorker*, December 3, 2012. https://www.newyorker.com/magazine/2012/12/03/land-of-the-seven-moles.

Trubek, Amy B. *The Taste of Place*. Berkeley: University of California Press, 2008.

Tsign, Anna Lowenhaupt. *The Mushroom at the End of the World*. Princeton: Princeton University Press, 2015.

Ulmer, Gregory. "The Unheimlich Maneuver." *Lusitania—A Journal of Reflection and Oceanography* 8 (Spring 1996): 131–41.

Unknown author. *The Cabinet of Curiosities, Or Wonders of the World Displayed: Forming a Repository of Whatever is Remarkable in the Regions of Nature and Art Extraordinary Events, and Eccentric Biography*. Vol. 1. New York: Piercy and Reed, 1840.

"URWHATUPOST—Bolthouse Farms." Accessed December 12, 2016. http://www.urwhatupost.com.

Vallee, Bert L. "Alcohol in the Western World." *Scientific American* 278, no. 6 (1998): 80–85.

Vats, Anjali. "Cooking Up Hashtag Activism: #PaulasBestDishes and Counternarratives of Southern Food." *Communication & Critical/Cultural Studies* 12, no. 2 (2015): 209–13.

Vickers, Brian. *In Defense of Rhetoric*. New York: Oxford University Press, 2002.

Vitanza, Victor. *Sexual Violence in Western Thought and Writing: Chaste Rape*. New York: Palgrave MacMillan, 2011.

Vivian, Bradford. *Being Made Strange: Rhetoric Beyond Representation*. Albany: State University of New York Press, 2004.

Wansink, Brian, and Jeffery Sobal. "Mindless Eating: The 200 Daily Food Decisions We Overlook." *Environment and Behavior* 39, no. 1 (2007): 106–23.

Warnick, Barbara. "Two Systems of Invention: The Topics in the Rhetoric and the New Rhetoric." In *Rereading Aristotle*, edited by Alan Gross and Arthur Walzer, 107–29. Carbondale: Southern Illinois University Press, 2008.

Weaver, Jacob. "Strength in the Pot." *Gastronomica* 6, no. 4 (2006): 5–6.

Weaver, Richard. *The Ethics of Rhetoric*. Davis, CA: Hermagoras Press, 1985.

"Welcome to Beaufort, Port Royal, and the Sea Islands of South Carolina." Vimeo video, posted by Visit Beaufort, SC, November 4, 2011. https://vimeo.com/31626474.

Wells, Pete. "Fast Food for Needy Neighborhoods, at Locol in California." *New York Times*, January 3, 2017.

Wilcox, Estelle Woods. *The Dixie-Cookbook*. Atlanta: L. A. Clarkson & Company, 1885.

Williams, Linda. "Film Bodies: Gender, Genre, and Excess." *Film Quarterly* 44, no. 4 (1991): 2–13.

———. *Hard Core: Power, Pleasure, and the "Frenzy of the Visible."* Berkeley: University of California Press, 1989.

Williams, Raymond. *Keywords: A Vocabulary of Culture and Society*. New York: Oxford University Press, 1983.

Winne, Mark. "To Solve Hunger First Solve Poverty." Civil Eats. April 20, 2017. https://civileats.com/2017/04/20/to-solve-hunger-first-solve-poverty/.

Wu, Frank H. "The Best 'Chink' Food: Eating and Dilemma of Diversity." *Gastronomica* 2, no. 2 (Spring 2002): 38–45.

Young, Anna M. "The Politics of Wine and the Style of Bullshit." *Rhetoric Society Quarterly* 45, no. 5 (2015): 472–76.

———. "Quaffable but . . . Far from Transcendent." In *The Politics of Style and the Style of Politics*, edited by Barry Brummett, 263–78. Lanham, MD: Lexington Books, 2011.

Young, Anna M., Justin Eckstein, and Donovan Conley. "Rhetorics and Foodways," *Communication and Critical/Cultural Studies* 12, no. 2 (2015): 198–99.

Young, Stephanie L. "Running Like a Man, Sitting Like a Girl: Visual Enthymeme and the Case of Caster Semenya." *Women's Studies in Communication* 38, no. 3 (2015): 331–50.

Zebrowski, Katie. "Alinea Phenomenology: Cookery as Flat Ontology." In Barnett and Boyle, eds, *Rhetoric*, 55–66.

Zizek, Slavoj. *Welcome to the Desert of the Real: Five Essays on September 11 and Related Dates*. London: Verso, 2013.

Contributors

Donovan Conley is associate professor of communication studies at the University of Nevada, Las Vegas, where he holds the Sanford Berman Chair in Language and Thought. His research explores the ways taste mediates influence, and so he pursues an ecologized approach to the study of rhetoric. His scholarship seeks to understand how taste and "the political" are historically interlinked. Driving this work is a premise: the forces which mold our sense of taste are those which enable or inhibit our capacity to make choices/changes.

Greg Dickinson is professor and chair in the Department of Communication Studies at Colorado State University. He is an award-winning scholar and teacher whose work advances critical and theoretical understanding of memory, place, materiality, race, gender, and everyday life. He has published in communication, cultural studies, and rhetoric journals on coffee shops, shopping malls, museums, and gentrified urban spaces. He is the author of *Suburban Dreams: Building and Imagining the Good Life*, coauthor of *The Twitter Presidency: Donald J. Trump and the Politics of White Rage* and is the coeditor of *Places of Public Memory: The Rhetoric of Museums and Memorials* and the *Routledge Reader in Rhetorical Criticism*. He is the editor of the 2019–2021 issues of *Communication and Critical/Cultural Studies*.

Katie Dickman received her PhD in English from Saint Louis University. Her research has appeared in *enculturation*, *Kairos*, and the *Journal of Interactive Technology and Pedagogy* as well as in the edited collection *Rhetoric, through Everyday Things*. She currently works as a developmental editor.

Justin Eckstein is assistant professor of communication and director of forensics in the Department of Communication at Pacific Lutheran University in Tacoma, Washington. He is an award-winning researcher who studies how the senses reason. His work has appeared in journals such as *Philosophy and Rhetoric* and *Communication and Critical/Cultural Studies*.

Casey R. Kelly is associate professor of communication studies at the University of Nebraska-Lincoln. He is the author of *Abstinence Cinema: Virginity and the Rhetoric of Sexual Purity in Contemporary Film* and *Food Television and Otherness in the Age of Globalization*. His work has appeared in journals such as *Quarterly Journal of Speech* and *Communication and Critical/Cultural Studies*.

Jeff Rice is Martha B. Reynolds Professor of Writing, Rhetoric, and Digital Studies and chair of the Department of Writing, Rhetoric and Digital Studies at the University of Kentucky. He is the author of *The Rhetoric of Cool: Composition Studies and New Media; Digital Detroit: Rhetoric and Space in the Age of the Network; Craft Obsession: The Social Rhetorics of Beer*, and numerous articles and chapters on rhetoric, new media, and writing.

Nathaniel A. Rivers is associate professor of English at Saint Louis University. His current research addresses topics such as environmentalism, locative media, and accessibility. He coedited *Thinking with Bruno Latour in Rhetoric and Composition* (SIUP, 2015). His recent work has appeared in journals such as *Rhetoric Society Quarterly*, *Enculturation*, and *Quarterly Journal of Speech*.

Anna Marjorie Young is associate professor and chair of the Department of Communication at Pacific Lutheran University. Her work centers on questions of expertise and public and political life, including her book, *Prophets, Gurus & Pundits: Rhetorical Styles & Public Engagement* (SIU Press, 2014). Most recently she's interested in food and wine politics and is pursuing a second book manuscript on conservative rhetorical style.

Index

Page numbers in italics refer to figures.